Tun-huang

Chiu-ch'üan

Chang-yeh

Wu-wei

Wu-yüan

Yün-chung

Lo-lang

Shang-ku

Tai

Yen-men

Shang chün

T'ai-yüan

Pei-ti

Yellow R.

An-ting

Lo-yang

Ch'ang-an

Han-chung

Shu

Pa

Yangtze R.

Wo-nu

K'un-ming

P'an-yü

Chiao-chih

Ho-p'u

Chiu-chen

Chu-yai

Jih-nan

Hsiung-nu

Hsien-pi

Wu-huan

Ch'iang and Ti

Southwestern Barbarians

Trade and Expansion in Han China

Trade and Expansion in Han China

A Study in the Structure of Sino-Barbarian Economic Relations

by Ying-shih Yü

UNIVERSITY OF CALIFORNIA PRESS

Berkeley and Los Angeles 1967

University of California Press,
Berkeley and Los Angeles, California

Cambridge University Press,
London, England

Designed by David Pauly

Library of Congress Catalog Card Number 67-12492
Printed in the United States of America

Foreword

As the first long-lasting bureaucratic empire, the Han dynasty (206 B.C.–A.D. 220) served for many centuries as the classical model of Imperial rule in East Asia. In China Han institutions were studied for their historical lessons by continuous generations of rulers and literati-officials, not only under the Chinese dynasties but also under the alien dynasties. The Han imperial order exerted a notable influence, too, on neighboring countries, especially Korea, Japan, and Viet Nam (Annam), both directly and through its modified T'ang model.

The major reason for the paramount influence of Han institutions was the success of their judicious amalgamation of various apparently contradictory elements in their legacy from pre-Han China. For instance, the conscious combination of Confucianism and Legalism in theory and practice allowed a wide range of variation and vibration between idealism and realism. The same reconciliation was applied to militarism and pacifism, laissez-faire and state control, and other conflicting forces. The whole imperial network was comparable to a large wine bottle, which, although filled with old wine most of the time, was able to accommodate some new wine and strong enough to tolerate further fermentation.

Dr. Ying-shih Yü's book discusses several sectors of this imperial network, centering around the theme of trade and expansion. Foreign relations between the Han Chinese and the other peoples are examined from various angles, based on thorough research of written documents as well as of archaeological materials. Economic and military problems faced by the Han dynasty are reviewed against the broad historical and cultural background. The result is a comprehensive picture, illustrated with concrete examples and illuminated with perceptive comments. Its scope and depth make this book the first full-scale study of the subject in any language, and it constitutes a substantial contribution to the understanding of Chinese history.

In a time of great cultural upheaval, the value of history may become extremely dubious. On the other hand, since what is present today will become past tomorrow, it is obviously futile for a nation or a people to deny all connection or continuity with the past. The ugly face reflected in the historical mirror may belong to our ancestor, but unfortunately it bears a resemblance to our face too. The Chinese people have been known for their historical-mindedness. It is unlikely that such a deep-rooted cultural trait can be totally erased in a generation or two, even with state coercion. As is said in a line by the T'ang poet, Li Po, "Sword may be drawn to cut the stream, but the stream will continue to flow."

LIEN-SHENG YANG

Cambridge, Massachusetts
September, 1966

Preface

I have tried in this book to give a systematic account of Sino-barbarian economic relations in Han times, making the interplay between trade and expansion the central theme. The undertaking can be justified on several grounds.

In the first place, we have available today a great deal of source material to which even Ssu-ma Ch'ien and Pan Ku, the two great Han historians, had no access. I refer particularly to the many recent archaeological finds. In the second place, although almost every aspect of the subject has been critically examined by modern scholars in the East as well as in the West, the findings of modern historical research yet require consolidation in terms of an interpretive scheme so that their significance can be more readily recognized.

Finally, there is a growing need for a better understanding of the traditional Chinese world order. Much has been written in recent years about the inadequacies of the Chinese tributary system in coping with the Western challenge to the Manchu dynasty. That the system collapsed beyond repair in the face of a new world order is well known; but it should be remembered that the Chinese tributary system has a long prior history. Any just evaluation of it must, I believe, take into account not only its decline and fall but also its establishment and growth. Since the system began to take shape in the Han dynasty period, I have undertaken to analyze its development against the background of the economic and political realities of the time.

In working out the general framework of the book, I

have relied primarily on accounts in the dynastic histories, where basic facts are reported in their chronological context. As my notes indicate, this work is deeply indebted to modern historical scholarship, without which no synthesis (even one as limited as this) can hope to succeed.

Archaeological finds have been used mainly to verify historical records. However, in the reconstruction of the trading relations, especially the silk trade, between Han China and the western countries the archaeological evidence plays a major role. Special mention should be made of the Han documents on wood, discovered at Tun-huang and Edsin Gol, which are sources no student of the period can afford to overlook; they were extremely helpful to me in clarifying, on a number of occasions, the institutional background of frontier trade.

Every book is a symbol of intellectual debt which its author owes to his teachers and friends. Mine is no exception. I must first mention Dr. Ch'ien Mu, who, during my undergraduate years at New Asia College, Hong Kong, initiated me into the field of Chinese studies and, at the same time, taught me to love Chinese history. I am particularly grateful to Professor Lien-sheng Yang, Harvard University, who not only guided the writing of the book at every stage but also honors it with his Foreword. My thanks are also due to Professors John K. Fairbank of Harvard University, Ping-ti Ho of the University of Chicago, and Lao Kan of the University of California at Los Angeles, who kindly read the first draft of my manuscript, in whole or in part, and generously offered suggestions for improvement.

Three research grants from the Rackham School of Graduate Studies, University of Michigan, during the period 1963–1966 enabled me to visit several Asian libraries in the United States in search of materials for this study. During the same period, the Center for Chinese Studies, University of Michigan, materially facilitated the preparation of the work not only by rendering extensive typing service, but also by according me research assistance, permitting the incorporation of important German and Russian archaeological sources into my study. To the Director of the Center, Professor Albert Feuerwerker, my friend and colleague, I am especially indebted for his constant encouragement. Without the enthusiasm of members of the staff of the University of California Press, the transformation of this manuscript into a book would have been much delayed.

Ying-shih Yü

October, 1966
Cambridge, Massachusetts

Contents

Chronology

The Ch'in Dynasty
The First Emperor 221–210 B.C.
The Second Emperor 209–206

The Former Han Dynasty
Emperor Kao-tsu 206–195 B.C.
Emperor Hui 194–188
Empress Lü 187–180
Emperor Wen 179–157
Emperor Ching 156–141
Emperor Wu 140–87
Emperor Chao 86–74
Emperor Hsüan 73–49
Emperor Yuan 48–33
Emperor Ch'eng 32–7
Emperor Ai 6–1
Emperor P'ing A.D. 1–5
Ju-tzu Ying 6–8

The Hsin Dynasty of Wang Mang, A.D. *9–23*

The Later Han Dynasty
Emperor Kuang-wu A.D. 25–57
Emperor Ming 58–75
Emperor Chang 76–88
Emperor Ho 89–105
Emperor Shang 106
Emperor An 107–125
Emperor Shun 126–144
Emperor Ch'ung 145
Emperor Chih 146
Emperor Huan 147–167
Emperor Ling 168–188
Emperor Shao 189
Emperor Hsien 189–220

The Three Kingdoms
Wei A.D. 220–264
Shu 221–263
Wu 222–280

Table of Equivalents

1 *hu* or *shih* = 10 *tou* = 100 *sheng* = 0.565 United States bushels

1 *p'i* = 4 *chang*

1 *chang* = 7 feet, 6.94 inches English measure

1 *li* = 1364.1+ English feet

1 catty (*chin*) = 244 grams

cash (*ch'ien*) = copper coins

10,000 copper coins = 1 catty of actual gold = 244 grams

chapter one

Introduction:
The Problem and Its Origins

I

As an historical period the greatness of Han China is especially marked, among other things, by it unprecedented achievements in trade and expansion. The creation of the Silk Route and the opening of the northwestern passage to Central Asia, though of paramount historical significance, constitute but a small part of the whole story. Trade, in its broadest sense, could embrace all kinds of exchange in which things of economic value are involved. Thus the voluntary exchange of gifts between ancient princes is taken by Max Weber as a form of trade—"gift trade," [1] whereas, in the case of traditional China, the exchange of the imperial gift and the barbarian tribute has long been labelled "tributary trade." [2] On the other hand, expansion is also manifold—military, political, economic as well as cultural. Therefore, in the present study it may range from the most concrete meaning of territorial expansion to the highly abstract one of cultural expansion—the acculturation of foreign ethnic groups by China, or, in a word, Sinicization.

Trade and expansion in Han China were so closely interwoven that they were hardly separable in reality, though distinguishable in conception. Throughout the period they developed side by side through mutual stimulation. But any attempt at determining which was the cause and which the effect would inevitably end in despair. As a

---

[1] Max Weber, *General Economic History*, p. 197.
[2] Owen Lattimore, *Inner Asian Frontiers of China*, pp. 482–483.

1

matter of fact, it worked in both directions: sometimes it was trade that paved the way for expansion and sometimes it was expansion that opened opportunities for trade. It is out of this consideration that attention here is focused more on the interplay of the two than either one in isolation from the other.

From the historical point of view, trade and expansion in this period began as a reaction to the barbarian threat of the Hsiung-nu on the northern and northwestern frontiers, and ended not only in the inclusion of various barbarian groups into the empire, such as the Southern Hsiung-nu, the Ch'iang, the Wu-huan, and the Southwestern barbarians, but also in the Sinicization of them to greater and lesser degrees. In between, China also expanded to the Western Regions and Central Asia, and even established trading relations, directly or indirectly, with countries farther west. The latter development, that is, western expansion, important as it was in the history of the Han empire, must nevertheless be understood as a side current. In the general realm of foreign relations of the empire, the central and immediate concern of the court was always how to deal successfully with all the barbarian groups along the Chinese frontiers with a view to preventing them from disturbing the imperial order. Western expansion was desirable only as far as it would serve this purpose. In short, it was a means to an end rather an end in itself. History of the period abounds in evidence on this point. For instance, Emperor Wu's excessive expansionistic policy incurred severe posthumous criticism at the court.[3] Even the expansionistic emperor himself issued a decree toward the end of his life expressing his regrets.[4] As will be shown below, several later emperors, especially Emperor Hsüan of the Former Han and Emperor Kuang-wu of the Later Han, much hesitated to follow an expansionistic policy toward the Western Regions. Some of the court officials even advanced interesting theories against expansion. The best proof, however, is to be found in the

---

[3] Lien-sheng Yang, *Studies in Chinese Institutional History*, p. 6.
[4] *HS*, 96B:5a–b.

proportion of Chinese aid to the various groups of tributary barbarians under the Later Han dynasty: the total annual payments made to all the tributary states of the Western Regions were 74,800,000 cash, whereas that for the Southern Hsiung-nu alone amounted to 100,900,000.

All these facts unmistakably indicate where the emphasis lay in the Han foreign policy. It is in the light of such an understanding that particular stress is placed in this study on the general economic relations between the Chinese and the frontier barbarians. Thus the settlement of the surrendered barbarians in China and China's trade with the various non-Chinese peoples, both at home and abroad, are treated as equally important aspects of the subject. The immediate aim here is to present a balanced picture of the basic facts relating to trade and expansion. Through an analysis of these historical facts, however, it is also hoped that the general structure of Sino-barbarian economic relations in Han China will be unveiled. By structure is meant not only the manner in which all types of economic intercourse took place, but also how this intercourse was anchored to the political and economic systems of the empire.

Traditional China has been persistently labelled in the West as a "Confucian" state or society, the meaning of which is by no means clear and well-defined. If by this is meant the establishment of a state or society along the lines, or according to the principles, set forth in the political and social writings of the pre-Ch'in Confucianism, then China in Han times may be considered as more typically Confucian than she was under any of the later dynasties. Moreover, institutionally speaking, the importance of the Han period lies in its being the formative stage in which the basic pattern of the Chinese imperial order took shape—a pattern that was to last, through various phases of change within tradition, until the end of the nineteenth century. From this point of view, a detailed analysis of the structure of Sino-barbarian economic relations under the Han dynasty may also throw some light on the nature of the so-called Confucian state or society.

2

The problem of a barbarian threat in Chinese history did not begin with the beginning of the Han dynasty. In order to understand the historical background we must trace its origins in earlier periods. The problem first became particularly grave in the Ch'un-ch'iu period (771–481 B.C.). First of all, we know that the eastern movement of the Chou capital from Hao, near the modern city of Sian in Shensi, to Lo-yang in Honan, which marked the beginning of the period, was directly related to, if not caused by, the invasion of the Jung barbarians on the northwestern frontier. Throughout the period, barbarians continued to invade the Chinese states from time to time. Repulsing the barbarians thus became one of the immediate political objectives, as well as obligations, of the leading states under the *Pa* or Hegemony system. During this period, it is important to bear in mind that a Chinese was differentiated from a barbarian more by cultural criteria than by ethnic ones. The Jung and Ti peoples in the north and northwest, on the one hand, and the underdeveloped and aggressive Ch'u people in the south, on the other hand, were therefore equally regarded as barbarians. The *Kung-yang Commentary to the Ch'un-ch'iu* says: "The Southern I (i.e., Ch'u) and the Northern Ti barbarians both made invasions [into China] and the existence of China hung by a thread." [5]

In terms of economic life the difference between a Chinese and a barbarian in the Ch'un-ch'iu period, as later in Han times, was essentially one between an agriculturalist and a nomad. As a nomad, the barbarian usually had greater interests in mobile wealth such as money and commodities, which were easy to carry, than in land, except for the purpose of grazing animals. [6] In long-time and close contacts with the barbarians, the Chinese not only had learned their particular pattern of economic behavior, but

---

[5] *Ch'u-ch'iu Kung-yang chu-shu, Shih-san ching chu-shu* edition, 10:14a. (Note: all translations not otherwise credited are the author's.)

[6] Lattimore, *op. cit.*, p. 66.

also had begun to take advantage of it in dealing with them as early as the sixth century B.C. For instance, in 568, Wei Chiang, a minister of the state of Chin (in modern Shansi) proposed a peace policy toward the neighboring Jung and Ti barbarians. In so doing he pointed out a number of advantages that would surely result from a peace agreement. Among them, the following two particularly bear on the topic of discussion—trade and expansion. First, both the Jung and Ti were mobile and, therefore, would prefer goods to land. Through peaceful means their land could be purchased, presumably for cultivation by the Chinese. Second, with the advent of peace the tension on the border would be relaxed, which in turn would make it possible for the frontier Chinese farmers to carry on their agricultural work.[7]

From the first point we know that even at this early stage, as in the Han period, trade was already used as a political weapon by the Chinese government to keep the frontier barbarians under control. Lattimore has made an interesting point when he emphasizes that in fighting barbarian wars, China in the Chan-kuo or Warring-States period (450?–221), was expanding rather than defending its territories.[8] Now the first point further suggests that the Chinese expansion not only took the form of war, but also that of trade, which sometimes proved even more effective and thorough. From the second point it seems clear that the barbarian threat in the Ch'un-ch'iu period, as will be fully shown below, foreshadowed that of Han China, namely, a nomadic menace to the sedentary life of the Chinese agriculturalists, which always found its expression in constant frontier raids.

As revealed in both historical records and archaeological finds, Sino-barbarian economic intercourse generally existed in many frontier areas during the Warring-States period, especially after the third century B.C. The northern

---

[7] James Legge, tr., *The Ch'un-Ts'ew with the Tso Chuen* in *The Chinese Classics*, 5:424. A similar but much shortened passage may be found in the *Kuo-yü, WYWK* edition, *Chin*, 7, p. 159.

[8] Lattimore, *op. cit.*, pp. 340–349.

Chinese state of Yen is reported to have had close contact
with its neighboring barbarians, notably the Wu-huan in
Manchuria. Trading relations of the Yen people are said to
have stretched as far, even, as to Korea.[9] This literary
record has been confirmed by modern archaeological discovery of large amounts of knife-coins known as *Ming-tao*
in northern Korea.[10] In 1958–1960, cemeteries in several
places in Manchuria, datable to the Warring-States period,
were excavated. The tombs are considered to have belonged to the so-called Eastern barbarians, possibly the Wu-
huan. Among the remains are bronze articles including
weapons, which clearly show traces of their having been
under the cultural influence of both the Chinese and the
Hsiung-nu. The presence of the Chinese *ko* halberd of the
Warring-States period, for instance, may very well be
taken as evidence that some sort of relations, especially
economic, must have been established between these barbarians and the people of interior China.[11]

In the frontier areas of southwestern China, especially
Szechwan, cultural and economic contacts of the native
barbarians with the Chinese in the interior may be traced
back to as early as Yin and Chou times. But such contacts
did not become very significant until the Ch'un-ch'iu and
the Chan-kuo periods, especially after the conquest of Shu
(upper Szechwan) by the state of Ch'in in 316 B.C.[12]
Archaeological investigations have shown that during the
Warring-States period, Chinese imports had been continuously brought to Szechwan from various Chinese states.
Items that have been found include bronze vessels from
Ch'in and lacquer works, bronze tripods and steamers, as
well as weapons from Ch'u. In eastern Szechwan are found

---

[9] *SC*, 129:5a; *HS*, 28B:13b. Cf. Burton Watson, *Records of the Grand
Historian of China*, 2:487.

[10] For a comprehensive study of the *Ming-tao* knife-coins found in Korea
and their possible bearing on trade see Fujita Ryōsaku, *Chōsen kōkogaku
kenkyū*, pp. 196–292; cf., also, Wang Yü-ch'üan, *Wo-kuo ku-tai huo-pi ti
ch'i-yüan ho fa-chan*, pp. 65–69.

[11] *HCKTKKSH*, p. 72.

[12] Hsü Chung-shu, "Pa-Shu wen-hua ch'u-lun," *Ssu-ch'uan Ta-hsüeh
hsüeh-pao, She-hui k'o-hsüeh*, pp. 21–44.

not only Chinese style products, bearing inscriptions, and iron implements, but also copper coins of the state of Ch'in, which are sure signs of exchange trade between the outside Chinese and the native barbarians.[13]

In this connection, archaeological finds can be most fruitfully studied in conjunction with literary sources. According to the latter, quite a few Chinese became wealthy through trading with the native barbarians of Szechwan and Yunnan toward the end of the third century B.C. For instance, the famous Cho family of Shu, who made a fortune by smelting and casting iron, eventually dominated the trade with the frontier barbarian peoples of southwestern China. At about the same time, another well-known merchant of Szechwan, Ch'eng Cheng, who also had a hand in the iron industry, frequently traded with a group of barbarians described in history as "wearing their hair in the mallet-shape fashion." [14] These barbarians are obviously identifiable with those tribes known collectively as the Southwestern barbarians under the Han dynasty.[15] It must have been through the intermediary of Chinese merchants like Cho and Ch'eng that Chinese objects, especially metal works, that have been recently discovered by archaeologists first found their way to the southwestern frontier.

On the northwestern frontier, similar activities of Chinese merchants are also observable. A merchant by the name of Lo of Wu-chih (in modern Kansu) is reported to have been made rich by his silk trade with a barbarian chief. Each time when he sold his cattle, he bought fine silk fabrics and other precious articles and presented them to the king of the Jung barbarians. The latter always repaid him ten times the original price and, in addition, returned the favor by giving him cattle and horses. In this way, as the story runs, he was able to accumulate so many

---

[13] *HCKTKKSH*, pp. 73–74; *KKTH* (1955:6), pp. 48–54.

[14] Watson, 2:495–496; Nancy Lee Swann, *Food and Money in Ancient China*, pp. 452–453.

[15] Because the Southwestern barbarians are also given a similar description in the *Shih Chi*. Cf. Watson, 2:290.

animals that their number was beyond counting.[16] To cite another example: In the late third century the ancestors of Pan Ku, the great Han historian, appeared in the northwestern frontier region as the leading family in the cattle business. The number of horses, oxen, and sheep of the family amounted to several thousand. Moreover, according to Pan Ku, the success of his family so inspired and encouraged the frontier Chinese that many of them followed in the Pan's footsteps.[17] It seems beyond doubt that this successful cattle business must also have had something to do with the frontier barbarians.

Viewed as a whole, the historical significance of Sino-barbarian frontier trade in the late Warring-States period, as indicated by the above instances, can hardly be overstressed. In the first place, as an historical phenomenon it must be placed in the context of the rapid industrial and commercial developments of the entire Warring-States period in general and in that of the interstate or interregional trade in particular. In the second place, frontier trade between individual Chinese and barbarians, as it was carried out in the Warring-States period, may be legitimately regarded as the prototype of one particular pattern of behavior that, as will be demonstrated below, characterized many of the frontier Chinese merchants in Han times.

---

[16] Watson, 2:483; Swann, p. 430. Kuo Mo-jo has wrongly identified this barbarian king with the Hsiung-nu. See his *Wen-shih lun-chi*, p. 156.
[17] *HS*, 100A:1a.

chapter two

Policy Background and Foundations of Trade

Trade and expansion in Han China cannot be fully understood without at least a brief examination of its changing policies, both foreign and economic, as well as its growing commercial conditions. In the first place, we must find out what was the general attitude of the Han government toward both the barbarians and the merchants, who undoubtedly played leading roles in the Sino-barbarian economic intercourse. In the second place, we must also know what Han China could offer to the non-Chinese peoples and how offers were made. This naturally leads to the discussion of Han China's agricultural and industrial resources, on the one hand, and on the other hand, its general trading facilities, such as the transportation system, which altogether constituted what we call the foundations of trade. This chapter is devoted to answering some of these basic questions.

1 Foreign Policy

Foreign policy under the Former Han dynasty (206 B.C.–A.D. 8) hinged almost entirely on the empire's relations with the Hsiung-nu. Thus a review of its Hsiung-nu policy would be sufficient to reveal its basic attitude toward the barbarians in general.

When the Han dynasty eventually unified China in 202 B.C., it inherited from the Ch'in not only the empire but also all its problems. One of the most acute problems was the Hsiung-nu threat on the northern and northwestern

9

frontiers, which had troubled the Chinese from the fourth century B.C. on.[1] A typical example of this threat occurred only one year later. The first large-scale military encounter between the Han and the Hsiung-nu forces in 201–200 began with the surrender of a Chinese general to the Hsiung-nu and ended in the narrow escape of Han Kao-tsu, the founding emperor, from capture after a seven-day siege at P'ing-ch'eng (in modern Ta-t'ung, Shansi).[2]

平城

Immediately after the defeat at P'ing-ch'eng, Emperor Kao-tsu adopted the famous ho-ch'in policy and concluded peace with the Hsiung-nu at the suggestion of one of his assistants by the name of Liu Ching.[3] This first ho-ch'in agreement assured the Hsiung-nu a fixed amount of annual imperial "gifts" and the hand of a Han "princess" to their Shan-yü, the barbarian counterpart of the Chinese Son of Heaven. On the other hand, the Hsiung-nu made the pledge that they would stop raiding the Chinese border areas.[4] A similar line of foreign policy was generally followed, not without difficulties or sometimes even

刘敬

---

[1] Owen Lattimore, *Inner Asian Frontiers of China*, pp. 450–468.

[2] *SC*, 8:16a, 93:1b–2a; HS, 1B:5a, 33:3b–4a. Cf. Burton Watson, *Records of the Grand Historian of China*, 1:110, 235–236; H. H. Dubs, *The History of the Former Han Dynasty*, 1:115–116. For a modern interpretation of Kao-tsu's expedition see Lattimore, *op. cit.*, pp. 479–480.

[3] *SC*, 99:2b; Watson, 1:289–290. By *ho-ch'in* I refer to the type of relations between China and the Hsiung-nu that marked the early Han dynasty up to about 135 B.C. As will be fully analyzed in the next chapter, *ho-ch'in* may be considered as a kind of peace which the Chinese court bought from the Hsiung-nu at a high price without actually obtaining anything from them in return except their easily breakable promise of non-aggression. This may very well be taken as another type of "unequal treaty" in Chinese history, which, in a modified form and to a different extent, was also to reappear occasionally in later periods when the Chinese empire was militarily weak and therefore was unable to maintain the equilibrium of tributary relations with the powerful barbarians. This was especially true with the case of Sung China's (960–1279) relations with the barbarian Liao [Ch'i-tan] (907–1125) and Chin [Jurchen] (1115–1234) dynasties. It must be pointed out that after 135 B.C. the term *ho-ch'in* was sometimes also used in Chinese history in a very broad sense meaning simply "peaceful and friendly relations." In this sense, it could equally apply to the case in which good relations were maintained between China as the suzerain state and the barbarians as the submissive vassals under the tributary system. Throughout this study, however, *ho-ch'in* is used only in its original narrow sense.

[4] *SC*, 110:6b; Watson, 2:166–167.

* according to Lattimore: when Han Wang Hsin surrendered to Hsiung Nu, Liu Pang took field against him, this was to prevent such defection from spreading & resulting in general disturbance of empire.

disgrace, under the reigns of Emperor Hui (194–188
B.C.), Empress Lü (187–180), Emperor Wen (179–157)
and Emperor Ching (156–141). A drastic change, however, eventually took place in the time of Emperor Wu
(140–87) after the *ho-ch'in* policy had repeatedly proved
no remedy to the barbarian disease. The change can by no
means be taken as having come suddenly. As early as under
the reign of Emperor Wen, Chia I, the young political
thinker, had already severely criticized the *ho-ch'in* policy
in a long memorial, which may be partly translated as follows: 治安策

The situation of the empire may be described just like a person
hanging upside down. The Son of Heaven is the head of the empire.
Why? Because he should remain on the top. The barbarians are the
feet of the empire. Why? Because they should be placed at the bottom. Now, the Hsiung-nu are arrogant and insolent on the one
hand, and invade and plunder us on the other hand, which must be
considered as an expression of extreme disrespect toward us. And
the harm they have been doing to the empire is extremely boundless.
Yet each year Han provides them with money, silk floss and fabrics.
To command the barbarian is the power vested in the Emperor on
the top, and, to present tribute to the Son of Heaven is a ritual to be
performed by vassals at the bottom. Now the feet are put on the top
and the head at the bottom. Hanging upside down like this is something beyond comprehension. . . . In your minister's estimation, the
population of the Hsiung-nu does not exceed that of a large Chinese
hsien or district. That a great empire has come under the control of
the population of a district is something your minister feels very
much ashamed for those who are in charge of the affairs of the empire. Why doesn't Your Majesty try to employ me, your minister, as
an official in charge of the *shu-kuo* or subject states? Should your
minister's plan be adopted, your minister would be able to, on the
one hand, tie the neck of the *Shan-yü* and put his life at our mercy,
and, on the other hand, force Chung-hang Yüeh[5] to prostrate himself in order to receive flogging on his back. Moreover, the entire
Hsiung-nu people would also be made to obey only the Emperor's
order.[6]

---

[5] Chung-hang Yüeh was a Chinese eunuch who was sent to the Hsiung-
nu against his will as an escort with a Chinese princess under the reign
of Emperor Wen. Out of hatred he therefore devoted himself to the
interests of the Hsiung-nu as against those of Han China. He was very
much hated by the Chinese as a traitor. His activities may be found in
Lattimore, *op. cit.*, pp. 487–488, where his name is not given and in
Watson, 2:170–171 where his name is misread as Chung-hsing Shuo.

[6] *HS*, 48:6a–b.

Here, Chia I's criticism of the *ho-ch'in* policy probably reflects the psychology of many of his contemporaries. What is actually suggested in this memorial is no less than 1) a change from the defensive foreign policy to one of expansion by force, and 2) the replacement of the *ho-ch'in* system by the tributary system. His suggestions, however, did not receive serious consideration at the court until about one generation later.

In 135 B.C., the Hsiung-nu sent envoys to the court requesting renewal of the *ho-ch'in* agreement, on account of which a court conference was summoned by the Emperor. In that conference opinions were divided between two groups represented by Han An-kuo, the Imperial Secretary, and Wang Hui, a frontier official versed in barbarian affairs. The former vigorously defended the traditional *ho-ch'in* policy while the latter strongly urged the use of force. As Han An-kuo's opinion won the support of the majority, Emperor Wu agreed rather reluctantly to continue the *ho-ch'in* peace line. The complete break with the Hsiung-nu came in 133 as a result of another court conference, in which prolonged and hot debates between the peace and war parties finally led the Emperor to reverse his previous decision.[7] From these debates it is clear why the change to an entirely new line of foreign policy was considered necessary. Financially, the ever-increasing demand of annual "gifts" by the Hsiung-nu under the *ho-ch'in* agreement had already been no small burden for the empire. Politically, the fact that disloyal Chinese generals and other undesirable elements often sought support from, or defected to, the Hsiung-nu, presented itself as a constant threat to the Han imperial order.[8] But even at such a price there was still no prospect of securing a lasting peace. From time to time, reports of the Hsiung-nu incursions were rushed to the court from the frontiers. To pull out, once and for all, this barbarian thorn from the flesh of the

---

[7] *HS*, 52:7a–8b. For the importance of the court conference for policy discussions and decisions in Han China, see Yü-ch'üan Wang, "An Outline of the Central Government of the Former Han Dynasty," *HJAS*, pp. 173–178.

[8] Cf. Lattimore, *op. cit.*, pp. 478–480.

empire by resorting to naked force thus was believed to be the only alternative.

This change of policy toward the Hsiung-nu produced far-reaching consequences in the foreign relations of the empire. In order to separate the Hsiung-nu from the peoples in Central Asia whom they dominated and, at the same time, to seek allies for China, imperial envoys were sent to establish diplomatic relations between the Han empire and many small states in what was then known as the Western Regions. Thus began the Chinese western expansion. This expansionistic foreign policy, it may be noted, was generally carried out to the end of the Former Han period with only minor modifications.

The Later Han dynasty faced very different barbarian problems, and, therefore, had to formulate its foreign policy along different lines. The Hsiung-nu in this period were now permanently split into two groups respectively known as the Southern and Northern Hsiung-nu. The Southern Hsiung-nu meekly submitted themselves to the Chinese tributary system and lived along the imperial frontiers. Inside or on the frontiers also settled other barbarians, notably the Ch'iang, the Wu-huan, and the Hsien-pi. In short, the Later Han had to deal with a number of barbarian peoples, some of whom were within the Chinese territory. The immediate concern of the empire was not to expand further but how to embrace all of these barbarian groups into the imperial arms without disturbing the internal order. At its beginning, the founding emperor Kuang-wu's (A.D. 25–57) foreign policy is described as "closing the Yü-men Gate to reject hostages from the states of the Western Regions and humbly using words and money to entertain envoys from the Hsiung-nu." [9] Even toward the very end of his reign, he still flatly put aside a plan of his generals to launch a large-scale military expedition against the Northern Hsiung-nu. In his opinion, the empire already had enough troubles to worry about and expansion was simply out of the question.[10]

[9] *HHS*, 48:8b. For more details see *ibid.*, 118:6b and 119:1a–b.
[10] *HHS*, 48:8a.

以夷 制夷
攻夷 法夷

晁 錯

Under the general policy of a more defensive and conservative than expansionist nature, the Later Han dynasty made extensive use of the famous tactics known in Chinese history as *i-i-chih-i* or *i-i-fa-i*, "using barbarians to check barbarians" or "using barbarians to attack barbarians." This method was no Later Han innovation. It was probably first suggested to Emperor Wen by Ch'ao Ts'o (d. 155 B.C.). In a long memorial Ch'ao said that the situation of the empire was such that it was to its best advantage to use barbarians to attack barbarians. By this he meant especially to arm the surrendered Hsiung-nu as cavalrymen and incorporate them into the Chinese forces so that they could be effectively used to fight against their own tribesmen.[11] Thus, from Emperor Wu's time on, barbarian elements began to be introduced into the Han military system, notably the *shu-kuo* soldiers of the surrendered Hsiung-nu and the Hu (also Hsiung-nu) and Yueh (Southern barbarians) cavalrymen.[12]

Under the Later Han dynasty, however, this method was further refined and elaborated to meet the need arising out of a new barbarian situation. The slogan *i-i-fa-i* or "using barbarians to attack barbarians," for instance, appears in a number of the Later Han memorials.[13] Owing to the general relaxation or abolition of the military service system, especially frontier garrison duties,[14] surrendered or inner barbarians such as the Southern Hsiung-nu, the Wu-huan, and the Ch'iang were equally employed either in wars of expansion or in wars of barbarian rebellion. Toward the end of the period and in the age of the Three Kingdoms (221–265), they even played an important role in civil

---

[11] *HS*, 49:5a–b.

[12] Sun Yü-t'ang, "Hsi-Han ti ping-chih," *Chung-kuo she-hui ching-chi shih chi-k'an*, pp. 33–35. *HS*, 94A:12a–b also mentions that at one time General Li Kuang-li sent 2,000 Hsiung-nu cavalrymen of a *shu-kuo* to fight against the invading Hsiung-nu. The problem of barbarian constituents in the Han army is recently discussed in Ch'un-shu Chang, "Military Aspects of Han Wu-ti's Northern and Northwestern Campaigns," *HJAS*, 26 (1966), esp. p. 172.

[13] For instance see *HHS*, 46:4b and 119:6a.

[14] For labor and military services under the Former Han, see Lien-sheng Yang, *Studies in Chinese Institutional History*, pp. 108–116.

wars.[15] As we shall see below, this also partly explains why the Later Han government encouraged barbarians to settle down inside the Chinese territory as well as why the inner barbarians were always required to render heavy labor services to the local governments.

The meaning of *i-i-fa-i* was much broadened in scope under the Later Han. Sometimes it amounts to what we may call "divide and rule." [16] For instance, in A.D. 137, barbarians in Jih-nan (in modern Vietnam) rose in arms against the Chinese local government. In a court conference held in the following year, an official named Li Ku proposed, instead of sending Chinese forces to put down the rebellion, the use of the "divide and rule" method. According to him, the most effective and convenient device was to use money and honor to drive a wedge into the barbarians so that they would be turned to fight against each other. This proposal not only won a general acceptance at the court, but actually led to the expected results.[17] The same method was also adopted in dealing with other barbarians. On several occasions Chinese frontier officials found it effective to use money as a weapon to pulverize a Ch'iang united front and cause them to busy themselves with mutual attacks.[18] The split of the Hsiung-nu is a case too well-known to require further comment. As one memorialist put it in A.D. 88: "We are fortunate to have such an opportunity given by Heaven that the northern barbarians (i.e., the Hsiung-nu) have split into two groups and engaged in wars against each other. It is to the advantage of our state to use barbarians to attack barbarians." [19]

Moreover, very often the Later Han government also encouraged one barbarian people to attack another—a method which not only had a Former Han origin, but, interestingly enough, also found its contemporaneous west-

[15] Ho Ch'ang-ch'ün, "Tung-Han keng-i shu-i chih-tu ti fei-chih," *LSYC*, pp. 96–115.

[16] Lien-sheng Yang, *Topics in Chinese History*, p. 10.

[17] *HHS*, 116:4a–b.

[18] *HHS*, 117:5b–6a.

[19] *HHS*, 119:6a.

ern counterpart in the Roman Empire.[20] For instance,
when the Hsien-pi defeated the Northern Hsiung-nu in
A.D. 88, a Chinese official at the court applauded and con-
gratulated the Emperor for having won a war without
losing a single Chinese soldier. Of course, he fully realized the fact that this was possible only because the Hsien-
pi were greedy for the attractive imperial rewards.[21] In
the same year, it is interesting to note, the Yüeh-chih barbarians in Chang-yeh (in modern Kansu) were also under
the attack of the Ch'iang. When the former turned to the
Han court for help and protection, almost all the court
officials considered the situation rather advantageous to
China, and therefore disapproved of the idea of Chinese
intervention of any sort.[22]

Obviously, the fact that the *i-i-fa-i* policy under the
Later Han could serve the Chinese interests so admirably
must be understood against the background of a new barbarian reality of the time, which was characterized not by
the constant threat from a unified, powerful, and aggressive steppe empire, but by face-to-face confrontations with
many small and divided, but no less troublesome, barbarian groups both inside and outside the Chinese frontiers.

2 Economic and Commercial Policy

Foreign policy was closely connected with economic
policy. Change of the former often had repercussions in
the latter. Thus the reign of Emperor Wu is also known in
Chinese history for the adoption of a new economic policy
characterized particularly by the establishment of government monopolies of salt, iron, liquor etc. As clearly stated
in the famous Han work, *Yen-t'ieh lun:*

> When the Hsiung-nu rebelled against our authority and fre-
> quently raided and devastated the frontier settlements, to be con-
> stantly on watch for them was a great strain upon the soldiery of the
> Middle Kingdom; but without measures of precaution being taken,
> these forays and depredations would never cease. The late emperor

---

[20] Cf. Camila Trevor, *Excavations in Northern Mongolia,* pp. 16–17.
[21] *HHS,* 71:8a.
[22] *HHS,* 46:4b.

(i.e., Emperor Wu), grieving at the long suffering of the denizens of the marches who live in fear of capture by the barbarians, caused consequently forts and signal stations to be built, where garrisons were held ready against the nomads. When the revenue for the defence of the frontier fell short, the salt and iron monopoly was established, the liquor excise and system of equable marketing introduced; goods were multiplied and wealth increased so as to furnish the frontier expenses.[23]

This connection is also emphasized in the *Han Shu*:[24]

Gifts were sent as far as over ten thousand *li* to the states in the Western Regions; and the costs involved in the military expeditions against the Hsiung-nu were beyond calculation. When it eventually came to the point that expenditure was deficient, the government therefore established monopoly of liquor, salt, and iron, cast white metal as money,[25] made leather money,[26] collected taxes on carts and boats,[27] and even levied impositions on domestic animals.[28]

The economic policy of the Former Han period has been noted for its emphasis on agriculture as the fundamental occupation, on the one hand, and its corresponding disregard for commercial and industrial pursuits as of only secondary importance, on the other hand. Within the domain of non-agricultural economic activities, the underlying principle of the policy, especially under the reign of Emperor Wu, was that the government should control all the important productions and put commerce under regulation.[29] At first glance it appears as if the Former Han policy were extremely unfavorable to the merchants. But this was much more apparent than real. Not only were the general economic conditions conducive to the growth of trade, but the law itself was no sooner established than it was relaxed. Evidence tends to show that in spite of such a

---

[23] *Yen-t'ieh lun,* p. 1. English translation by Esson M. Gale, *Discourses on Salt and Iron,* pp. 3–4.
[24] Pan Ku's remark in *HS,* 96B:10b.
[25] This 'white metal' was an alloy of silver and tin. See Lien-sheng Yang, *Money and Credit in China,* p. 42.
[26] *P'i-pi* refers to the "white deerskin money." Cf. Yang, *ibid.,* p. 51.
[27] Cf. Nancy Lee Swann, *Food and Money in Ancient China,* pp. 279–280.
[28] Cf. Dubs, *op. cit.,* 2:167, n. 7.1; Li Chien-nung, *Hsien-Ch'in Liang-Han ching-chi shih kao,* pp. 250–251.
[29] Cf. Li Chien-nung, pp. 271–276.

policy, trade, both domestic and foreign, never ceased to grow throughout the period.[30]

If the Former Han policy was not so harmful to the merchants, the general economic policy of the Later Han may even be considered as favorable to the development of trade. This is certainly not too surprising when we bear in mind the fact that Emperor Kuang-wu's success in eliminating all the other power contenders in the early stage of his imperial career owed much to the support, not only of the intellectual-landlord class in general, but also of some rich and powerful merchant families.[31] This background probably explains why no significant restrictions were made on the merchant class under Kuang-wu's reign.[32]

---

[30] Legal restrictions on the merchant class were, on the one hand, loosened after the death of Emperor Kao-tsu (Swann, p. 231) and, on the other hand, were actually defied by the early Han society (*ibid.*, p. 166). On how the Han policy may have affected the merchants and the development of commerce see, however, Ku Chi-kuang, "Chan-kuo Ch'in-Han chien chung-nung ch'ing-shang chih li-lun yü shih-chi," *Chung-kuo she-hui ching-chi shih chi-k'an*, esp. pp. 13–17.

[31] Yü Ying-shih, "Tung-Han cheng-ch'üan chih chien-li yü shih-tsu ta-hsing chih kuan-hsi," *Hsin-Ya hsüeh-pao*, p. 240.

[32] The well-known regulation under the Later Han which prohibited one person from engaging in "two occupations" (*erh-yeh*) at the same time was probably introduced sometime in the early years of Emperor Ming's reign (58–75) rather than in Kuang-wu's time. It is true that Huan T'an memorialized between 26 and 30 to Emperor Kuang-wu, suggesting the prohibition of practising two occupations by the same person, but Huan's biography in the *Hou Han Shu* says that the emperor took no heed of Huan's words (58A:1b–2a). (For an excellent annotated English translation of the entire biography of Huan T'an, see Timoteus Pokora, "The Life of Huan T'an," *Archiv Orientalni*, pp. 16–35. The memorial mentioned above may be found on pp. 23–29.) This regulation has been generally understood as being intended to prevent the merchants from encroaching on the lands of the poor, which is probably the case. But it may be pointed out that Li Hsien, the commentator of the *Hou Han Shu*, seems to have understood the term *erh-yeh* somewhat differently. According to him, it means "those who are engaged in agriculture are not allowed to pursue trade" (69:5a). Of course, we can assume that the law would probably also apply vice versa, but even so there is already a difference in emphasis.

Moreover, almost as soon as the regulation was put into effect, it turned out to be something harmful to the poor peasants rather than to the merchants. Sometime after A.D. 68, Liu Pan memorialized to Emperor Ming reporting that because of the misapplication of the regulation by the local authorities, poor peasants were barred from fishing, which added

The commercial policy of the Later Han dynasty, if any, may be legitimately labelled laissez-faire. The founding emperor simply refused to do anything to check the activities of the aggressive merchants of his time.[33] Later emperors were also on the whole lenient with them. Sometimes the emperor even wanted the officials to see to it that regulations should not be enforced so strictly as to hinder their normal economic activities.[34]

The loosening of government restrictions over the merchants in the Later Han period may further be seen in the change of the government monopoly system. The centralized monopoly of salt and iron of the preceding age was not reintroduced with the founding of the dynasty. Instead, a localized system was adopted later. The *Hou Han Shu* says: "Salt and iron officials of various provinces and principalities originally were under the control of the *Ssu-nung* or Ministry of Agriculture in the central government, but after the Restoration they were all made officials of the *chün* and *hsien* local governments." [35] This system

---

much to their hardship. Liu, therefore proposed the repeal of the law, which was in turn approved by the emperor (*HHS*, 69:5a). Probably as a result of the removal, or at least relaxation, of this prohibition, concurrent engagement in trade became almost a general practice among the rich landlords. It has been shown that these landlords were actively involved in commercial pursuits nine months out of a year. (See Yang Lien-sheng, "Tung-Han ti hao-tsu," *CHHP*, 11:4 (1936), pp. 1028–1029.) Hu Chi-ch'uang, *Chung-kuo ching-chi ssu-hsiang shih*, vol. 2, pp. 188–191, misinterprets the term *erh-yeh* as referring to any two occupations. This is probably due to his misunderstanding of a sentence in Huan T'an's memorial which reads, "Emperors of earlier times prohibited the practising of two occupations by the same person and forbade traders and merchants to serve as officials." (*HHS*, 58A:2a; Pokora, pp. 26–27.) Hu seems to have taken the barring of the merchants from office as an illustration of the prohibition of people practising two occupations at the same time, but in fact they refer to two different regulations. The so-called *erh-yeh* was very strict in meaning, referring to agriculture and trade respectively. This explains why Liu Pan argued forcefully in his memorial that fishery should not be considered as having anything to do with "two occupations." Li Chien-nung (p. 288) has understood the term correctly, but erred in saying that Liu Pan memorialized in Emperor Chang's time (76–88).

[33] *HHS*, 58A:2a.
[34] See, for instance, the imperial edict of A.D. 99 in *HHS*, 4:6a.
[35] *HHS*, 36:1b.

is further explained elsewhere as follows: "In those *chün* and *hsien* where a large quantity of salt is produced, a salt official is to be established to take charge of the salt gabelle; and [in those *chün* and *hsien*] where a large quantity of iron is produced, an iron official is to be established to take charge of iron casting." [36] Even this localized system, it must be noted, existed only for several short intervals rather than throughout the period. Discussion of its establishment began in A.D. 81,[37] but no action was taken until sometime in the Yüan-ho (84–86) period.[38] It is, however, interesting to add that no sooner had Emperor Chang (76–88) adopted the system than he regretted it. In 88 his successor, Emperor Ho, issued an edict which read:

> Our former Emperor (i.e., Emperor Chang) . . . again restored the salt and iron monopolies from the consideration of meeting unexpected expenditure as well as of stabilizing the frontiers. Unfortunately, officials in charge of the matter were mostly bad and whatever they did the system was invariably deprived of its advantages, contrary to the will of the Emperor. The former Emperor therefore strongly disliked it and in his posthumous instructions he ordered the abolition of salt and iron monopolies of the various provinces and principalities. The people should be given freedom to engage in salt production and iron casting and pay taxes to the Emperor, as in former cases.[39]

From this edict at least three important points bearing on our discussion may be stressed: First, the phrase "as in former cases" (*ju ku-shih*) indicates that under both Emperors Kuang-wu and Ming (58–75), salt and iron production had been open to private competition. Second, the establishment of the localized monopoly system on a na-

---

[36] *HHS*, 38:4a. For a general picture of the geographical distribution of the localized salt and iron monopolies, see Yen Keng-wang, *Chung-kuo ti-fang hsing-cheng chih-tu shih, shang-pien*, 1:195–202.

[37] *HHS*, 66:3b.

[38] *HHS*, 73:2a. Ma Tuan-lin's *Wen-hsien t'ung-k'ao* is mistaken in assuming that the system was set up earlier in Emperor Ming's time (*T'u-shu chi-ch'eng* edition, 15:3b). On this point see Su Ch'eng-chien, *Hou-Han shih-huo chih ch'ang-pien*, pp. 86–87. Hu Chi-ch'uang, however, believes that the system was adopted sometime between 81 and 83 (p. 226, n. 37).

[39] *HHS*, 4:1b.

tional scale under Emperor Chang lasted altogether no more than eight years (81–88). Of course, it is possible that partial revival of the system may have been made in later times, but such reestablishments, if ever, were probably of no important consequences as can be judged by the almost complete silence of history on this matter.[40] Third, "the people" to whom freedom to engage in salt and iron production was given consisted mostly, if not entirely, of merchants. Obviously, not any ordinary person could participate in this kind of private competition which required both capital and technological knowledge. Under such a liberal and encouraging economic policy, it is certainly no wonder should the merchants have become more acquisitive and aggressive than ever before in Han China.

3 Agricultural and Industrial Resources

With the unification of China under the Han dynasty, agriculture also entered into a new era, owing largely to the extensive use of iron implements. It has been archaeologically established that new and more effective agricultural implements of iron had been in the process of invention throughout the Han period. Wide utilization of ox-drawn ploughs capable of turning up soil deeply has now been amply verified by archaeological excavations. Other newly-invented or -improved tools of the time have also been continuously coming to light.[41] Moreover, the spread of new agricultural implements and new methods of land cultivation was further facilitated by the Han policy of appointing experts to teach people how to use them.[42] It was especially characteristic of the *hsün-li* or Confucian-type model officials of the Han times to introduce such new implements and methods to the underde-

---

[40] See Yen Keng-wang, 1:195–196; Su Ch'eng-chien, pp. 87–88. Cf. also *Tung-Han hui-yao*, *WYWK* edition, p. 338.

[41] *HCKTKKSH*, pp. 75–76; Wang Chung-shu, "Han-tai wu-chih wen-hua lüeh-shuo," *KKTH*, pp. 57–58.

[42] Two famous Former Han agriculturalists were Chao Kuo and Fan Sheng-chih. Cf. Li Chien-nung, pp. 155–158. On Chao Kuo's contribution, see Swann, pp. 184–191. On Fan Sheng-chih, see Lien-sheng Yang, *Studies in Chinese Institutional History*, p. 182.

veloped frontier areas, thus contributing directly to the economic and cultural expansion of China.[43]

Irrigation systems were also taken good care of by various local governments, especially under the Later Han dynasty. Traces of water constructions of the period have been discovered in many places. One of the most important of such recent discoveries is that of Shou-hsien, Anhwei, which was a work initiated by the local government of Lu-chiang province in the late first century A.D. It has been suggested that the work was possibly completed under the supervision of one of the best-known hydraulic engineers in Chinese history, Wang Ching, who served as the governor of Lu-chiang during Emperor Chang's reign.[44] Improvement of irrigation systems may also have been facilitated by the use of iron. For instance, in North China irrigation relied very much on wells. It was probably the use of iron tools that made the digging of large numbers of wells possible.[45]

Such technological advances must have generally enhanced agricultural productivity in China, especially from Emperor Wu's time on.[46] Opening up of more wastelands for cultivation and repeated abundance of harvests are actually reported as having characterized the reigns of both Emperors Chao and Hsüan (86–49 B.C.).[47] Archaeology further shows that the Han farmers cultivated a great variety of crops including rice, barley, wheat, millet and soy beans.[48] Some of these products, such as millet and rice, it is important to bear in mind, were very much in demand by the Hsiung-nu.[49]

Of all Han industrial products, silk was far more famous

---

[43] For a few Later Han examples, see Hisayuki Miyakawa, "The Confucianization of South China," *The Confucian Persuasion*, pp. 30–31.

[44] *HCKTKKSH*, p. 77; Yin Ti-fei's article in *Wen Wu*, pp. 61–62. On Wang Ching see *HHS*, 106:3a–4a.

[45] Wang Chung-shu, *op. cit.*, p. 58.

[46] *HCKTKKSH*, p. 77.

[47] Swann, p. 191.

[48] See the article by Huang Shih-pin in *KKTH* (1958:1), pp. 36–41.

[49] For instance see *HS*, 94A:12b; A. Wylie, "History of Heung-noo in Their Relation with China," *The Journal of the Royal Anthropological Institute*, 3:3, p. 440.

than anything else as an export article. The silk textile industry was not only an important government business but also a favored private enterprise. Under the Former Han dynasty, the central government established two workshops for the weaving of silk fabrics, respectively known as *Tung Chih-shih* and *Hsi Chih-shih* or East Weaving Chamber and West Weaving Chamber. In 25 B.C., however, the East Weaving Chamber was closed down because of expenses and the name of the West Weaving Chamber was accordingly changed to *Chih-shih* or Weaving Chamber.[50] A similar workshop was maintained under the Later Han.[51] In the provinces where sericulture was well developed, large-scale local workshops were also founded to manufacture silks by the government. The most famous of such provincial factories were those of the Ch'i (Shantung) area. In Emperor Yüan's time (48–31 B.C.) it was reported that government workshops for making imperial silk clothes in Ch'i employed several thousand workers each season, which cost the government annually several tens of thousands cash. On the other hand, the same report also reveals that the two Weaving Chambers in the capital were maintained at the cost of some fifty million cash each year.[52]

Apart from Shantung, Szechwan was another center of silk production. The *chin* or silk brocade of Szechwan later won a nationwide reputation, especially during the period of Three Kingdoms.[53] It is not known whether there were local government workshops.[54] Nevertheless, textile industry as a private household business was highly developed in Szechwan at the beginning of the Later Han dy-

---

[50] *HS*, 19A:4b. It may be noted that in the early years of the Former Han when the capital was still in Lo-yang, there had already existed a Weaving Chamber. *HS*, 97A:3a and Ying Shao, *Feng-su t'ung-i, SPTK* edition, 2:9a.

[51] *HHS*, 36:5a.

[52] *HS*, 72:5b.

[53] *HHS*, 112B:7b.

[54] Another place famous for silk brocades was Hsiang-i, Ch'en-liu (in Honan) where government workshops are known to have existed (*HS*, 28A:9a). See also Ch'en Chih, *Liang-Han ching-chi shih-liao lun-ts'ung*, p. 82.

nasty.[55] This industry, it may be conjectured, consisted
not only of the manufacturing of cloths (hemp or linen),
for which Szechwan was particularly known in Former
Han times,[56] but also of silk fabrics.

Lacquer work was another important export article of
the time.[57] Archaeologically it has a wide distribution
ranging, for instance, from Lo-lang in modern North
Korea [58] to Noin-ula in Northern Mongolia.[59] In terms
of technology, archaeologists are even of the opinion that
lacquer manufacturing reached the stage of perfection under the Han dynasty.[60] Both Szechwan and Honan were
then the regions where lac trees grew and thus naturally
developed into centers of the trade. In Szechwan alone
three government workshops partly produced lacquer
wares. Altogether there were no less than ten such workshops in the empire.[61] Of the lacquers excavated thus far,
many bear inscriptions but more do not. The uninscribed
ones, it has been suggested, probably came not from the
government workshops, but were manufactured under
private enterprise.[62]

Iron manufacturing was by far the most important
sector in the Han industry. It not only indirectly accelerated agricultural development, but also directly strengthened the military power of the empire. Archaeology has
amply shown that even in the early years of the Former
Han, iron weapons had already begun to replace bronze
ones to a rather astonishing extent.[63] And this Chinese
military superiority, it may be further noted, was clearly

[55] HHS, 43:7b.

[56] Yen-t'ieh lun, p. 3; Gale, p. 11.

[57] For a Western account of lacquer in ancient China, see O. Mänchen-
Helfen, "Zur Geschichte der Lackkunst in China," Wiener Beiträge zur
Kunst- und Kultur- Geschichte Asiens, pp. 32–64.

[58] Harada Yoshito and Tawaza Kingo, Lo-Lang, pp. 36–49.

[59] Trevor, pp. 47–48; Umehara Sueji, Mōko Noin-Ura hakken no ibutsu,
pp. 28–34.

[60] Wang Chung-shu, op. cit., p. 60.

[61] Ch'en Chih, op. cit., pp. 97–98.

[62] William Willetts, Chinese Art, 1:193.

[63] HCKTKKSH, p. 78.

understood by the contemporary strategists [64] and thus provided the empire with a strong basis for expansion.

Han China was resourceful with iron. After the adoption of the monopoly system by Emperor Wu, government iron workshops were established in no less than forty provinces.[65] Instances seem to show that the number of workers in a Han iron workshop varied from a few hundred to a thousand.[66] As in other public works, manpower of government workshops normally came from two sources: conscripts and convicts.[67] This was especially the case with iron workers. As the *Yen-t'ieh lun* says, "Both conscripts and convicts receive food and clothing from the government and they make and mould iron implements in great plenty to meet the need." [68]

In the last decade, quite a number of iron workshop sites of Han date have been found, of which some are of considerable size possessing as many as twenty furnaces.[69] One large iron workshop was excavated at Nan-yang, Honan, which is the old site of the Han city of Wan.[70]

---

[64] For instance see *HS*, 49:5a–b.

[65] Ch'en Chih, *op. cit.*, p. 116; Li Chien-nung, pp. 170–171. As for the total number of iron workshops in Han China, Ch'en gives 50 while Li gives 44. Actually both are incorrect. The correct number should be 48 as enumerated in Yen Keng-wang, 1:198–202.

[66] The number of iron workers can be seen from the following instances: in 22 B.C. a group of 180 workers in a government iron workshop at Ying-ch'uan (in Honan) rose in arms (*HS*, 10:4a; Dubs, *op. cit.*, 2:391) and in 13 B.C. another group of 228 iron workers started a revolt at Shan-yang (in Shantung), which later affected altogether nineteen provinces (*HS*, 10:6a; Dubs, *op. cit.*, 2:406–407). According to Ch'en Chih, *op. cit.*, pp. 117–118, however, a large Han iron workshop probably needed more than a thousand men to take care of its production. For government iron workers and their revolts in Han China, see Chang Cheng-lang, "Han-tai ti t'ieh-kuan t'u," *Li-shih chiao-hsüeh*, pp. 17–22.

[67] Lien-sheng Yang, *Les aspects économiques des travaux publics dans la Chine impériale*, pp. 19–21.

[68] *Yen-t'ieh lun*, p. 10. Gale's translation (p. 34) is not exactly followed because it not only fails to distinguish *tsu* (conscripts) from *t'u* (convicts) but also misrenders the term *hsien-kuan*, or government, as district magistrates.

[69] *HCKTKKSH*, pp. 77–79.

[70] "Nan-yang Han-tai t'ieh-kung-ch'ang fa-chüeh chien-pao," *Wen-wu* (1960:1).

This discovery completely confirms the historical records that the Han government had established iron factories there.[71] On the other hand, private operations in iron industry also occasionally existed. Before the creation of the monopoly system, a private iron worshop could employ even as many as over one thousand workers.[72] At the beginning of the Later Han, due to the relaxation of the monopoly system, private iron manufacturing is reported to have been in operation at least in some areas.[73]

Along with iron, copper was still used extensively and often for the same purposes, as was the case in late medieval Western Europe.[74] Although copper continued to render services to the daily life of the Chinese in this period,[75] it was, nevertheless, mainly used to make large quantities of mirrors and coins.[76] Studies of the existing Han bronze vessels show that in the Former Han times the area of modern Anhwei and Kiangsu was known for its resourcefulness with copper ores, whereas under the Later Han, Szechwan became famous for copper mining.[77] For the making of bronze articles, especially mirrors, the government also established workshops both at the capital and in various localities. At the capital, such workshops fell under the control of two offices known as *Shang-fang* and *K'ao-kung* respectively, both belonging to the *Shao-fu* or Small Treasury. It was, however, the *Shang-fang*, the Imperial Workshop, that particularly produced refined bronze mirrors and many of the Han mirror inscriptions begin with the name of that office.[78] As for the local workshops, they were as a rule set up in places where rich copper ores were found.[79] Since the bronze industry was not a

---

[71] *HS*, 28A:10b.
[72] *Yen-t'ieh lun*, p. 11; Gale, p. 35.
[73] For instance see *HHS*, 106:1b.
[74] M. M. Postan and H. J. Habakkuk, eds., *The Cambridge Economic History of Europe*, 2:434.
[75] Ch'en Chih, *op. cit.*, pp. 134–169.
[76] Wang Chung-shu, *op. cit.*, pp. 61–62, 65–67.
[77] Ch'en Chih, *op. cit.*, pp. 241–245.
[78] For examples, see *CHHW*, 97:9b–10b.
[79] For instance, Tan-yang (in Anhui) is reported to have had government factories for manufacturing bronze wares (*HS*, 28A:16b), which probably

state monopoly, a list of government workshops would probably be far from complete. One Later Han workshop at Wu-tu (in southern Kansu), for example, is mentioned, not in the *Hou Han Shu,* but in a stone inscription.[80]

Concerning the Han bronze mirrors, a favorite commodity in the market of the day both at home and abroad, two interesting points may be observed. First, in terms of decorative design, the Han mirror seems to show a clear continuation of style as developed in the preceding, that is, the Ch'un-ch'iu and the Chan-kuo, periods. There is, however, an important innovation, namely, it bears inscriptions.[81] Second, from its changing inscriptions during the Han period it can be detected that the bronze mirror was increasingly becoming a popular commodity. The earlier inscriptions seem to have been more literary in flavor, which would indicate that it was a luxury of the nobility. Later on, however, they were gradually replaced by stereotyped popular expressions of blessing, which tend to point to the fact that it had found its way to the commoners. At any rate, the bronze mirror seems to have been fully transformed into a common trading article under the Later Han dynasty.[82]

In the above we have analyzed certain aspects of the agricultural and industrial developments in Han China on the basis of available historical and archaeological evidence. The analysis is necessarily selective, because emphasis has been laid on the immediate relevancy of such developments to trade and expansion of the time. Even from this incomplete picture it is clear that the productive forces of Han China were much released and the general agricultural and industrial output, accordingly, seem to have been considerably increased so as to be able to meet the vast demand of both Chinese and foreign consumers.

---

resulted from the fact that the copper there was of superior quality. Thus, some Former Han mirrors often bear the inscription "Han China has good bronze from Tan-yang." (See examples cited in Ch'en Chih, *op. cit.,* p. 242.)

[80] *CHHW,* 102:8b.

[81] Ch'en Chih, *op. cit.,* pp. 156–157.

[82] Wang Chung-shu, *op. cit.,* p. 61.

Our analysis also reveals that the Han government, apart
from controlling the salt and iron monopolies, played a
leading role in promoting practically all the major industries. In this way it created a tradition that remained characteristic of the economic structure of China until the end
of the imperial age.[83] It is very interesting to observe that
the Han local workshops were invariably established in regions which produced the raw material. In such conscious
efforts to develop industries against the geographical background of specific resources on the part of the government,
we can discern the beginning of what may be called a rudi-
mentary form of planned economy. In this respect, the
Han empire contrasts interestingly to its western counterpart, the Roman Empire. In the Roman Empire there existed a very obvious line of distinction between the various
provinces—its eastern part was the region of industry and
manufacture, and its western part the great storehouse of
raw material.[84] Finally, it must be emphatically pointed
out that it was the large number of government-controlled
workshops that furnished the Han emperor with the enormous quantity of imperial gifts made to the barbarians,
and, it was also these workshops that provided the Han
empire with a solid economic basis on which tributary
trade was carried out throughout the period.

4 Transportation System

Trade, of course, depends very much on transportation
facilities. As Max Weber has pointed out, "For the existence of commerce as an independent occupation, specific
technological conditions are prerequisite. In the first place
there must be regular and reasonably reliable transport
opportunities." [85] Although transportation systems had

---

[83] For general studies of government control of industries in imperial
China see Pai Shou-i and Wang Yü-ch'üan, "Shuo Ch'in-Han tao Ming-
mo kuan shou-kung-yeh ho feng-chien chih-tu ti kuan-hsi," *LSYC*, pp.
63–98, also reprinted in Pai Shou-i, *Hsüeh-pu chi*, pp. 35–73; T'ang
Chang-ju, *Wei-Chin Nan-pei Ch'ao shih lun-ts'ung hsü-pien*, pp. 29–92.
[84] M. P. Charlesworth, *Trade-Routes and Commerce of the Roman Empire*, p. 237.
[85] Max Weber, *General Economic History*, p. 199.

already been considerably developed in ancient China prior to the unification in 221 B.C.,[86] it was under the Ch'in and Han dynasties that large-scale road construction projects were executed with vigor and enthusiasm. As a result, there came into existence in the empire an effective highway system. Under the Han, road-building activities were even more widespread. Records concerning such matters abound in both dynastic histories and stone inscriptions of the time.[87] Road construction and repair was made the responsibility of all the local governments at both provincial and district levels. Failure to take good care of the roads under his jurisdiction often made a local official subject to impeachment.[88]

Apart from land routes, water transportation was also tremendously improved. Canals were built in many areas of the empire not only for irrigation but for transportation of grain as well.[89] The famous Lin-ch'ü canal constructed under the Ch'in dynasty played a particularly important role in the overseas trade throughout the Han period. It connected the Li River of Kwangsi with the Hsiang River of Hunan and thus made it possible for foreign commodities received at P'an-yü (modern Canton) to be transported to the Yangtze River region, all by water routes.[90] As a matter of fact, all the major rivers of China such as the Yellow River in the north and the Yangtze and Huai in the south were considerably exploited by the merchants for the furtherance of trade, both domestic and foreign. Most of the commercially prosperous and industrially active cities of the time, for instance, were situated either

---

[86] See Ch'ü Shou-yüeh, "Chung-kuo ku-tai ti tao-lu," *CHHP*, pp. 143–151; Kuo Pao-chün, *Chung-kuo ch'ing-t'ung ch'i shih-tai*, pp. 144–155; Cho-yun Hsu, *Ancient China in Transition*, pp. 117–118.

[87] See examples given in Lao Kan, "Han-tai chih lu-yün yü shui-yün," *CYYY*, pp. 71–74.

[88] Sun Yü-T'ang, "Han-tai ti chiao-t'ung," *Chung-kuo she-hui ching-chi shih chi-k'an*, p. 26. For a general discussion of the construction of the imperial highway system in China after 221 B.C. see Karl A. Wittfogel, *Oriental Despotism, A Comparative Study of Total Power*, pp. 37–38.

[89] Swann, pp. 260–261.

[90] Wang Yü-hu, "Ch'in-Han ti-kuo chih ching-chi chi chiao-t'ung ti-li," *Wen-shih tsa-chih*, p. 34.

on or near these waters.[91] Traffic by sea was of course much more risky. Nevertheless, it, too, was developed to a certain extent in Han China. Transportation along the sea coast was by no means uncommon. Under the Later Han, for instance, up to A.D. 83, tributes from Chiao-chih (in modern Annam) and other neighboring provinces invariably took the unsafe sea route through the Fukien coast to Lower Yangtze, wherefrom they were then forwarded to Lo-yang.[92] Needless to say, efforts made by the Han government to improve the transportation system both on land and on water were primarily motivated by political and military considerations. But the profit-seeking merchants never failed to use public facilities to serve their private ends.

The vehicles employed in transportation must also be taken into consideration. On land, carts were most often used. Two kinds of Han carts may be distinguished: those drawn by horses and those by oxen and donkeys. The former were mostly used by the government for official purposes.[93] But, on the other hand, people of the time also had private horses of their own, sometimes even in large numbers.[94] This was especially true with people on the northern frontier who often possessed horses of good stock.[95] Although the merchants were prohibited by law to ride in horse-drawn carts under the reign of the founding emperor of the Former Han dynasty, the prohibition,

---

[91] Such as Loyang of Honan, Lin-tzu of Shantung, Han-tan of Hopei, Shou-ch'un of Anhui, Chiang-ling of Hupei, Ch'angsha and Kuei-yang of Hunan and P'an-yü of Kwangtung. See Sun Yü-t'ang, "Han-tai ti chiao-t'ung," pp. 27–28.

[92] HHS, 63:7a.

[93] The government carts were classified into four categories differing from each other in number and quality of horses. See Swann, pp. 207–208, n. 328; Hamaguchi Shigekuni, "Kandai no den," Wada Hakase koki kinen Tōyōshi ronsō (hereafter, Wada ronsō), pp. 741–751.

[94] For instance, in 119 B.C. soldiers sent to fight the Hsiung-nu brought with them 140,000 private horses (HS, 94A:9a and Yen Shih-ku's commentary; cf., also, Lü Ssu-mien, Ch'in-Han shih, 2:601). Private horses are also recorded in the newly-discovered Han documents on wood (see Ch'en Chih, op. cit., p. 38).

[95] See a famous story in the Huai-nan tzu, Che-chiang shu-chü edition, 18:8a–b.

hardly survived him.[96] But horse-drawn carts were mainly
used to carry people, not cargoes. It was rather the ox- or
donkey-drawn cart that was by far the most important
means of transportation for the merchants because of its
inexhaustible carrying capabilities.[97] In A.D. 135 the Wu-
huan barbarians held up a Chinese caravan consisting of
more than one thousand carts and oxen somewhere on the
northwestern frontier, which may be taken as sufficient
proof of the large-scale use of ox-drawn carts in frontier
trade by the Han merchants.[98] The newly-discovered Han
documents on wood also reveal that ox-drawn carts were
extensively utilized on the frontiers for a variety of purposes.[99] Instead of drawing loaded carts, animals, including donkeys, oxen, and horses sometimes also carried goods
on their back.[100] But whenever this was the case, donkeys
were always the best choice. Only recently imported to
China from Hsiung-nu, they were soon to become a
favorite animal of the Chinese, from the emperor down to
the common people.[101] As an animal, the donkey was ap-
preciated mainly for its low price, its ability to carry a
heavy load, as well as its patience in travelling long and
difficult journeys.[102]

In water, transport media of the time also fell under two
general categories: boats propelled by oars, and rafts made
of either wood or bamboo. We know comparatively little
about the art of shipbuilding in this period.[103] That it
must have been much advanced can nevertheless be inferred from the famous sea-going *lou-ch'uan* or storied

[96] Swann, p. 231.
[97] Ch'ien Ta-hsin, *Nien-erh shih k'ao-i*, 1:409–411. Cf., also, Lao Kan, *Chü-yen Han-chien, k'ao-cheng*, p. 20.
[98] *HHS*, 120:2b.
[99] See examples collected together in Lao Kan, "Han-tai chih lu-yün yü shui-yün," *CYYY*, pp. 79–80.
[100] Sun Yü-t'ang, "Han-tai ti chiao-t'ung", p. 27.
[101] For a general discussion see Ku Yen-wu, *Jih-chih lu, chi-shih* edition by Huang Ju-ch'eng, 29:2b–4a.
[102] For instance, see *HHS*, 46:4a and 52:3b; Yüan Hung, *Hou-Han Chi, SPTK* edition, 18:18b.
[103] For a brief discussion, however, see Chang Sun, *Wo-kuo ku-tai ti hai-shang chiao-t'ung*, pp. 14–16.

boat, which was built for military purposes.[104] In terms of capacity, an ordinary transport boat could be very large. In one particular case it is said that the capacity of a boat was greater than that of a cart by several tens of times.[105] Recent archaeological excavations, however, throw considerable light on the boat used in Han times. In several ports in south China, notably Canton, wooden and pottery models of ships have been found among the mortuary objects in tombs of Han date. These models clearly show that the Han ship had an anchor in the front and a helm in the rear, and that it could have had as many as sixteen oars.[106] These finds seem to fit very well with the historical account that trade by water transportation, both overseas and inland, was quite common during the Han period.[107] A word may be said about the raft. Astonishingly enough, even at a very early stage, bamboo rafts had been developed along the coast of southeastern China to the extent of being capable of deep sea navigation.[108] Down to the Han times, this primitive means of transportation, generally known under the name of fang-p'ai, was still resorted to occasionally on a fairly large scale.[109]

Along with the transportation system, Han China also provided travellers with sufficient housing facilities along the highways. Let us first take a look at the public side of the picture. As is widely known, both the Ch'in and Han dynasties maintained a highly efficient system of housing accommodation and horse stations.[110] These public services were originally reserved for official use only. As time

---

[104] Swann, pp. 298–299.

[105] SC, 118:6a. Watson's translation gives "twenty or thirty" times, 2:376.

[106] This brief summary is made on the basis of the following archaeological reports: HCKTKKSH, p. 82; KKTH (1957:4), pp. 26–27; Chung-kuo K'o-hsüeh Yuan K'ao-ku Yen-chiu So, Ch'ang-sha fa-chüeh pao-kao, pp. 154–160. For illustrations of the Han ship models see HCKTKKSH, Plates LXXIX and LXXX.

[107] See some of the data collected together in Lao Kan, "Han-tai chih lu-yün yü shui-yün," pp. 84–90.

[108] Ling Ch'un-sheng, "T'ai-wan ti hang-hai chu-fa chi ch'i ch'i-yüan," Min-tsu-hsüeh Yen-chiu So chi-k'an, 1 (1956), pp. 1–23.

[109] For examples see HHS, 46:5a and 47:8a.

[110] Wittfogel, p. 38.

went on, however, evidence tends to show that the official guest houses, variously known as *t'ing*, *t'ing-chuan* and *chuan-she*, could also be used by private itinerants.[111] In this way the *t'ing* actually performed the function of a private inn. That they must have been places frequented by merchants can be seen from the fact that markets sometimes grew in their neighborhoods.[112]

The story of private inns is a different one. The origin of the private inn is at least as old as its public counterpart. In ancient China it was known under a variety of names such as *ni-lü* or "traveller's lodge," [113] *k'o-she* or "guest house," [114] and *kuan-she* or "hostel." [115] Down to our

---

[111] Literature on *t'ing* and *chuan-she* is enormous and the problem of *t'ing* is especially controversial. Generally speaking, three kinds of *t'ing* may be distinguished in Han China. (Cf. Yen Keng-wang, *op. cit.*, 1:58–66.) For our purpose, however, only the *t'ing* that provided houses for travellers is important. This kind of *t'ing*, it may be noted, sometimes may be identified with *chuan-she*, *she* meaning house. All such *t'ing* were built along the highways and, in most cases, near cities. Private travellers could also make occasional use of the *t'ing* but were required to pay a certain amount of money to the government as rent. (See Yen Keng-wang, 1:63–64; Sun Yü-t'ang, "Han-tai ti chiao-t'ung," pp. 33–35; Lao Kan, "Han-tai ti t'ing-chih," *CYYY*, p. 138.) For more details on both *t'ing* and *chuan-she* the reader is referred to the following studies: Lao Kan, "Han-tai ti t'ing-chih," *CYYY*, pp. 129–138; Wang Yü-ch'üan, "Han-tai t'ing yü hsiang-li pu-t'ung hsing-chih pu-t'ung hsing-cheng hsi-t'ung shuo," *LSYC*, pp. 127–135; Hamaguchi Shigekuni, "Kandai no densha," *Tōyō gakuhō*, pp. 45–68; Hibino Takeo, "Kyōteiri ni tsuite no kenkyū," *Tōyōshi kenkyū*, pp. 23–42; Sogabe Shizuo, "Kandai ni okeru yū-tei haichi no kankaku ni tsuite," *Bunka*, pp. 20–26; R. A. Stein, "Remarques sur les mouvements du Taoisme politico-religieux au IIe siècle ap. J-C," *TP*, especially pp. 59–76.

[112] It is interesting to note that in one case, a local official even took part in helping the establishment of a regular fair near a *t'ing* for people's shopping convenience (*CHHW*, 101:3a). The term *t'ing-shih* or *t'ing*-market appears in a stone inscription of Later Han date (*CHHW*, 103:11b), which indicates the close connection between the *t'ing* and the market place.

[113] James Legge, tr., *The Ch'un Ts'ew with the Tso Chuen*, in *Chinese Classics*, 5, p. 136. In the *Shang-chün shu* (*WYWK* edition, p. 3), a book attributed to Lord Shang (390?–338 B.C.), *ni-lü* is also twice mentioned, which is rendered as "hostelries for the reception of travellers" by J. J. L. Duyvendak, *The Book of Lord Shang*, p. 178.

[114] *SC*, 68:5a.

[115] Ch'ü Shou-yüeh, pp. 146–147; Hamaguchi Shigekuni, "Kandai no densha," p. 55.

period, it is interesting to note that such private inns are rarely mentioned in records of the Former Han, but may be found amply in those of the Later Han. It would seem to suggest that the well-developed public housing accommodation system under the Former Han probably had left little room for the growth of private inns. What is even more interesting is the fact that the prosperity of the private inn business under the Later Han contrasted sharply to the contemporaneous decline of the government-controlled *t'ing-chuan* system.[116] The following instance particularly reveals the critical shortage of public guest houses on the one hand, and their replacement by private inns on the other hand: In A.D. 95, Ying Shen memorialized to Emperor Ho complaining that when the Accountants of all provinces came to the capital to make their annual reports, on their way they had to stay in *ni-lü* or "traveller's lodges" and *ssu-kuan* or "private hotels," and the inadequacy of conditions in these private inns was such that it often caused damages, in one way or another, to the tributary articles under their care. Ying, thereupon, proposed that public guest houses be established to accommodate these officials.[117]

Finally it is important to point out that the growing prosperity of the private inn business during the Later Han period seems to have had a close correlation with the increasingly developing trade of the time, in general. At the beginning the business was probably not very lucrative. Therefore only poor people occasionally cared to make a meager living from it.[118] In the middle of the second century when the empire enjoyed general prosperity of trade, the inn business also became profitable enough to

---

[116] In the Later Han period, the government horse stations provided official travellers with only horses but no longer carriages because of financial consideration. (Preface to *Wei hsin-lü* quoted in *Chin Shu*, T'ung-wen edition, 30:11b; cf. the discussion by Hamaguchi Shigekuni, *Wada ronsō*, p. 746.) Along with the cutting down of carriages, it has been suggested, went probably also the reduction of the number of public inns (Lao Kan, "Han-tai ti t'ing-chih," p. 138).

[117] *CHHW*, 35:1b. The same story may also be found in a commentary to the *HHS*, 35:4b, where the year is given as A.D. 98.

[118] For instance see *HHS*, 109A:6a.

attract the rich and powerful.[119] As Chung-ch'ang T'ung
(A.D. 180–?) remarked, "The powerful and rich people
[plunge themselves into] commercial pursuits. [Their]
hotels and inns spread all over the country." [120] Toward
the end of the Later Han dynasty, it may be noted as an
amusing finishing touch, private inns became in the eyes of
the contemporaries something which may be described as
"of the merchants, by the merchants, and for the merchants." In this connection, the following two lines from a
poem of Ts'ao Ts'ao (155–220) may be most fittingly
quoted to conclude this discussion:

Keep [your] traveller's lodges nicely furnished,
Traders and merchants would come for commercial intercourse.[121]

---

[119] For instance see *HHS*, 66:9a.

[120] *CHHW*, 88:5a. The political and social ideas of Chung-ch'ang T'ung
are discussed in Etienne Balazs' excellent article, "La crise sociale et la
philosophie politique à la fin des Han," *TP*, 34 (1949–1950), pp. 81–131.
For an English translation see his *Chinese Civilization and Bureaucracy*,
pp. 187–225.

[121] *Ts'ao Ts'ao chi*, p. 11.

chapter three

General Sino-Barbarian Economic Relations under the Tributary System

In the realm of foreign relations, as in many other areas, the Han dynasty marks the beginning of a new era. It was in this period that the well-known tributary system, which basically regulated Chinese foreign relations throughout the imperial age until the middle of nineteenth century,[1] fully took shape. The establishment of a system of such lasting historical value was by no means an easy task. The system went through many difficulties before it reached maturity, as the following discussion will show.

Barbarian submission was an inseparable part of the Confucian political order. It also characterized, at least in theory, what may be called *Pax Sinica*. From this point of view, the *ho-ch'in* system was probably not different from the tributary system in its ultimate objective of bringing about a general Hsiung-nu submission. Therefore, in the early part of the Former Han when there was still no clear notion as to what should be the specific components of the tributary system, several interesting schemes had been proposed by leading Confucian scholars at the court concerning how to keep the Hsiung-nu under control within the *ho-ch'in* framework. There was first the famous suggestion of the so-called "five baits" from Chia I (201–169 B.C.):

---

[1] For the last stage of the Chinese tributary system see J. K. Fairbank and S. Y. Teng, "On the Ch'ing Tributary System," *HJAS*, pp. 135–246.

To give them (i.e., the Hsiung-nu) elaborate clothes and carriages in order to corrupt their eyes; to give them fine food in order to corrupt their mouth; to give them music and women in order to corrupt their ears; to provide them with lofty buildings, granaries and slaves in order to corrupt their stomach (i.e., general desire or appetite); and, as for those who come to surrender, the emperor [should] show them favor by honoring them with an imperial reception party in which the emperor should personally serve them wine and food so as to corrupt their mind. These are what may be called the five baits.[2]

Obviously, what is suggested here is no less than using the superior material culture as well as the luxurious way of life of Han China to paralyze the barbarous Hsiung-nu through the *ho-ch'in* system. That the *ho-ch'in* system must actually have had a malicious intent of this kind is fully confirmed by the following counter-proposal made to the *Shan-yü* by Chung-hang Yüeh, the Chinese traitor:

The strength of the Hsiung-nu lies in the very fact that their food and clothing are different from those of the Chinese, and they are therefore not dependent upon the Han for anything. Now the *Shan-yü* has his fondness for Chinese things and is trying to change the Hsiung-nu customs. Thus, although the Han sends no more than a fifth of its goods here, it will in the end succeed in winning over the whole Hsiung-nu nation. From now on, when you get any of the Han silks, put them on and try riding around on your horses through the brush and brambles! In no times your robes and leggings will be torn to shreds and everyone will be able to see that silks are no match for the utility and excellence of felt or leather garments. Likewise, when you get any of the Han foodstuffs, throw them away so that the people can see that they are not as practical or as tasty as milk and kumiss! [3]

Thus, both sides were equally aware of what was really behind the *ho-ch'in* system. Its very fruit for the Hsiung-nu—Han gifts of silk and grain, sweet as it tasted, was nevertheless poisonous. Unfortunately, at this time the Hsiung-nu were already too much intoxicated by the Han goods to be able to take Chung-hang Yüeh's advice. And even Chung-

[2] As quoted in Yen Shih-ku's commentary to the *HS*, 48:13a. A much longer but very difficult version may be found in Chia I, *Hsin shu, Ssu-pu pei-yao* edition, 4:2b–4b.

[3] *SC*, 110:8a; translation by Burton Watson, *Records of the Grand Historian of China*, 2:170.

hang Yüeh himself eventually realized that the best service he could render to his barbarian master was no more than asking the Han to bring to the Hsiung-nu silks and grain-stuffs of the right measure and quality.[4]

On the other hand, Han China's dissatisfaction with the *ho-ch'in* system was of a different kind. The increasing amount of annual payments made to the Hsiung-nu was not used of course entirely in vain. But, without other measures of check, it simply failed to have the effect ex-pected, or, sometimes even served only to stimulate the Hsiung-nu's appetite. It was probably out of this sort of consideration that Tung Chung-shu (179?–104? B.C.), the arch-Confucianist of Han times, proposed to Emperor Wu his scheme to improve the *ho-ch'in* system. According to him, sense of propriety could touch the *chün-tzu*, or man of principles, but, as for the greedy people like the Hsiung-nu, they could only be delighted by material gains. Tung, therefore, did not hesitate to urge the court to increase the annual payments as the Hsiung-nu requested. He was nevertheless practical enough to add that in doing so China should, at the same time, conclude a treaty with the Hsiung-nu by taking together a solemn oath before Heaven. Moreover, in order to make sure that the Hsiung-nu would observe the treaty, Han must require the *Shan-yü* to send a son to China as hostage. Thus, through triple bondages—economic, religious, and personal—it was calcu-lated that the Hsiung-nu would be forced to submit them-selves to the Han rule under the *ho-ch'in* system.[5]

Both Chia and Tung's suggestions as discussed above must not be taken merely as empty words of individual scholars. As a matter of fact, they were not only more or less embodied in the *ho-ch'in* system, but also contributed particularly to the formation of the tributary system in later days. For instance, the use of Han goods as an eco-nomic weapon was fully incorporated into the tributary system whereas the taking of a hostage from the barbarians also turned out to be an important symbol of the tributary

---

[4] *SC*, 110:8b; Watson, 2:172.
[5] *HS*, 94B:12b

submission. From a dynamic angle, the whole development from the *ho-ch'in* system to the tributary system may be viewed as a continuous quest on the part of the Han empire, for a proper form in which Sino-barbarian relations could be regulated in keeping with the general imperial order. Chia I's idea of taming the Hsiung-nu through the use of the superior Han material culture is certainly ingenious. Being devoid of a proper form, however, it could hardly function in an institutional vacuum. Tung Chung-shu, on the other hand, came much closer to the problem of form. And yet religious and personal ties alone were still too feeble to serve as an institutional basis on which the economic weapon of Han China could exert its utility to the utmost to bring about the desired barbarian submission. The superiority of the tributary system over its *ho-ch'in* predecessor, from the point of view of the Han court, lay primarily in the fact that the former, and only the former, could *politically* fit the various neighboring barbarians into the Chinese imperial order. Thus considered, the tributary system, as was applied to the barbarians in Han times, may be legitimately understood as no less than a logical extension of the Han imperial system to the realm of foreign relations. This dominant political feature of the system, it must be emphatically pointed out, is of vital importance to our understanding of Sino-barbarian economic relations in Han China. It explains, for example, why the ever-increasing demand for Chinese gifts on the part of the Hsiung-nu was considered unbearable by the court under the earlier *ho-ch'in* system, but acceptable, undesirable notwithstanding, under the later tributary system. It also explains why barbarians in Han China were differentiated into various categories and received different treatment according to their respective political status.

Under the tributary system, Sino-barbarian economic intercourse took two main forms: the exchange of "tributary products" and "imperial gifts," and normal trade both legal and contraband. Although in a broad sense both forms can be taken as trade, it is nevertheless desirable to distinguish the one from the other for the purpose of analysis. Therefore, I shall confine the discussion in this chapter to the general tribute-gift exchange to the exclusion of normal trade, which will be taken up later.

1 The Hsiung-nu

Almost throughout the Former Han period the Hsiung-nu on the northern border were a constant source of trouble for the Chinese people. Aggressiveness and even, indeed, avariciousness, as the Chinese characterizations of the Hsiung-nu go, cannot, however, be simply understood as inherent in their very barbarian nature. Such characteristics had their roots deep in the Hsiung-nu's cultural and economic backgrounds. The following passage from the *Discourses on Salt and Iron* gives us a general picture of the Hsiung-nu's life: "The Hsiung-nu live in the desert and grow in the land which produces no food. [They are the people who] are abandoned by Heaven for being good-for-nothing. They have no houses to shelter themselves, and make no distinction between men and women. They take the entire wilderness as their villages and the *ch'iung-lu* tents [6] their homes. They wear animal's skins, eat meat raw and drink blood.[7] They wander to meet in order to exchange goods and stay [for a while] in order to herd cattle." [8]

---

[6] For a detailed study of the *ch'iung-lu* tent see Egami Namio, *Yūrashiya kodai hoppō bunka*, pp. 39–79; an excellent recent discussion of the Hsiung-nu huts based on new archaeological finds may be found in Serg Ivanovich Rudenko, *Kul'tura khunnov i noinulinskie kurgany*, pp. 30–31.

[7] Egami Namio, pp. 81–121.

[8] *Yen-t'ieh lun*, p. 70. Not translated in Esson M. Gale, *Discourses on Salt and Iron*. This description of the Hsiung-nu's life is generally true and reliable, and agrees with other sources of the time including both the *Shih Chi* and the *Han Shu*. In another place the *Yen-t'ieh lun* further reports that the Hsiung-nu had no walled cities, nor did they have granaries for grain storage (p. 91). The *Shih Chi* also says that the Hsiung-nu "move and migrate following water and grass and have no walled cities, places for permanent settlement or agriculture" (110:1b); (Watson, 2:155). Lack of cities and granaries was probably characteristic of the earlier life of the Hsiung-nu when their nomadism was in its full swing. Later on, probably due to the Chinese influence, it seems that they also began to build cities. Lattimore is right when he says "Certainly the later Hsiung-nu Khans had a capital that was undoubtedly a city"

Economic dependence seems to have been always the main cause for Hsiung-nu's frontier raids as well as wars of conquest. As a Japanese expert has pointed out, the Hsiung-nu economy relied on three things apart from pastoral industry: exactions from conquered peoples, gifts or tributes from friendly states, and trade with foreign countries.[9] With the possible exception of the last one, the rest obviously entailed the use of force in greater or lesser degrees. Han China's early economic relations with the Hsiung-nu fall mainly into the second category: China sent annual tribute (which the Han court called "gifts") to the Hsiung-nu in order to buy border peace. The first peace agreement, under the name of *ho-ch'in*, was reached between China and the Hsiung-nu in the year 198 B.C.[10] Although as a general policy line it was followed by the Han court until 133 B.C., the details did not always remain the same. As time went by, the Hsiung-nu required China to make more and more concessions, especially in economic terms. The original peace agreement contained the following items:

a. A Chinese princess to be married to the *Shan-yü*.
b. Chinese annual payments to be made to the Hsiung-nu, including silk, wine, rice, and other kinds of food, each in fixed amounts.
c. The Han and Hsiung-nu to be equal ("brotherly") states.[11]

(*Inner Asian Frontier of China*, p. 524). Actually the *Han Shu* already tells us a story of how a surrendered Chinese suggested to the Hsiung-nu that they erect walled cities for defense and construct towers for grain storage (94A:13b). And another surrendered Chinese, by the name of Chao Hsin, also built a city for the Hsiung-nu (*SC*, 110:12b). Modern archaeological excavations have shown conclusively that the Hsiung-nu had cities of their own. Several of their cities have been unearthed by Russian archaeologists in Outer Mongolia. The Hsiung-nu city usually consisted of walls and four gates and within the walls the buildings, sometimes including a palace, were modelled on the Han Chinese style, covered with even typical Han tiles. (Chinese translation in *Shih-hsüeh i-ts'ung*, 1957:6, pp. 81–82.)

[9] Egami Namio, p. 28.
[10] According to the *Tzu-chih t'ung-chien*, Ku-chi ch'u-pan she edition, 1:382–383.
[11] *SC*, 110:6b; *HS*, 94A:4b.

d. The Great Wall to be the border between the Han and the Hsiung-nu.[12]

The economic insufficiency of the Hsiung-nu is fully indicated by the fact that food and clothes constituted the main body of the annual payments, which was also true of all the later treaties.[13] Under Emperor Wen, however, the total amount of "gifts" was considerably increased, and cash (gold or coins) also formed part of the "gifts."[14] It was also in Emperor Wen's time that border trade between China and the Hsiung-nu was, for the first time, formally included as an integral part of the ho-ch'in agreement.[15] The payments were periodically augmented down to the early years of Emperor Wu's reign, and the trade further expanded in the Hsiung-nu's favor.[16] The ever-increasing economic demands of the Hsiung-nu, coupled with their ability to destroy the peace along the border, must have precipitated the decision of the Chinese court to abandon the ho-ch'in policy and substitute punitive expeditions. At any rate, it seems quite obvious that all important court discussions with regard to the Hsiung-nu policy that took place under the reigns of Emperors Wen and Wu respectively resulted from new requests from the Hsiung-nu for more "gifts" or trade.[17] Under the ho-ch'in policy, economic intercourse between the Han court and the Hsiung-nu was rather a one-way traffic. The annual imperial gifts were normally not matched by barbarian tribute. Only occasionally did the Hsiung-nu present to the Chinese emperor one or two camels or horses,[18] merely as a token of "friendship." In reality, the ho-ch'in policy had turned the Chinese tributary system in reverse. As shown in Chia I's

---

[12] SC, 110:9a–b; HS, 94A:7a.
[13] See the interesting statement of Chung-hang Yueh in SC, 110:8a and HS, 94A:6a. Cf., also, Lattimore, op. cit., pp. 487–488.
[14] The term chin (gold or copper coins) is first mentioned in Emperor Wen's letter to the Shan-yü of the Hsiung-nu, SC, 110:9b; HS 94A:7a.
[15] This point is clear only when we read the tsan or "remarks" made by Pan Ku at the end of the Hsiung-nu section, HS, 94B:12b.
[16] SC, 110:10a; HS, 94A:7b.
[17] For instance, see HS, 94A:5a, 9a.
[18] For instance, see SC, 110:7a; HS, 94A:5b, 7a.

memorial cited in Chapter II, by annually sending cash and silken fabrics to the Hsiung-nu the Han Empire was playing the role of a tributary state to the barbarians. The most important concern of the Han court was, herefore, how to put an end to the *ho-ch'in* relations, and to bring the Hsiung-nu into the framework of a Chinese-dominated tributary system. This, however, was possible only after the Hsiung-nu were militarily much weakened and economically more dependent on Chinese aid.

The transformation from *ho-ch'in* relations to tributary relations involved several radical changes. First, China required a hostage prince from the Hsiung-nu as a surety of their submission. Second, the *Shan-yü*, or some Hsiung-nu nobles representing him, should come to China to pay homage. Third, the Hsiung-nu should send tribute to China to return the favor of the imperial gifts. The first two conditions, hostage and homage, proved to be the most insoluble difficulties of several abortive peace negotiations after the complete break between the two parties. The problem of the hostage was particularly acute.[19] In 107 B.C., after having heavily defeated the Hsiung-nu, Emperor Wu sent Yang Hsin to negotiate peace with the *Shan-yü* on the condition that the latter should send his heir-apparent to the Chinese court as a hostage. The negotiation yielded no result at all because the *Shan-yü* was still talking in the outdated *ho-ch'in* terms and flatly rejected the idea of sending a hostage on the ground that it did not accord with any of the former agreements.[20] The "homage" controversy equally stood in the way of fruitful negotiations. Sometime in 119 B.C., the Hsiung-nu, newly defeated and badly in need of Chinese supplies, requested China, in softened language, to renew the former *ho-ch'in* agreement. The Emperor called a court conference to discuss the matter. In that conference one group of officials favored the resumption of the *ho-ch'in* relations while the other group, presumably the majority, insisted that China

---

[19] On hostage see Lien-sheng Yang, "Hostages in Chinese History," reprinted in *Studies in Chinese Institutional History*, esp. pp. 45–46.

[20] *SC*, 110:13b; *HS*, 94A:10a–b.

should take the opportunity to put the Hsiung-nu under the regulation of the tributary system. It was also necessary that the latter should come to the Chinese border, if not the court, to pay homage to the emperor. Emperor Wu's opinion was fully in line with the latter group. The *Shan-yü* was so enraged that he even kept the Chinese envoy a prisoner.[21] Later, still hoping to obtain money and goods from China, the *Shan-yü* made a false promise that he would come to China and send the heir-apparent as a hostage. The emperor was very pleased and a special house was built in Ch'ang-an to accommodate the *Shan-yü*. Neither father nor son, however, arrived because they never intended to.[22] In many ways the negotiations between China and the Hsiung-nu at this stage remind us of those between China and the Western countries in the nineteenth century. While Han China was mainly interested in placing the Hsiung-nu under the tributary system, the latter were still anxious to resume the former *ho-ch'in* relations, just as when the West was breaking into China with its sharp weapon of the treaty system, the Ch'ing court was still trying to bring the maritime barbarians in line with the old tributary relations. In both cases, it may be noted, both sides were not on speaking terms. There is, however, one important difference: in the former case it was China that prevailed over the barbarians.

The incorporation of the Hsiung-nu into the Chinese tributary system eventually took place in Emperor Hsüan's time (73–49 B.C.). After 60 B.C., the Hsiung-nu broke up into five groups and waged suicidal wars against each other. As a result, not only their military power as a whole was much weakened, but they became irretrievably divided into two larger branches in 54, one in the north and the other in the south. The southern branch in Inner Mongolia, hard pressed and defeated by the northern branch from Outer Mongolia, offered their allegiance to the Han court in 53. The decision to demote themselves from the status of China's "brotherly" state to that of a

---

[21] *SC*, 110:13a; *HS*, 94A:9b; *Tzu-chih t'ung-chien*, 2:645.
[22] *SC*, 110:14a; *HS*, 94A:10b.

tributary state was indeed a painful one to make. The Hsiung-nu nobles were mostly opposed to the idea of surrendering themselves to China. Only after prolonged hot debates did *Shan-yü* Hu-han-yeh make up his mind to accept China's terms.[23] The submission of the southern branch was partly a result of the internal power struggle of the Hsiung-nu, and partly, as we shall see, precipitated by economic considerations.

To fulfill tributary obligations, Hu-han-yeh first sent a son to Ch'ang-an, in 53 B.C., as hostage [24] and then in 51 he attended the imperial court in person, with tribute, to pay his first homage to the Han emperor. The surrender of the Hsiung-nu was by far the most important single event in the history of foreign relations of the Han period. On the one hand, it enhanced the prestige of Han China in the Western Regions to an unprecedented degree and, on the other hand, it also marked the formal establishment of tributary relations between the Hsiung-nu and Han China. This probably explains why Hu-han-yeh, the *Shan-yü* of the southern branch, was treated with unusual honors during his stay in the Han capital.[25]

Under the tributary system, economic relations between China and the Hsiung-nu began to take a new course. After a long interruption of over eighty years, Chinese gifts were again showered on the Hsiung-nu. In the very year when Hu-han-yeh was in the capital, he was given, together with a number of other things which signified honors, 20 catties of gold, 200,000 cash, 77 suits of clothes, 8,000 pieces of various kinds of silken fabrics, and 6,000 catties of silk floss. Some 34,000 *hu* of rice were forwarded to Hu-han-yeh after he returned to his homeland. The next year, Hu-han-yeh again came to the court and received an additional increase of 110 suits of clothes, 9,000 pieces of silken

---

[23] *HS*, 94B:1b–2a.

[24] According to *HS*, 8:9b, the *Shan-yü* already sent a brother to China as a hostage in 54 B.C. Since at that time there were three *Shan-yü*, it is rather difficult to identify him with Hu-han-yeh. Cf. *Tzu-chih t'ung-chien*, 2:876, esp. the *K'ao-i* and Hu San-hsing's commentary.

[25] The best single account of this event is that of the *Tzu-chih t'ung-chien*, 2:885–888.

fabrics, and 8,000 catties of silk.[26] Since we are here
concerned more with the structure of Sino-barbarian intercourse than with its detailed contents, it is unnecessary
to list all such figures.

The ways in which "gifts" were now sent to the Hsiung-
nu differed considerably from the former *ho-ch'in* policy.
Two obvious points may be made. First, Chinese "gifts"
were given, at least in theory, on a reciprocal basis. The
Hsiung-nu also presented tribute to the Chinese court each
time when their *Shan-yü* made his homage trip to China.
From the point of view of the Chinese court, however, it
was the symbolic value of submissiveness rather than the
actual economic worth of the Hsiung-nu tribute that was
important. Second, unlike the *ho-ch'in* system, Chinese
"gifts" were not sent to the Hsiung-nu annually at a fixed
amount agreed upon by both sides [27] but only upon request or when the *Shan-yü* attended the court. For instance,
in 48 B.C., Hu-han-yeh sent a written petition to Emperor
Yuan for economic aid; the latter then ordered two frontier provinces to forward 20,000 *hu* of grain to the Hsiung-
nu.[28] There was also some kind of correlation between the
frequency of the *Shan-yü*'s visits at the court and the
amount of imperial gifts.[29] That the *Shan-yü* preferred to
attend the Chinese court in person instead of sending envoys may easily be explained by the fact that this produced
many more gifts from the emperor. For instance, in 3 B.C.,
when the *Shan-yü* sent a written petition to the court expressing the desire to come to pay homage in the next year,
a court conference was held to discuss the matter. Most
ministers supported the idea of turning down the request
on the ground that the *Shan-yü*'s homage trip would cost
China too much. The emperor at first approved the deci-

[26] *HS*, 94B:2a–b.

[27] *Chin Shu*, 97:17b, however, says that the *Shan-yü* was given annual
payments including silk, money, and grain, but this information cannot
be confirmed by the extant sources of the Han period.

[28] *HS*, 94B:2b–3a.

[29] Hu-han-yeh made his last trip to Ch'ang-an in 33 B.C. (*HS*, 9:6b; 94B:
3b). He was succeeded in 31 by his son Fu-chu-lei-jo, who attended the
court in 25. In 12, another new *Shan-yü*, who succeeded Fu-chu-lei-jo in
20, requested to come to the court the next year; unfortunately, he did
not live long enough to make it (*HS*, 94B:5b).

sion of the conference but changed his mind only after Yang Hsiung memorialized against such an unfriendly attitude. In his long memorial Yang Hsiung did not deny that the homage trip exhausted much of the state treasury, but convincingly argued that its political necessity weighed far above its economic undesirability.[30] This instance seems to give us a clue as to why the Hsiung-nu always took the initiative in requesting the homage trip, as well as why China did not welcome too frequent attendance of the *Shan-yü* at the court.

The economic motive behind the *Shan-yü*'s homage trip may further be seen in the size of his retinue. The Han court limited the number normally to two hundred. In 1 B.C., however, the *Shan-yü* requested that he be allowed this time to bring with him five hundred followers, to which the emperor eventually agreed. Consequently, there was a tremendous increase of gifts that year.[31] As has been keenly observed by the Sung historian, Ssu-ma Kuang, from 49 B.C. on, each time the *Shan-yü* attended the court he received an additional increase of imperial gifts.[32] Such a trend is particularly traceable in the increase of Han gifts of various kinds of silk to the tributary Hsiung-nu:[33]

YEAR (B.C.)	SILK FLOSS (CATTIES)	SILK FABRICS (PIECES)
51	6,000	8,000
49	8,000	9,000
33	16,000	18,000
25	20,000	20,000
1	30,000	30,000

As the tabulation shows, the increase reached its peak in 1 B.C. and probably stayed at the same level in the early years

---

[30] *HS*, 94B:6b–8a.

[31] *Ibid.*, 94B:8a.

[32] *Tzu-chih t'ung-chien*, 3:1123.

[33] For instance, in 33 B.C., the gifts (including silk clothes, silken fabrics, refuse silk, etc.) for Hu-han-yeh, it is reported, increased once again as much as he received in 49 (*HS*, 94B:3b); in 25, an additional increase of 20,000 pieces of silken fabrics and 20,000 catties of refuse silk was made to the Hsiung-nu (*HS*, 94B:5b); and in 1 B.C., the number of clothes was increased to 370 suits, that of silken fabrics to 30,000 pieces, and refuse silk to 30,000 catties (*HS*, 94B:8a).

of Wang Mang's reign.[34] It must be pointed out that these are only the figures clearly recorded in the *Han Shu,* and cannot be taken as the total amount of silk given to the Hsiung-nu during this period. It is not likely that every such payment is recorded in the dynastic history.

Interestingly enough, these Han gifts of silk have been more or less borne out by modern archaeological discoveries. Among the famous finds of Noin-ula in Northern Mongolia are a large number of silk fabrics of Chinese origin. The tombs excavated are generally considered as belonging to the Hsiung-nu of the late first century B.C., or rather at the turn of the Christian era.[35] The inscriptions of two lacquer cups dated 2 B.C. indicate, on the one hand, the general date of these tombs and, on the other hand, the fact that the Han goods buried there came probably from the Chinese court as imperial gifts.[36] One silk fabric bearing the Chinese characters "Hsin shen ling kuang ch'eng shou wan nien" has drawn attention of scholars from the very beginning of its discovery. Various readings have been suggested.[37] Recently some Japanese experts have come to the conclusion that the first character, *Hsin,* refers most likely to the Hsin dynasty of Wang Mang (A.D. 9–23) as in the case of many bronze mirrors of the same period.[38] If so, it would then seem that at least some of the Chinese silks found in Noin-ula were given to the tributary Hsiung-nu under the reign of Wang Mang. At any rate, these archaeological finds fit remarkably well with the period in which Chinese silks are reported to have been sent to the Hsiung-nu in an ever-increasing amount under the newly-established tributary system.[39] Judging from the relative border peace during the half-century covered by the above

---

[34] See the table in Egami Namio, p. 38. The unit and quantity of silk given there, however, are not entirely reliable.

[35] W. Perceval Yetts, "Discoveries of the Kozlov Expedition," *Burlington Magazine,* pp. 168–185; G. Borovka, "Die Funde der Expedition Koslow in der Mongolei, 1924/25," pp. 341–368.

[36] Camila Trevor, *Excavations in Northern Mongolia,* pp. 19–21; Umehara Sueji, *Mōko Noin-Ura hakken no ibutsu,* esp. pp. 99–100.

[37] Yetts, p. 181.

[38] Egami Namio, pp. 295–306; Umehara Sueji, *op. cit.,* pp. 74–75.

[39] Umehara Sueji, *op. cit.,* pp. 81–82.

tabulation, it may be safely concluded that the Former Han dynasty must have effectively turned the irregular but ever-increasing gifts into an economic weapon to keep the Hsiung-nu well under control with a view to achieving the political aim of the tributary system.

Furthermore, the figures also reveal how strongly the Han court considered the tributary system a political necessity, despite its economic undesirability. This point will become immediately clear when we compare the relative costs at which both the *ho-ch'in* and the tributary systems were maintained respectively. Although we do not know the exact amount of annual payments made to the Hsiung-nu under the previous *ho-ch'in* policy, there is, however, an important clue which indicates that the tributary system was probably more expensive. For as late as 89 B.C. the *Shan-yü*, only, requested of the Han court, as a price to resume the *ho-ch'in* relations, an *increased* annual payment of 10,000 *shih* of wine, 5,000 *hu* of grain and 10,000 *p'i* of silk.[40] It can therefore be assumed that the previous payments must have been below these figures.

Toward the end of Wang Mang's reign and at the beginning of the Later Han, the Hsiung-nu, newly-reunited, took advantage of China's internal turmoil to start frontier raids again. They even tried to revive *ho-ch'in* relations with China. Fortunately, the prudent policy of Emperor Kuang-wu saved China from entering into open conflict with the Hsiung-nu and succeeded in gradually bringing them back into the tributary system.[41] In A.D. 47, the Hsiung-nu once more broke into two branches known respectively as the Southern Hsiung-nu and Northern Hsiung-nu, this time permanently. In 50, the Southern Hsiung-nu, following in the wake of their ancestors of one century ago, sent a hostage prince, plus envoys representing the *Shan-yü* and carrying tribute, to the Han court to pay homage, for

---

[40] *HS*, 94A:12b.

[41] For Emperor Kuang-wu's policy toward the Hsiung-nu and the Sino-Hsiung-nu relations in the Later Han period see Uchida Gimpū, "Gōkan Kōbutei no tai-Minami Kyōdo seisaku ni tsuite," *Shirin*, 17:4, pp. 59–90 and 18:1, pp. 97–139. Cf., also, Hans Bielenstein, *Emperor Kuang-wu and the Northern Barbarians*.

which they received in return, among other gifts, 10,000 pieces of silken fabrics, 10,000 catties of silk, 25,000 *hu* of rice and 36,000 head of cattle.[42] From this year on the tributary relations between China and the Hsiung-nu became regularized. At the end of each year the *Shan-yü* sent his tribute-bearers, together with a hostage prince to the court, and at the same time China returned the hostage prince of the preceding year. Often, we are told, the new and old hostage princes met on their way to and from China. The gifts to the Hsiung-nu nobility were also regularized and made annual. After each New Year, the Hsiung-nu envoys were sent back with specified gifts for the envoys themselves as well as for the Hsiung-nu nobility, including the royal house.[43] Probably partly as a result of the decline of the Hsiung-nu economy, it seems that the Southern Hsiung-nu in the Later Han became much more dependent on China for provisions of daily necessities than ever before. The best proof is to be found in the fact that they even received from China large numbers of cattle, which were supposed to be their economic specialization. We have just seen that in A.D. 50 China sent the Southern Hsiung-nu 36,000 heads of cattle. Only three years later they were again given several tens of thousands of sheep.[44] The total annual payments for the Southern Hsiung-nu toward the end of the first century A.D. were amazing. In 91, Yuan An reported that according to the established practice of the Later Han the annual provisions for the Southern Hsiung-nu alone amounted to more than 100,-900,000 cash in value.[45] This scale is further confirmed by a memorial of the *Shan-yü* dated A.D. 88, in which we read:

---

[42] *HHS*, 119:2b.

[43] *HHS*, 119:2b–3a. The silken fabrics for the envoys totalled 1,000 pieces and for the entire Hsiung-nu nobility, 10,000 pieces. It must be pointed out, however, that this amount can by no means be taken as the total annual payments made to the Hsiung-nu. As a matter of fact it did not include even the gift for the *Shan-yü*. The regular payments for the whole Southern Hsiung-nu will be discussed presently.

[44] *HHS*, 119:4a.

[45] *HHS*, 75:2b. This must be a real number because it is followed immediately by the figure of annual expenses for the Western Regions, which amounts to 74,800,000.

"In the past 40 years, your subjects have been growing on the Han soil and have depended entirely on [China] for food. Each year we received both regular and occasional gifts which can be counted only by hundreds of millions." [46] The tremendous increase of the gifts for the Southern Hsiung-nu in Later Han times was probably related to their population growth. In Hu-han-yeh's time their population was only around fifty to sixty thousand but by the year A.D. 90 the total number of the Southern Hsiung-nu, including those who were newly attached to them, increased to 237,300 individuals. [47]

Under the regularized tributary system of the Later Han, it may be further noted, the Hsiung-nu received regular annual provisions from China, but had to present tribute to the Chinese court every year. Moreover, they were loaded with still another kind of financial burden: bribes to the Chinese officials with whom they had dealings from time to time. Ying Shao, the second-century scholar, reports that the *Yeh-che,* or reception officials, who escorted the Hsiung-nu hostage princes and envoys as they came and left every year, usually received bribes, in the course of time, that amounted to more than a million cash. [48]

2 Other Barbarians—Ch'iang, Wu-huan, and Hsien-pi

The Hsiung-nu were by far the most formidable enemies of Han China. Other minor barbarians, including the Ch'iang, Wu-huan and Hsien-pi, were actually jammed between the Hsiung-nu and Han China—then the two greatest East Asian powers. These three barbarian peoples had been at first subject to the economic exploitation of the Hsiung-nu at one time or another. During the Han period, the Ch'iang spread widely along the Chinese frontiers—from the Western Region to Kansu and even Szechwan

---

[46] *HHS,* 119:6a. The text has *i-wan.* For the number *i* and the combination *i-wan* see the discussion in Nancy Lee Swann, *Food and Money in Ancient China,* pp. 264–265, n. 482.

[47] *HHS,* 119:6b. Cf. Lü Ssu-mien, *Yen-shih cha-chi,* Shanghai, 1937, pp. 128–131.

[48] *CHHW,* 35:6b.

and Yunnan.[49] In the early days of the Former Han, it was the Ch'iang of the Kansu area that were particularly troublesome. Around 200 B.C. when the Hsiung-nu military power was at its peak, they forced the Ch'iang into submission and made them important allies. One of the immediate objectives of Emperor Wu's conquest and consolidation of the so-called Ho-hsi area was to separate the Ch'iang from the Hsiung-nu.[50]

Since the Ch'iang were scattered all around and never became a unified people, it was scarcely possible to incorporate them fully into the tributary system. In A.D. 98, nevertheless, presumably attracted by the material gains of the tributary system, a powerful Ch'iang tribe did come to the court to present tribute as well as to pay homage to the Emperor and, in return, they received large amounts of gifts from China.[51] From Emperor Hsüan's time on the Ch'iang gradually moved into the Chinese border [52] and thus began to have direct contacts with the Chinese. Although the Ch'iang did not become great frontier problem until the Later Han, they, nonetheless, seem not to have been on good terms with the Chinese from the very beginning. The basic cause of the Chinese-Ch'iang conflicts was always the excessive Chinese economic exploitation. As early as 88 B.C., the Hsiung-nu urged the Ch'iang to rise against China by using the pretext that the latter had drained too much labor service from the Ch'iang people.[53] The truth, however, has been well revealed by the words of Hou Ying in 33 B.C.: "The Western Ch'iang of late offered to guard [our] frontier. Thus, they were in daily intercourse with the Chinese. The Chinese frontier officials as well as [powerful] people, bent on gains, often robbed the Ch'iang of their cattle, women, and children. This incurred

---

[49] During the Ch'in and Han period, the Ch'iang people tended to move from the northwest to the southwest. See Li Shao-ming, "Kuan-yü Ch'iang-tsu ku-tai shih ti chi-ko wen-t'i," *LSYC*, pp. 165–169.

[50] *HHS*, 117:3a; *Yen-t'ieh lun*, p. 81.

[51] *HHS*, 4:6a; 117:6a–b.

[52] *HS*, 69:7b; 79:2a.

[53] *HS*, 69:1b.

the hatred of the Ch'iang and consequently they revolted against China from time to time." [54]

As a matter of fact, it is exactly the same kind of exploitation or encroachment that was repeated but much aggravated in the Later Han period. In A.D. 33, Pan Piao pointed out the danger of the Ch'iang living face to face with the Chinese as follows:

> Now in Liang-chou (Kansu) there are surrendered Ch'iang people who still lead a barbarian way of life. Nevertheless, they are living together with the Chinese. Since the two peoples are different in social customs and cannot communicate in language, very often the Chinese petty officials and crafty people take the advantage to rob the Ch'iang of their belongings. Extremely enraged and yet helpless, they thus rise in revolt. We can almost say that this is the cause of all barbarian rebellions.[55]

This general observation is amply confirmed by various reports of the time. For instance, in An-ting, one of the Liang-chou provinces, the Ch'iang people settled here and there. They were all forced to render labor services to the local officials as well as powerful Chinese residents. Their sorrows and hatred increased with the passing of each day.[56] Ma Fang, an experienced frontier general, had been several times blamed by Emperor Chang (76–88) for having squeezed levies from the Ch'iang barbarians.[57] It would seem that Huang-fu Kuei, an expert of the Ch'iang affairs of the day, is justified when he came to the conclusion, in A.D. 141, that all Ch'iang rebellions resulted from the fact that the frontier officials, as a rule, ceaselessly encroached upon properties of the Ch'iangs.[58]

The Wu-huan people, who lived mostly in Southern

---

[54] *HS*, 94B:4a.

[55] *HHS*, 117:3b–4a.

[56] *HHS*, 117:7a.

[57] *HHS*, 54:10b.

[58] *HHS*, 95:1a. Cf., also, the commentary of Hu San-hsing, *Tzu-chih t'ung-chien*, 4:1690. The rebellions of the Ch'iang have not been adequately studied. Toward the end of the Later Han the Ch'iang also took part, though not very significantly, in the Liang-chou rebellion. See G. Haloun, "The Liang-chou Rebellion, A.D. 184–221," *Asia Major*, pp. 119–130.

Manchuria, were defeated and conquered by the Hsiung-nu early in the beginning of the Han period. Thereafter they were required to present to the Hsiung-nu annual payments, which included cattle and furs. When Emperor Wu defeated the Hsiung-nu, however, the Wu-huan were brought under the protection of the Chinese tributary system, under which their chieftain came to pay homage at the court every year.[59] Toward the end of the Former Han, as the Hsiung-nu became once more powerful, they seized the opportunity of the political chaos in China to impose a sort of "fur and cloth tax" on the Wu-huan. Later, when the Wu-huan refused to pay the taxes at the instigation of the Chinese, the Hsiung-nu captured about one thousand Wu-huan women and children and asked the Wu-huan people to pay a large amount of ransom including cattle, furs and cloth, with which the latter eventually complied.[60]

In the early years of Emperor Kuang-wu's reign, the Wu-huan became again the Hsiung-nu's military ally and invaded Chinese frontiers from time to time.[61] In A.D. 46, however, when the Hsiung-nu's power was much weakened by their internal struggles, Emperor Kuang-wu succeeded in buying the Wu-huan over with a large amount of cash and silk payments. Therefore, a large group of them attended the court to pay homage in 49. They presented to the emperor, as tribute, slaves, cattle, bows, and various kinds of animal skins, which may be taken as a good indication of their economic life. In return, they received imperial gifts and a great number of them were settled along the frontiers with regular Chinese food and clothes provisions. Moreover, the office of *Hu Wu-huan Chiao-wei* [62] was reestablished at Ning-ch'eng of Shang-ku

---

[59] *HHS*, 120:1b.

[60] *HS*, 94B:8b–9a. See also Uchida Gimpū, "Ugan [Wu-huan] zoku ni kansuru kenkyū" (hereafter "Wu-huan"), *Man-Mō shi ronsō*, pp. 30–31.

[61] On this point see examples given in Uchida Gimpū, "Wu-huan," pp. 39–40, n. 14.

[62] The *Wu-huan Chiao-wei* was first established in Emperor Wu's time. Similar offices were also set up to take charge of the affairs of other barbarians. For instance, there was a *Chiao-wei* for the Ch'iang and

(in modern Chahar) to take care of the affairs of both the Wu-huan and Hsien-pi, which consisted of forwarding gifts to them, arranging regular trade for them as well as taking hostages from them.[63] From this time onward, Chinese–Wu-huan relations went on rather smoothly until toward the middle of the second century. Other aspects of economic intercourse between the Chinese and Wu-huan will be examined below in connection with the problem of surrendered barbarians and that of frontier trade.

The Hsien-pi people, who were probably also scattered in Manchuria, were very close to the Wu-haun but did not become active on Chinese frontiers until the Later Han dynasty. Like the Wu-huan, they, too, had been conquered by the Hsiung-nu and were subject to their direct control at the beginning of the Former Han. Even as late as in the second century A.D., some Hsien-pi tribes still had to render military service to the Hsiung-nu.[64] Militarily, the Hsien-pi were much stronger than the Wu-huan, but economically they were just as unable to support themselves. Trade and plunder underlined their activities throughout the Later Han period. In this period, they probably made more border invasions than any other barbarian peoples. Especially between A.D. 156 and 178, under the able leadership of T'an-shih-huai, they plundered northern and northeastern frontier provinces almost every year.[65] Alternation of submission and rebellion characterized their relations with Han China.

In A.D. 54, two Hsien-pi chieftains led their tribesmen to pay homage at the court. Both of them were amply rewarded with honors as well as gifts. Following their examples, in 58, other Hsien-pi chieftains all submitted them-

---

another one for the Western Regions. The full title was *Hu Wu-huan chiao-wei* or "official protecting the Wu-huan." Cf. *HHS*, 38:4a.

[63] For the above account see *HHS*, 120:1b–2b; *Wei Shu* of Wang Ch'en, quoted in *SKC, Wei*, 30:3a–b. Cf., also, Ma Ch'ang-shou, *Wu-huan yü Hsien-pi*, pp. 133–134 and p. 135, n. 1.

[64] For instance the father of T'an-shih-huai, the great Hsien-pi leader, served three years in the Hsiung-nu army. *HHS*, 120:4b; *Wei Shu* quoted in *SKC, Wei*, 30:6a. Cf. Ma Ch'ang-shou, *op. cit.*, p. 179.

[65] Ma Ch'ang-shou, *op. cit.*, pp. 183–188.

selves to China. In return, they received from China altogether a regular annual payment of 270,000,000 cash, which was almost three times as much as that made to the Southern Hsiung-nu—an unmistakable indication of their superiority in power and position among other barbarians. Such an expensive peace lasted only about thirty years.[66] In 91, when the Northern Hsiung-nu were heavily defeated by the Chinese and fled further westward, the Hsien-pi not only moved into their lands but also absorbed more than one hundred thousand of the Hsiung-nu people.[67] Such a sudden expansion in both territory and manpower made the Hsien-pi strong enough to start anew incursions along the frontiers. They did not return to the Chinese tributary system until the Yung-ch'u period (107–113), when they were offered much better economic terms. This time, trade was regularly opened to them and two *chih-kuan* or "hostage hostels" were built at Ning-ch'eng to accommodate hostages from the Hsien-pi. As a result, some 120 Hsien-pi tribes are reported to have joined the Chinese tributary system of their own accord by sending hostages to China.[68] In the next hundred years, as the Han power was steadily on the decline, the Hsien-pi became accordingly more aggressive than submissive. Occasionally, they still presented tributes to the court when circumstances were not favorable for open attacks,[69] but for most of the time the northern and northeastern frontier provinces of China felt their blows.

To conclude the discussion of Sino-barbarian economic relations thus far, I offer the following succinct statement by Fan Yeh:

The violent power of the four [groups of] barbarians took turns in rise and fall. The flame of the Hsiung-nu flared up during the

[66] *HHS*, 120:3b; *Wei Shu* quoted in *SKC, Wei,* 30:5b.

[67] Uchida Gimpū, *Tōyōshi kenkyū,* 2:1, pp. 19–20.

[68] *HHS*, 120:3b–4a. According to *Wei Shu* quoted in *SKC, Wei,* 130:5b, however, only twenty Hsien-pi groups sent hostages to Ning-ch'eng. These two *chih-kuan* are also mentioned in Lien-sheng Yang, "Hostages in Chinese History," p. 46.

[69] For instance, the Hsien-pi presented tribute to China in A.D. 120 and 127, respectively (*HHS*, 120:4a–b).

Former Han, whereas the Western Ch'iang rose suddenly after the Restoration (i.e., the Later Han). Under the reigns of Emperors Ling and Hsien (68–220), however, two [other] barbarians (i.e., Wu-huan and Hsien-pi) became powerful one after another: The brave and fierce [T'an] shih-huai [of Hsien-pi] took over all the lands previously possessed by the *Shan-yü* [of the Northern Hsiung-nu] and the cruel and ambitious T'a-tun (i.e., a great Wu-huan chieftain) openly occupied the territories of Liao-hsi (South Manchuria and part of Hopei). [From this time on to the end of the Later Han] they (i.e., Wu-huan and Hsien-pi) never ceased to ravage Chinese soil as well as to bring disaster to the [Chinese] people.[70]

This changing barbarian threat throughout the Han period indicates sufficiently the instability of the Chinese tributary system. From the above general survey of Sino-barbarian economic relations, it is also clear that stabilization of the system involved many factors such as the superior military and economic strength of the Chinese empire on the one hand, and the weakened barbarian power on the other, both of which depended on the interplay of a variety of other conditions normally beyond the control of the imperial government. It is interesting to note that with all his efforts to pacify the Hsiung-nu, backed by the military and economic strength which was at its peak in Han China, Emperor Wu failed to force the Hsiung-nu into a tributary submission. This simple fact tends to show that Chinese military and economic superiority alone was not sufficient to bring about the establishment of tributary relations with such powerful barbarians as the Hsiung-nu. The Hsiung-nu under Emperor Wu's reign, though several times defeated, remained a unified tribal confederation strong enough to defy the Chinese domination. Nor can the participation of the Southern Hsiung-nu, under *Shan-yü* Hu-han-yeh, in the Chinese tributary system during Emperor Hsüan's reign be simply explained on the ground of their tribal schism as a result of internal power struggle. The Chinese side of the picture must also be taken into full account. In the history of the Former Han, Emperor Hsüan's reign has been considered

---

[70] *HHS,* 120:6b.

as the age of restoration (*chung-hsing*) marked by both political stability and economic prosperity. As a matter of fact, an excellent explanation of this event has already been given by Pan Ku, the great Han historian, in the *Han Shu*:

> [The fundamental principle in] the government of [Emperor] Hsiao-hsüan was [to make] rewards dependable and punishments certain and to examine and confront names with realities. His gentlemen [who were concerned] with government business, who were Literary Scholars, or [were concerned with] law and principles were all excellent in their capacities. Even his artists, craftsmen, workmen, and artisans, his vessels and utensils could seldom be matched in the time of [Emperors] Yuan and Ch'eng, [which fact] is indeed sufficient to indicate that his officials were worthy of their positions and that the common people were satisfied in their occupations.
>
> He happened [to live at a time when] the Huns (i.e., Hsiung-nu) were acting contrary to reason and were in disturbance, [hence he was able] to "overthrow those who should perish, to strengthen those who should be preserved," and to display his majesty to the northern barbarians. The *Shan-yü* longed [to perform] his duties of fealty, bowed his head to the ground, and called himself a feudatory.[71]

Maintaining a well-balanced tributary system in imperial China required the presence of a number of specific conditions (political, military, economic, etc.) on both the Chinese and barbarian sides. As these conditions were variables rather than constants, the system was, by its very nature, unstable. In this sense, the system may be conceived as a state of delicate equilibrium, generally sensitive to the change of conditions on either side. And this delicacy also explains why the system has been traditionally taken by historians as one of the criteria by which the prosperity and decline of a given dynasty is judged, thus bearing importantly on the problem of the dynastic cycle.

Even the inclusion of the minor barbarians into the tributary system was no easy task. Generally speaking, they were very much under the influence of the rise and fall of other, especially the major, barbarian powers of the time.

---

[71] *HS*, 8:11b, "tsan." Translation by Dubs, *History of the Former Han Dynasty*, 2:265.

But no valid generalization is possible. Sometimes it was the rise of another barbarian group that alienated them from the power orbit of the Han empire, and the fall of the same group that forced them to return to the Chinese tributary system, but sometimes it was vice versa. In our case, we have seen that the Wu-huan twice became, willingly or unwillingly, the auxiliaries of the Hsiung-nu when the latter were militarily strong enough to establish and maintain a political and economic center of gravity in the steppe, and that they submitted once again to Han rule as the power of the Hsiung-nu declined. On the other hand, the Hsien-pi in the Later Han period availed themselves of the opportunity of the fall of the Northern Hsiung-nu for self-aggrandizement and therefore were able to break away from Chinese domination. Perhaps the only safe conclusion we can draw from such complicated Sino-barbarian relations is what Ch'en Yin-k'o calls the "interlocking nature of the rise and fall of foreign races" as in the case of the T'ang dynasty.[72] In other words, tributary relations between the Han empire and any of its neighboring barbarian groups can be properly understood, not in unilateral or even bilateral terms, but in multilateral terms. Needless to say, this interlocking nature worked only toward further weakening of the stability of the tributary system.

From the economic point of view, it is well known that the barbarians always took the tribute as a cloak for trade. While Sino-barbarian trade will be fully covered in a later chapter, suffice it to say here that permission to trade directly with the Chinese was one of the main attractions of the system for the barbarians. This point seems to have been borne out by the fact that the opening of barbarian markets at Ning-ch'eng in the early years of the second century succeeded admirably in bringing a large number of Wu-huan and Hsien-pi groups into the system. Under the Han dynasty, however, it must be emphatically pointed out that direct Chinese economic aid to the barbarians,

---

[72] Ch'en Yin-k'o, *T'ang-tai cheng-chih shih shu-lun kao*, p. 94. Cf. Lien-sheng Yang, *Studies in Chinese Institutional History*, p. 6.

normally in the guise of imperial gifts, played an equally important role in upholding the tributary system. Thus the ever-increasing imperial gifts showered on the Hsiung-nu encouraged the frequency of homage by their *Shan-yü* toward the end of the Former Han. That such gifts must have considerably drained the state treasury is clearly shown in the case of the court conference of 3 B.C., which flatly turned down, on economic grounds, the *Shan-yü's* request to attend the court. It must, also, have been partly out of economic considerations that Emperor Kuang-wu, in A.D. 45 firmly refused to enlarge the tributary system by declining the offer of eighteen states of the Western Regions to send hostages with tribute to China.[73] As will be discussed toward the end of the book, the possibility cannot be entirely ruled out that occasionally imperial economic interest may also have found its expression in the system. But on the whole, it, nevertheless, seems obvious that the system was a liability rather than an asset for Han China as far as the state finance was concerned. Its economic value, if any, was far outweighed by its political significance. This probably explains why Wang Mang never hesitated to squander gold, valuables, and silks on various barbarians in order to obtain their submission within the framework of tributary relations.[74]

Finally, by way of conclusion, let us make a rough estimate of the total annual expenditure involved in the maintenance of the tributary system against the revenue of the Han empire, just to see to what extent the system affected the state finance. But this is easier said than done, because statistics for such an estimate are either lacking or incomplete. In the following discussion, it must be pointed out emphatically, we can only be content with a general indication rather than statistical precision. Since imperial gifts made to the tributary barbarians under the Former Han dynasty were highly irregular, I prefer to cover in the following tabulation the Later Han period from about A.D.

---

[73] See note 9 to Chapter II.
[74] For instances see *HS*, 94B:10a, 11b; 99A:12b–13a.

50 to 100, in which payments made to the various tributary barbarians were generally regularized:

BARBARIANS	TOTAL ANNUAL AMOUNT (CASH)
Hsien-pi	270,000,000
Hsiung-nu	100,900,000
Western Regions	74,800,000
Total Amount	445,700,000

Before we can proceed with the discussion, a few points must be clarified. First, the figures given can by no means claim completeness, because payments made to other barbarians such as the Ch'iang and the Wu-huan are simply not known. Second, the above figures refer probably only to regular payments and do not include occasional gifts, like silks, grain and cattle, as we have seen earlier in this chapter. Third, administrative costs of the tributary system must also be taken into consideration. To keep the system working a number of offices were created, among which were the *shu-kuo tu-wei*, the *Hu Ch'iang chiao-wei*, the *Hu Wu-huan chiao-wei*, the *Hsi-yü tu-hu*, as well as the *chih-kuan* or "hostage hostels." Fourth, military expenses should not be overlooked, either. Sometimes wars had to be fought in order to bring the rebellious barbarians to the tributary terms. Such expenses could be incredibly enormous. For instance, punitive expeditions against the Ch'iang barbarians, from 107 to 118, cost the Later Han government 24,000,000,000 cash and from 136 to 145 an additional amount of 8,000,000,000. Altogether, a total amount of 32,000,000,000 was used in these twenty years.[75] With all these modifications in mind, we must say that the total amount in the tabulation constitutes but a small portion of the total annual expenditure for the maintenance of the tributary system.

Let us now turn to the problem of the revenue of the empire, which is even more difficult than that of the tributary expenditure. The annual revenue of the Later Han

---

[75] *HHS*, 117:9a and 11b. Cf. Lien-sheng Yang, *op. cit.*, p. 155, n. 51; Su Ch'eng-chien, *Hou-Han shih-huo chih ch'ang-pien*, p. 29.

period is not reported in the *Hou Han Shu*. Fortunately, the well-informed scholar, Huan T'an (ca. 43 B.C.–A.D. 28), has provided us with a clue, which may lead to breaking the otherwise hopeless deadlock. According to him, from Emperor Hsüan's time on (73–49 B.C.), the totality of annual *fu-ch'ien* or tax money collected by the Han government amounted to more than 4,000,000,000 cash, of which, he further states, half was used to pay the salaries of all the officials of the empire. On the other hand, as for the total annual revenue of the *Shao-fu*, or the emperor's purse, Huan gives the amount of 8,300,000,000, which was used for the upkeep of the imperial palace as well as for various kinds of imperial gifts.[76]

But, for the discussion here, Huan T'an's statement seems to raise more questions than it can answer. First, there is a problem of time. He is obviously talking about the Former Han, not the Later. Then to what extent can these figures be taken as true, also, for the Later Han dynasty? Since, however, there is neither a report of a significant increase of tax quotas nor that of noticeable price fluctuations in the early part of the Later Han,[77] we have good reason to believe that the total tax revenue of the Later Han, before the end of the first century, must have been around this amount. Second, there is the problem of the inclusiveness of the so-called tax money or *fu-ch'ien*. The term *fu-ch'ien* seems to indicate that it refers to such levies as *suan-fu*, or poll tax, and *keng-fu*, or commutation taxes for labor services, but does not include land tax, which was normally levied in kind in Han times.[78] Thus

---

[76] *CHHW*, 14:2b; cf. Su Ch'eng-chien, pp. 22–23. For a comprehensive discussion of the distinction between the revenue of the empire and that of the emperor in Han times see Katō Shigeshi, *Shina keizaishi kōshō*, 1:35–156.

[77] This point can be best proved by the fact that the price of grain remained on the whole fairly stable throughout the two Han dynasties, with only occasional fluctuations. See Utsunomiya Kiyoyoshi, *Kandai shakai keizai shi kenkyū*, pp. 227–228; Lao Kan, *Chü-yen Han-chien, k'ao-cheng*, pp. 58–59.

[78] Li Chien-nung, *Hsien-Ch'in Liang-Han ching-chi shih kao*, pp. 244–256. For a brief discussion of the term *fu* used in Han China to indicate all kinds of taxes see, however, Lien-sheng Yang, *op. cit.*, pp. 105–107.

considered, the totality of *fu-ch'ien* still cannot be taken as the total revenue of the empire. The next question, therefore, is how much was the total revenue from land tax under the Later Han dynasty? Due to the lack of records, we cannot give a direct answer to this question. But, again there is an interesting clue which enables us at least to make a reasonable guess. In A.D. 159, when the wealthy imperial in-law, Liang Chi, was executed, all his properties were confiscated and sold by the government, which amounted altogether to more than 3,000,000,000 cash in value. All the money was then transferred to the state treasury for government use, and, at the same time, the land tax of the empire for that year was cut down by half.[79] This instance seems to indicate that the totality of land tax, if converted into cash, would be around 6,000,-000,000. Thus, we can probably put the regular total revenue of the Later Han government at about 10,000,000,000 a year. This total amount, it must be immediately added, however, includes *fu-ch'ien* and land tax, the two main sources of government revenue, but excludes the revenue of the *Shao-fu*, which was in theory the personal income of the emperor.[80]

Now, the known figures of regular annual payments to the three groups of tributary barbarians (i.e., Hsien-pi, Hsiung-nu and the Western Regions) are 445,700,000 at an average of about 150,000,000 for each group. But there are at least two more groups of barbarians (i.e., Ch'iang and Wu-huan) that must be added to the list. Let us assume that an additional amount of about 300,000,000 was made to these two groups, an assumption which is by no means unreasonable, especially in view of the fact that the Ch'iang barbarians were by far the most powerful as well as troublesome of all under the Later Han dynasty. With this addition, the total annual payments made to the tributary barbarians would be increased to around 750,000,000 in cash value. Therefore, the tributary system was main-

---

[79] *HHS*, 64:8a.

[80] On the various items of revenue of the *Shao-fu* see Katō Shigeshi, 1:40–82.

tained in Han China at the cost that was about one third of the annual government payroll or 7 percent of the total revenue of the empire, still without taking into account the military and administrative expenses that necessarily went along with the system. Indeed, it must have constituted one of the major items of government expenditure.

chapter four

Surrendered Barbarians and Their Treatment

The treatment of the surrendered barbarians under the Han dynasty forms an important part of the Sino-barbarian economic intercourse of the time, and, therefore, deserves further investigation. As the problem of surrendered barbarians is very diverse by itself, nothing like a comprehensive treatment will be possible here. In what follows, I shall attempt a preliminary analysis of Han China's general policy toward the surrendered barbarians as well as its administrative apparatus with which various kinds of surrendered barbarian groups were kept under control. Emphasis, however, will be laid on the economic aspects of the problem.

Generally speaking, the surrendered barbarians were people *sui generis* and, as such, they occupied a rather unique place in the Chinese imperial order. On the one hand, though surrendered, they still shared the barbarian nature of all other, including the tributary, barbarians, but differed from them in being accepted by the Han government as candidates for full membership in the Chinese civilization. On the other hand, like the Chinese they now, too, were subjects of the Han emperor, but unlike the Chinese, they were yet to be transformed into regular members of the Chinese state. Their half-barbarian and half-Chinese status thus made it necessary for the Chinese government to invent new administrative devices by means of which they could be properly taken care of without damaging the original political structure of the empire. The result, as we shall see, was what may be regarded as a sort of compromise between the tributary system and the *chün-hsien* administrative system.

1 The Inner and Outer Dichotomy

In terms of both frontiers and barbarians, there existed in Han China a general inner-outer distinction, which was obviously an application of the old Confucian *nei* (inner) and *wai* (outer) principles in the domain of frontier and foreign policies.

Owen Lattimore has long ago keenly discerned in Chinese frontier history an inner and outer division. In his own words: "Another characteristic of the frontier as a whole is its division into an "inner" and "outer" region. . . . Briefly, it may be said of this "inner" and "outer" structure that the "inner" region is more closely associated with Chinese, alternately as the garrison territory of barbarian holding power in China, or as the outpost region of Chinese power beyond the Great Wall in periods of Chinese ascendancy. The "outer" region is that which less frequently took part in direct assaults on China, and was less affected by Chinese control in the periods of reaction." [1]

Here Professor Lattimore is probably talking about the later periods of Chinese history because he elsewhere applies this principle particularly to the case of Mongolia under the Manchu rule.[2] Such a general inner-outer division of frontier regions, nevertheless, may be equally applicable to Han China. First, the ancient view that China, as a geographical entity, was the "inner region," hence the center of the known world, whereas all the lands beyond the Chinese boundaries constituted the "outer region," in which barbarians of all kinds resided, received further emphasis in the Han period. As Ts'ai Yung explicitly stated in A.D. 177, both the Great Wall built by the Ch'in, and the frontier barriers erected under Han, were intended to dis-

---

[1] "Chinese Turkestan," originally published in *The Open Court*, XLVII, no. 921 (March, 1933), reprinted in *Studies in Frontier History*, p. 183.

[2] Owen Lattimore, *Inner Asian Frontiers of China*, pp. 86–87.

tinguish the inner region from the outer region. The outer
region was to be left to the barbarians while the inner region was to be entrusted to the care of the Chinese officials.[3]
It is also interesting to note that this inner-outer distinction
was sometimes even used by Han scholars as an argument
against expansion. According to them, the natural geographical boundaries that separated China from the outside world were the very limits set forth purposely by
Heaven and Earth to distinguish the inner region from its
outer counterpart. Therefore, it was as unnatural, as it was
unnecessary, for the Chinese to expand beyond these
limits.[4]

Second, the inner-outer geographical division in the
Han times had a further application within the established
Chinese boundaries, which is unmistakably indicated in
the provincial system of the empire. An imperial edict of
73 B.C. mentions the term *nei-chün* (*kuo*), which may be
rendered as "inner provinces." According to a third century scholar, Wei Chao, provinces in interior China were
called *nei-chün,* while those along the frontiers with for-
tresses and barriers against the barbarians were generally
classified as *wai-chün* or "outer provinces." [5] The same distinction was also maintained during the Later Han period.
The *Hou Han Shu* clearly distinguishes the *nei-chün* from
such frontier regions as An-ting, Pei-ti, Shang-chün, Lung-
hsi and Chin-ch'eng, which were undoubtedly the *wai-
chün* of Han China.[6]

Let us now proceed to see how the same dichotomy was
extended to the barbarians. The above-mentioned Ts'ai
Yung's neat classification of an inner Chinese world and an
outer barbarian world, however, remained in Han China,
as in other periods of Chinese history, always a dream as
naïve as it was unrealizable. As a matter of fact, in the Han

---

[3] Yüan Hung, *Hou Han Chi,* 24:3a; *Ts'ai Chung-lang wen-chi, SPTK
so-pen,* p. 37.

[4] As summarized by Pan Ku in *HS,* 96B:10b–11a.

[5] *HS,* 8:2b. This commentary is translated in H. H. Dubs, *The History
of the Former Han Dynasty,* 2:208, with the commentator's name wrongly
given as Yen shih-ku.

[6] *HHS,* 117:10a.

period, as previously in Chou China,[7] barbarians were actually active on both sides of the Chinese frontiers. Thus, from almost the very beginning, the Han government found it useful to make a distinction among the surrendered barbarians between the inner and the outer barbarians. For instance, in 177 B.C., it was reported that the Hsiung-nu invaded Shang-chün (in modern Suiyuan and northern Shensi) and plundered the *Pao-sai Man-i* or "frontier-guarding barbarians" there.[8] The name *Pao-sai* here must have been a technical term of the time because it appears not only frequently in various Han texts, but also occasionally in the newly-discovered Han documents on wood.[9] In the same year, Emperor Wen also issued an edict charging the Hsiung-nu with having broken the peace agreement by invading the frontier and driving away the *Pao-sai Man-i* from their homes. Here the commentary of Yen Shih-ku defines the term as follows: "Those [barbarians] who had already been dependents of Han and lived along the frontiers to guard themselves." [10] The fact that these barbarians settled in Shang-chün is sufficient proof of their having been treated as inner barbarians by the Han dynasty.

This point becomes further clarified when we consider the following two cases. 1) The Chinese adventurer, Wei Man, who had fled to Korea at the beginning of the dynasty and established himself as king there, was appointed a *wai-ch'en* or "outer vassal" by the Han court under

---

[7] Ch'ien Mu, "Hsi-Chou Jung-huo k'ao," *Yü-Kung*, 2:4, pp. 2–5 and 2:12, pp. 27–32. For further discussion see Lattimore, *Inner Asian Frontiers of China*, pp. 364–365.

[8] *SC*, 110:6b. Burton Watson, *Records of the Grand Historian of China*, translates *Pao-sai Man-i* as "the loyal barbarians of Shang Province who had been appointed by the Han to guard the frontier," 2:167.

[9] Lao Kan, *Chü-yen Han-chien, shih-wen*, no. 3479, p. 69. It is highly interesting to note that in some cases the character *pao* is used as a prefix to frontier place-names in these documents. (See Ch'en Chih, *Liang-Han ching-chi shih-liao lun-ts'ung*, p. 44 and Michael Loewe, "Some Notes on Han-time Documents from Chüyen," *TP*, p. 302.) It seems to me that in such cases *pao* can be better understood as *pao-sai* indicating either that such places were constantly under the threat of barbarian invasions or that in such places there were "frontier-guarding" barbarians.

[10] *HS*, 94A:5a.

Emperor Hui and Empress Lü. In both the *Shih Chi* and *Han Shu,* he is mentioned together with the term *Pao-sai wai man-i,* which may be possibly interpreted as another technical term meaning "outer frontier-guarding barbarians." [11] 2) In Emperor Wu's time, the surrendered Wu-huan people were placed in regions outside five northern and northeastern frontier provinces to guard against the Hsiung-nu invasions for China.[12] Both cases seem to point to the fact that there existed side by side with the inner barbarians, also the outer barbarians. The latter, it may be noted however, were probably not too much different from the regular tributary barbarians. Because, in the case of the Wu-huan, it is said that their tribal chieftain came to pay homage at the court every year. That the so-called "frontier-guarding barbarians" were in most cases inner barbarians may be further illustrated by the case of the Ch'iang. In the Later Han period, some of the Ch'iang people were known by the name *Pao-sai* or "frontier-guarding" Ch'iang. And the commentator of the *Hou Han Shu* explains that they were so called because they had surrendered to China and lived within the imperial territory to guard the frontiers.[13] In another instance, it is interesting to find that the Later Han government made a very clear distinction between the "invading Ch'iang barbarians" on the one hand and the "frontier-guarding Ch'iang barbarians" on the other.[14] The fact that the frontier-guarding Ch'iang were inside the empire is also fully borne out by the statement of Hou Ying cited in the preceding chapter, which relates that ever since the Western Ch'iang offered to guard the frontier, they came into daily intercourse with the Chinese people.

保塞

In many ways the inner barbarians were distinguished from the outer barbarians in their treatment by the Han government.[15] As we shall deal with this problem in further detail later on, it is sufficient here to call attention

---

[11] *SC,* 115:1b; *HS,* 95:9a.
[12] *HHS,* 120:1b. Cf. Uchida Gimpū, "Wu-huan," pp. 26–27.
[13] *HHS,* 54:9b.
[14] *HHS,* 53:1b.
[15] An interesting recent article by Kurihara Tomonobu in *Kodaigaku,* pp. 10–15, gives details which throw light on this discussion.

to one important fact, namely, whenever the surrendered barbarians were classified as inner barbarians, the frontier barriers that had been previously established to separate them from the Chinese were removed. For instance, during the reign of Emperor Wu, both chieftains of some of the Southwestern barbarian tribes [16] and the king of Southern Yueh [17] asked to become inner barbarians of China. As a result, frontier barriers in both regions were abolished. The removal of frontier barriers in such cases actually means that the frontier-guarding task was then entrusted to the inner barbarians. This point becomes at once clear when we consider the following case. In 33 B.C. the surrendered Southern Hsiung-nu offered of their own accord to guard the Chinese frontiers from Shang-ku to Tun-huang and requested the removal of frontier barriers as well as the Chinese garrison. After much consideration, however, the court decided not to accept this generous offer, obviously because it did not trust the Hsiung-nu enough to leave the entire northwestern frontiers to their care. The Hsiung-nu, therefore, had no other alternative but to continue being outer barbarians of China.[18]

2 *The Classification of Surrendered Barbarians into Various Categories*

Before we discuss the various administrative categories into which surrendered barbarians of different origins were fitted, it is desirable to see how the barbarians generally became inner barbarians through surrender. To begin with, we must introduce a key term used in this period. In numerous cases, the barbarian surrender is described in the dynastic histories of the period as *nei-shu*, literally, "to become inner subjects" of China. Although occasionally *nei-shu* is also used loosely to indicate the establishment of tributary relations between China and the barbarian states beyond the Chinese frontiers, such as those of the Western Regions, in most cases, however, the

---

[16] *SC*, 113:3a; Watson, 2:245.
[17] *SC*, 117:15a; Watson, 2:325.
[18] *HS*, 94B:3b–4b.

term refers to the inclusion of surrendered barbarians along the frontiers into the Chinese territory and, as such, it was rather rigorously defined. It seems that whenever the barbarians became the inner subjects they surrendered to China, not as individuals, but as tribal groups together with their lands. Generally speaking, the origin of *nei-shu* is traceable to the Former Han, but it occurred most frequently during the Later Han dynasty, owing obviously to the inclusive barbarian and frontier policy of the latter.

Let us first discuss a typical *nei-shu* case during the reign of Wang Mang. In order to show that his New Dynasty had received the Mandate of Heaven, Wang Mang sent envoys to the various outer barbarians with large amounts of money to buy their submission. A group of Ch'iang people outside the northwestern border, attracted by the price, offered to become "inner subjects" on the following conditions: 1) they would surrender to China as a tribe of about 12,000 people; 2) they would present all their fertile lands to the Chinese; and 3) they themselves would take residence in the strategic points along the border to guard the frontier for China, presumably from inside.[19] From this instance we see not only the two basic elements of *nei-shu,* people and land, but also the identification of the "inner subjects" with the "frontier-guarding barbarians." As both land and people constituted the very basic elements of the *nei-shu* type of barbarian submission, therefore in the Later Han times, *nei-shu* was always given in the official reports in the combination of *chü-t'u nei-shu,* "surrender as inner subjects together with their land" [20] or, sometimes *chü-chung nei-fu,* "come to adhere [to China] as inner subjects with the entire people or race." [21] And it

---

[19] *HS,* 99A:12b.
[20] *HHS,* 116:3b, 4a, 5a, 8a, 9a, 9b, 10a, 11a; 117:12a.
[21] *HHS,* 116:9a. It is interesting to add, however, that a similar practice was followed in later periods. For instance, under the Mongolian dynasty of Yuan, we find such expressions as *chü-kuo lai-fu* and *chü-pu lai-kuei,* which may be rendered as "come to adhere with entire nation" and "come to submit with entire tribe," respectively. (Cf. Francis Woodman Cleaves, "The Sino-Mongolian Inscription of 1362," *HJAS,* 12: 1–2 (1949), n. 31 to Part 1 on pp. 43–44. In tracing the origin of such expressions,

may be further noted, under the Later Han dynasty it seems to have been a well-established practice that in becoming inner subjects the chieftains of the surrendered tribes always reported to the Chinese government the exact number of their people. This is, however, quite understandable since, as we shall see later, these inner barbarians were also subject to taxation and corvée levies. As a result, population figures given in such reports all seem to be real and reliable.[22]

It is now time to come to the more complicated problem of classification of surrendered barbarians into different categories. In many cases when a large number of barbarians surrendered to China as inner subjects, they were immediately organized into a *shu-kuo,* "subject state" or "dependent state." *Shu-kuo,* as an institution, had already been in use under the Ch'in dynasty,[23] but it was under the Han, especially during the reign of Emperor Wu, that the *shu-kuo* was used extensively to accommodate the rapidly increasing number of surrendered barbarians.[24] In 121–120 B.C., five *shu-kuo* were established on the northern border to give habitations to the newly-surrendered 40,000 Hsiung-nu.[25] A Chinese official, under the title of *shu-kuo tu-wei,* together with a number of administrative assistants, was appointed to take care of each *shu-kuo.*[26] What is particu-

---

however, Professor Cleaves seems to be too much concerned with the *chü-kuo* combination. Actually, the expression of *chü-t'u nei-shu* and *chü-chung nei fu* in our case, probably the earliest forms of the kind, would suit his explanation much more analogously.)

[22] Instances of such reports are many. The following two are chosen because they particularly show how exact the figures could have been. In A.D. 51 when a group of the Southwestern barbarians in Yunnan submitted to China as inner subjects, the total population reported consisted of 2,770 households and 17,659 individuals. In A.D. 69 another group surrendered with a population of 51,890 households and 553,711 individuals HHS, 116:8a).

[23] HS, 19A:5b.

[24] For examples of the Former Han, see *Hsi-Han hui-yao,* Chung-hua shu-chü edition, pp. 599–600.

[25] Dubs, *op. cit.,* 2:62. It may be pointed out that *shu-kuo* had already existed in Han dynasty before the reign of Emperor Wu because Chia I already mentioned it in his *Hsin shu,* 4:6b.

[26] For details see Yen Keng-wang, *Chung-kuo ti-fang hsing-cheng chih-tu shih, shang-pien,* 2:172–175; Kamada Shigeo, *Shin-Kan seiji seido no kenkyū,* part 2, chapter 7, pp. 329–336.

larly interesting about the *shu-kuo* is the fact that under it, the surrendered barbarians were generally allowed to follow their own social customs as well as lead their own way of life.[27]

The exact geographical location of these five Hsiung-nu *shu-kuo* has been a matter of much controversy.[28] Here, however, we only need to be concerned with one specific point of general institutional significance, namely, whether a *shu-kuo* was normally established inside the Han empire or outside it. In the case of the above five *shu-kuo* most scholars tend to think that they lay beyond the Han frontiers.[29] This conjecture is quite reasonable when we consider a later case. In 60 B.C., a *shu-kuo* was established in Chin-ch'eng (in modern Kansu) to accommodate the surrendered Ch'iang barbarians.[30] According to a Sung scholar, it was also located somewhere beyond the Han territory.[31] It would then seem that at least some of the *shu-kuo* of the Former Han period were outside the empire and that, as the logic goes, such *shu-kuo* people should be considered as outer barbarians.

But the problem is not so simple. As a matter of fact, a different view may be found in the memorial of 33 B.C. of Hou Ying. As this document reveals, the Chinese frontier barriers and garrisons were established not only for border defense against the Hsiung-nu invasions, but also for the purpose of preventing the surrendered people of the *shu-kuo* who had originally belonged to the Hsiung-nu, from running away to join the Hsiung-nu again.[32] Thus, the words of Hou Ying seem to imply that the *shu-kuo* was rather within the Chinese frontier. But it must also be emphatically pointed out that the latter view, in spite of its

---

[27] *SC*, 111:5b–6a and commentary (Watson, 2:205); *HS*, 55:5a and commentary. Cf. the view of Tezuka Takayoshi cited in Kamada Shigeo, *op. cit.*, p. 329.

[28] For a summary of conflicting views see Kamada Shigeo, *op. cit.*, pp. 330–331.

[29] See Hu San-hsing's commentary to the *Tzu-chih t'ung-chien*, 2:634 and Dubs, *op. cit.*, 2:62, n. 15.4.

[30] *HS*, 8:8b; Dubs, *op. cit.*, 2:243.

[31] The view of Wang Ying-lin cited in the *k'ao-cheng* section at the end of *HS*, 69.

[32] *HS*, 94B:4b.

being a contemporary testimony, does not necessarily invalidate the former one.

Probably the two seemingly conflicting views may be reconciled through a reexamination of the concept "frontier." The so-called "frontier" in Han China, probably also true for later periods, must be conceived in terms of vast areas extending sometimes to hundreds of miles, rather than a thin defense line. Moreover, in such vast frontier areas it may well have been the case that there existed more than one defense line in terms of barriers as well as garrisons.[33] If this was the case, we would find the above-mentioned distinction between an "outer" and an "inner" frontier made by Lattimore very useful. In all likelihood, the *shu-kuo* was located somewhere beyond the inner frontier and between at least two Chinese defense lines. It was probably also in this way that they helped to guard the frontier for China. Recent studies of the Han military establishments along the northwestern border have fully shown that the long defense line there was constantly under the vigilant guard of the Chinese garrison forces.[34] No trace whatsoever has yet been found that the task was ever entrusted to the frontier guarding barbarians.

In the light of such an understanding of the Han frontier situation, the various *shu-kuo* on the border may be taken as having formed part of what Lattimore calls "outer frontier" or "trans-frontier," and, since the *shu-kuo* barbarians, to use the words of Lattimore,[35] "were under control but not under direct rule" of the Chinese government,

---

[33] Lao Kan, *Chü-yen Han-chien, k'ao-cheng*, p. 28.

[34] Literature on this subject is enormous. See, however, the following studies: Lao Kan, "Ts'ung Han-chien so-chien chih pien-chün chih-tu," *CYYY*, pp. 159–180; Lao Kan, "Shih Han-tai chih t'ing-chang yü feng-sui," *CYYY*, pp. 501–522; Ho Ch'ang-ch'ün, "Feng-sui k'ao," *Kuo-hsüeh chi-k'an*, pp. 77–102; Yoneda Kenjirō, "Kandai no hengun soshiki," *Tōyōshi kenkyū*, pp. 50–63; Ch'en Meng-chia, "Han-chien so-chien Chü-yen pien-sai yü fang-yü tsu-chih," *K'ao-ku hsüeh-pao*, pp. 55–109. Western readers may consult a review article by A. F. P. Hulsewé, "Han-time Documents," *TP*, esp. pp. 8–9, for more bibliographical information.

[35] Lattimore, *Inner Asian Frontiers of China*, p. 87. Cf. also, his illuminating article, "Origins of the Great Wall of China: A Frontier Concept in Theory and Practice," reprinted in *Studies in Frontier History*, esp. the section on "The Frontier Reservoir," pp. 115–116.

it may also be legitimate to regard them, in this specific sense, as "outer barbarians." Of course, "outer" and "inner" are, after all, relative terms. The *shu-kuo* barbarians were "outer barbarians" only in relation to those in interior China. Compared to the tributary states, for example, in the Western Regions they, however, had probably every reason to call themselves the "inner subjects" of the Han empire.

Under the Later Han, the *shu-kuo* system continued to grow, and geographically extended from northwestern to northeastern and southwestern frontiers. And, more significantly, they were now established in areas which may be considered as indisputably "inner frontiers" of China.[36]

---

[36] See Yen Keng-wang, 1:164–165; Kamada Shigeo, *op cit.*, pp. 333–334. In one sense, however, the *shu-kuo* barbarians, especially those on the northwestern frontiers of the Later Han, may still be considered as "outer barbarians." It must be remembered that the capital of the Later Han was no longer in Ch'ang-an, which was adjacent to the northwestern frontier, but in Lo-yang in the interior. Thus, both financial and military considerations, even led some officials at the court to toy seriously, in A.D. 107, with the idea of evacuating the northwestern frontier of China from the Liang-chou (Kansu) area to the Kuan-chung area around Ch'ang-an. In other words, they wanted to desert Liang-chou altogether as Chinese territory and leave it to the barbarians. Strong reasons were given as to why Liang-chou had no longer much strategic value to the empire as well as why it was the defending position of the Kuan-chung area that should be strengthened instead (*HHS*, 81:2a–3a). On the other hand, those who were opposed to this idea argued that withdrawal of the frontier was no solution to the problem of barbarian threat. For if Liang-chou were gone, then the Kuan-chung area would immediately become the northwestern frontier of China and, moreover, the Han imperial tombs around the former capital would be exposed to the invading barbarians (*HHS*, 88:1a–b; cf. a similar view in Wang Fu, *Ch'ien-fu lun*, p. 36). Two more things should be borne in mind when we discuss the northwestern frontier situation in Later Han China. First, during this period the Kuan-chung area was repeatedly invaded by the Ch'iang barbarians (*HHS*, 117:10b–11a). Second, Chinese population in both Liang-chou and Kuan-chung areas dropped considerably as compared to the Former Han period (Ch'ien Mu, *Kuo-shih ta-kang*, 1:142–143). The latter must have resulted, to some extent, from the fact that Chinese residents in these two areas gradually moved to interior China in face of a growing barbarian threat. Thus, putting all these considerations together, it would seem safe to conclude that under the Later Han dynasty, especially from the beginning of the second century onward, Liang-chou and Kuan-chung had been transformed into, in reality if not in name, what may be called "outer" and "inner" frontiers of China respectively. It is in this

Thus, many of the inner Ch'iang barbarians in Liang-chou (Kansu), as well as the Southwestern barbarians in modern Szechwan and Yunnan, were organized into *shu-kuo* based on the same principle of allowing each of them to preserve their own way of life. This phenomenon may be explained again by reference to the adoption of an inclusive barbarian policy in the period, which resulted in ceaseless armed revolts of the barbarians, especially the Ch'iang and the Southwestern barbarians, due, as we shall see, as much to maltreatment by the local governments as to excessive exactions by the powerful and rich in the respective localities.[37] As we know, at least in theory, the *shu-kuo* was primarily intended to keep a loose rein on barbarians of the most rebellious kind, who were obviously not yet ready to accept the regular Chinese rule under the *chün-hsien* administrative system.

Throughout the Han period, there were also cases in which surrendered barbarians were directly brought under the Chinese *chün-hsien* (province-district) administration. Normally, only submissive or more or less Sinicized barbarians were admitted to the empire in this way. Moreover, according to the Han regulation, a *hsien* was to be called a *tao* in case there were barbarians under its jurisdiction.[38] The regulation itself is an unmistakable sign that there must have been considerable numbers of barbarians under the regular *chün-hsien* system, though not all of them were necessarily surrendered barbarians. And the regulation is fully borne out by the geographical sections of the dynastic histories of the period, where many such *tao* may be found. The following two instances, from the Former and Later Han respectively, should be able to illustrate our point. In 128 B.C., after some 280,000 people in what is modern north Korea had requested to become "inner subjects" of China, a Chinese province was established there under the name of Ts'ang-hai Chün.[39] In A.D.

---

sense that the *shu-kuo* barbarians in Liang-chou may have well fallen into the category of "outer barbarians."

[37] Cf. Kamada Shigeo, *op. cit.*, pp. 334–335.

[38] *HS*, 19A:8a.

[39] *HHS*, 115:4b.

69 when the Ai-lao barbarians of modern Yunnan submitted themselves to the Han government as "inner subjects" two *hsien* were created out of their lands.[40] Thus,
we also see that the *nei-shu* type of barbarian surrender,
coupled with the incorporation of the newly-acquired
lands into the *chün-hsien* administrative system, was used
as a normal method of expansion in Han China.

Between the *shu-kuo* and *chün-hsien,* a third administrative category may be distinguished, that of *pu. Pu* was
originally a military subdivision of a province both under
the Ch'in and Han dynasties. A frontier province was
usually divided into several *pu,* each under the care of a
military *tu-wei.*[41] But evidence also tends to show that in
some cases, especially in the frontier or "outer" provinces,
the *pu* functioned independently as an administrative unit,
under which both Chinese and surrendered barbarians were
governed. Unlike the barbarians in the *shu-kuo,* barbarians
in the *pu* were under the direct control of a Chinese official
—*tu-wei,* but also unlike the barbarians in the *chün-hsien,*
they were treated differently and sometimes even separately
from the Chinese. For instance, in the western *pu* of Shu
(Szechwan), instead of one, two *tu-wei* were appointed, in
103 B.C., to take charge of the barbarians and Chinese respectively.[42] The military nature of the *pu* seems to show
that the barbarians there were probably not yet submissive
enough to be included in the regular *chün-hsien* system.
Generally speaking, the ultimate goal of the Han government was to gradually embrace all the barbarians within the
empire into the arms of Chinese civilization so that they
could be eventually treated just as the Chinese under the
chün-hsien system. It was in this way that many *shu-kuo* and
pu were transformed into *chün* in the course of time.[43] It

---

[40] *HHS,* 116:8a.

[41] For details on the *pu* and its *tu-wei* see Ch'iang Ju-hsün. "Han chou-
chün-hsien li-chih k'ao" in *Chung-kuo hsüeh-pao,* pp. 11–14; Yen Keng-
wang, *op. cit.,* 1:147–187; Kamada Shigeo, *op. cit.,* pp. 304–328.

[42] *HHS,* 116:10a; *Hua-yang Kuo chih, SPTK* edition, 3:7a.

[43] For instances of such transformation see *HHS,* 116:8b, 11a, 11b; *Hua-
yang Kuo chih,* 1:9b; 4:15b–16a. As the *Sung Shu* (T'ung-wen edition,
40:6b) remarks, from toward the end of the Later Han to the period of
the Three Kingdoms (221–265) most *pu* were organized into *chün.*

may further be noted that the *pu* was of such an intermediate nature that sometimes it could also be changed to *shu-kuo*. During the reign of Emperor An (A.D. 107–125), many frontier *pu* were reorganized into *shu-kuo*.[44] The reason for such changes is not altogether clear. Presumably they were made as a means of simplifying the local administration.

3 Economic Aspects of the Treatment of Surrendered Barbarians

After having analyzed the various categories into which the surrendered barbarians were classified, we can now proceed to examine how they were treated by the Han government, especially in terms of economic relations. Generally speaking, the "outer barbarians" were always treated more leniently and generously than the "inner barbarians." And viewed dynamically, surrendered barbarians on the whole received better treatment under the Former Han than the Later Han because of different policies as well as varied historical situations.

In the Former Han period, as Ku Yung and Tu Ch'in pointed out in 28 B.C., the general policy was to use both money and honorary titles to induce the surrender of barbarians, especially the Hsiung-nu.[45] Honorary titles such as king, marquis, or the like had attraction, however, only to the barbarian chieftains.[46] As for the common barbarian peoples, they were concerned mainly with whatever material gains they could get from China. Chia I once suggested to the court that China should use her wealth to vie with the Hsiung-nu leaders, and thus wrest their subjects from them. As Yen Shih-ku's commentary makes very clear, this would mean that emphasis in economic policy should be laid on agricultural production rather than commerce, so that China could have full granaries and

---

[44] See the commentaries to the following *shu-kuo* in the *Hou Han Shu:* Kuang-han, Shu Chün (33:3a), Chien-wei (33:3b), Chang-yeh, Chü-yen (33:5a), and Liao-tung (33:7a).

[45] *HS,* 94B:5a.

[46] For illustrations see *HS,* 8:2b and Su Lin's commentary; 55:4b–5a; 94B:4b.

surplus cloths and silks to attract barbarians to surrender.[47]

As early as in 135 B.C., T'ang Meng succeeded in obtaining the submission of the Yeh-lang barbarians (in modern Kweichow) by lavishing imperial gifts on them.[48] This method proved to be quite effective. When barbarians in Szechwan heard this, they requested of their own accord to become inner subjects of China in order to receive Han gifts.[49] On a much larger scale, the same method was applied to the Hsiung-nu people. In 121 B.C. the newly-surrendered Hsiung-nu people of the five "subject states," which numbered more than 40,000, it is reported, "all received liberal rewards, and they looked to the central government *hsien-kuan* for clothes and food. As the central government had not sufficient [for them], the Son of Heaven restricted [the cost of] imperial food; he left off use of the state equipage with four horses [of matched color]; and he gave from his own supplies [which were in the hands] of the *yü-fu* (palace subordinate), in order to provide for the deficiency."[50] The Emperor was even criticized by officials at the court for having treated the surrendered Hsiung-nu too nicely.[51] In this case we also see how much the *shu-kuo* barbarians were dependent on China for provisions.

On the other hand, however, the political and military control over the *shu-kuo* was rather loose. This explains why sometimes entire groups of the *shu-kuo* barbarians could revolt against China. For instance, toward the end of Emperor Hsüan's reign, a group of several thousand surrendered barbarians of the Hsi Ho *shu-kuo* went away in rebellion.[52] In 48 B.C., more than ten thousand *shu-kuo* bar-

---

[47] HS, 24B:3a; Nancy Lee Swann, *Food and Money in Ancient China*, p. 239. For more details of Chia I's suggestion see his *Hsin shu*, esp. 4:2b–3a.

[48] SC, 116:2a; HS, 95:1b. Cf. Watson, 2:292.

[49] SC, 117:15a; HS, 57B:2a. Cf. Watson, 2:324.

[50] SC, 30:4a; HS, 24B:4b. Translation is by Swann, p. 262; cf., also, Watson, 2:86–87.

[51] SC, 120:2b; HS, 50:4a.

[52] HS, 79:1b. It may be noted that, instead of Emperor Hsüan, the HS text has Emperor Chao (86–74 B.C.). The Ch'ing scholar, Ch'i Shao-nan, seems to be right in pointing out that *Chao* must be a corruption of

barians of Shang-chün also escaped to join the Hsiung-nu.[53] Such large-scale barbarian revolts and freedom in action fully indicate the extent to which the surrendered barbarians were left independent and self-determining in their "subject states." In selecting officials to take charge of the surrendered barbarians, the Former Han government also showed considerable carefulness because the appointment of a wrong person often led to estrangement and even open rebellion.[54]

In theory, surrendered barbarians who were incorporated into the *chün-hsien* administration system were required to pay taxes to the Chinese government, just like the Chinese subjects. Under the Former Han dynasty however, the *chün-hsien* barbarians were so leniently treated that sometimes they were freed from such financial obligations. In Emperor Wu's time, for instance, "After three years of continuous fighting, the Han forces managed to suppress the Ch'iang barbarians and wiped out the kingdom of Southern Yüeh. On the southern border, from P'an-Yü on the coast to the south of Shu, seventeen new provinces were set up. These were governed in accordance with the old customs of the inhabitants and were not required to pay taxes." [55] The leniency of the Former Han government toward the surrendered barbarians may further be seen in the following instance. In 67 B.C., Wen Shan province (in modern Szechwan) was abolished at the request of the native barbarians there who complained to the court that it was too heavy a burden for them to support the administrative costs of an independent province.[56]

Hsüan, because the Hsi Ho *shu-kuo* was established under Emperor Hsüan's reign. Unfortunately, in making this correction Ch'i himself also commits a mistake when he says that the Hsi Ho *shu-kuo* was established in 54 B.C. (See *K'ao-cheng* at the end of *HS,* 79.) Actually, it was set up in 55 B.C., together with the Pei Ti *shu-kuo.* (*HS,* 8:9b; Dubs, *op. cit.,* 2:253.) Having obviously overlooked Ch'i's *K'ao-cheng,* Yen Keng-wang (1:163) is rather puzzled about the date of its establishment because of the two contradicting dates given in the *Han Shu.*

[53] *HS,* 9:1b; Dubs, *op. cit.,* 2:305.
[54] *HS,* 69:7b.
[55] *SC,* 30:9a–b; translated in Watson, 2:102.
[56] *HHS,* 116:11a.

Under the inclusive barbarian policy of the Later Han dynasty, surrendered barbarians were treated somewhat differently. The contrast in treatment between the powerful and aggressive barbarians, like those of the *shu-kuo*, and the weak and submissive ones, like those under the *chün-hsien*, became now much more striking. While the former continued to receive regular economic aid from the Chinese government, the latter generally suffered greatly from the exploitation and oppression of the Chinese local officials. To illustrate the former case, we can cite the instance of the aggressive Hsien-pi people. When the Hsien-pi surrendered to China at the Liao-tung *shu-kuo*, each year the Later Han government ordered both Ch'ing Chou and Hsü Chou to forward to them large payments in order to prevent them from causing disturbances. The practice lasted throughout the reigns of Emperors Ming and Chang (A.D. 58–88).[57] Similar treatment seems to have been also accorded some groups of the Southwestern barbarians. A Chinese translation of three long poems attributed to some barbarian poets reveals that their submission was made possible mainly because the Han court sent them large amounts of silk cloths, wine, and food.[58]

During the Later Han period, however, it was the treatment of the "inner barbarians" under direct Chinese administration that was of primary importance and therefore calls for further examination. The "inner barbarians" were now generally subject to taxation. In some cases, taxes were imposed on those who had been previously exempted from regular levies under the Former Han dynasty. For instance, three districts of Kuei-yang (in modern Hunan), which were populated by the surrendered Yueh people, were not required to pay land taxes when Emperor Wu first conquered that area. But in the early years of the Later Han, governor Wei Li was able to fully

---

[57] *HHS*, 116:11a; Wang Ch'en's *Wei Shu* quoted in *SKC, Wei,* 30:5b.

[58] *HHS*, 116:10b. For a general account of the various groups of the Southwestern barbarians see Yu Chung, "Han-Chin shih-ch'i ti Hsi-nan I," pp. 13–26 and Cheng Te-k'un, *Ssu-ch'uan ku-tai wen-hua shih,* pp. 96–111.

bring these people into the *chün-hsien* system and thus transformed them into regular taxpayers.[59] In more cases, tax impositions on the barbarians were increased during this period, and such increases often caused them to revolt against the local authorities. This situation is particularly well illustrated by the barbarians of Wu-ling (in modern Hunan). Under both Ch'in and the former Han dynasties, they were required to pay to the government a special kind of cloth tax known as *tsung-pu,* one entire roll (*p'i*) for each adult and twenty feet for each child. In A.D. 115, some two thousand barbarians there had already attacked cities and killed local officials because of unjust and excessive extortions imposed on them. In A.D. 136, however, the governor of Wu-ling proposed to the court a tax increase for the barbarians because they were now as submissive and obedient as the Chinese. The proposal was accepted by Emperor Shun in spite of the strong opposition of another official. Consequently, a large-scale barbarian rebellion broke out at the end of the year.[60] On the other hand, light taxation often had the effect of keeping the barbarians peaceful and obedient. This is exactly the case of the Ai-lao barbarians in Yunnan under the administration of Cheng Ch'un, who was appointed governor of Yung-ch'ang in Emperor Ming's time. An agreement was reached between Cheng and the Ai-lao barbarians that the regular annual taxes for the latter consisted only of two pieces of cloths and one *hu* of salt for each rich and powerful family. The barbarians were so much satisfied with the arrangement that they did not make any trouble throughout the period when Cheng was in office there.[61]

Tax levies on the barbarians generally varied from group to group and from region to region. Compared to the Chinese subjects, however, theirs were rather light since economically they were still in a much inferior position.[62] But, on the other hand, it must be also emphasized

---

[59] *HHS,* 106:1b.

[60] *HHS,* 116:1b–2b. Cf., also, 116:5a–b; 5b–6b.

[61] *HHS,* 116:8b; cf., also, Yu Chung, p. 28.

[62] Li Chien-nung, *Hsien-Ch'in Liang-Han ching-chi shih kao,* pp. 256–258.

that in terms of labor services the barbarians were generally under heavy Chinese exploitation. As Fan Yeh has pointed out, the *nei-shu* barbarians under the Later Han dynasty were forced to work as hard as slaves by the powerful Chinese.[63] The traditionally submissive Pan-tun barbarians of Szechwan, for instance, suffered so severely from the excessive labor drafts at the hands of the local officials that they revolted repeatedly against the Chinese government during the reign of Emperor Ling (A.D. 168–188).[64] As has been discussed previously in chapter II, during the Later Han the Chinese subjects were released from some of the labor and military services. Much of these services were now rendered by the surrendered barbarians. The *nei-shu* barbarians, such as the Ch'iang, were often drafted by the local officials to do hard work. Along the frontiers they were sometimes also relied upon as "ears and eyes" to watch all invasions from outside, thus performing the function of Chinese frontier guards.[65] Numerous instances show that the revolt of surrendered barbarians was caused primarily by such exactions. In A.D. 121 too much imposition of military services incurred deep hatred and therefore unrest among the newly-surrendered Hsiung-nu on the northern border.[66] In A.D. 45, a whole group of *shu-kuo* barbarians, possibly the Ch'iang, in An-ting, rose in arms and joined the Hsiung-nu also as a result of excessive corvée levies.[67] Under the *i-i-fa-i* or "using barbarians to attack barbarians" policy of the time, surrendered barbarians were also used to fight against their own tribesmen who remained hostile to the empire.[68] Barbarian soldiers thus used in both foreign and domestic wars were not even adequately provided with food. For instance, during the Liang-chou rebellion of A.D. 184, 3,000 Wu-huan cavalry men were

---

[63] *HHS*, 117:12b.

[64] *HHS*, 116:6a.

[65] For instance, see *HHS*, 117:4a; 119:3a–b; 120:2a.

[66] *HHS*, 119:8b; cf. Ma Ch'ang-shou, *Pei-Ti yü Hsiung-nu*, p. 89.

[67] *HHS*, 42:6b–7a.

[68] For instance, in the southwest, the local government often succeeded in using one group of I barbarians to crush the revolt of another. *HHS*, 116:9a; cf. Yu Chung, p. 29.

summoned from Yu-chou to fight the rebels. Lack of food provisions, however, eventually made them all desert and return home.[69] As a contemporary Chinese official rightly pointed out, the Wu-huan's desertion and subsequent insurrection rather resulted from the fact that their military services had been so excessively levied that they could no longer bear it.[70]

In the early years of the third century, the Wu-huan cavalry became more fully incorporated into the Chinese army and won a still greater reputation after Ts'ao Ts'ao moved them from the frontier provinces to interior China and reorganized them militarily.[71] In order to guarantee the loyalty of barbarian soldiers, the Han government found it necessary to require them to put their wives and children under the custody of Chinese officials as hostages. This practice has an earlier origin. Already in Wang Mang's time the Wu-huan and other barbarian soldiers had to send their families to the Chinese *chün* and *hsien* as hostages. Later on, when the Wu-huan deserted, the local government executed all these hostages.[72] The same method is found still in use in A.D. 217 under Ts'ao Ts'ao. For instance, when Lu Hsi, the king of the Wu-huan of T'ai-yuan was on military duty to guard the northwestern frontiers in Shensi with his tribesmen, his beloved wife was kept as a hostage in the city of Chin-yang in Shansi.[73] It is certainly legitimate to conjecture that hostage was prob-

---

[69] *HHS*, 103:1a; cf. Ma Ch'ang-shou, *Wu-huan yü Hsien-pi*, p. 142 and n. 3. In "The Liang-chou Rebellion," G. Haloun mentions this army as composed of Wu-huan and other barbarians but says nothing about the Wu-huan's later desertion (p. 121, n. 15). Uchida Gimpū, "Wu-huan," p. 78, however, mistakes these Wu-huan cavalrymen for "a sort of mercenaries" and thus misinterprets their desertion as a result of China's failure to pay them as promised. Actually, these Wu-huan were the *shu-kuo* barbarians, and, as such, were under obligation to render military services to China when called upon.

[70] Yüan Hung, *Hou Han Chi*, 25:5a–b.

[71] *SKC, Wei chih*, 30–5a. It may be pointed out that the Later Han government had such a high regard for the Wu-huan cavalry that some 736 Wu-huan and other barbarian cavalrymen were regularly used to guard the capital under the command of the *Ch'ang-shui Chiao-wei* (*HHS*, 37:3a–b).

[72] *HHS*, 120:2a.

[73] *Wei Lüeh*, quoted in *SKC, Wei chih*, 15:7b.

ably required of most, if not all, Wu-huan soldiers on active military duty.[74]

Toward the end of the Later Han and in the period of the Three Kingdoms (A.D. 221–265), Chinese control over the surrendered barbarians tended to be further tightened, and accordingly, their obligations to China in terms of taxes and labor services also became more or less regularized. For instance, with the decline of the power of their *Shan-yü* in A.D. 216 the Southern Hsiung-nu were divided by Ts'ao Ts'ao into several smaller groups. On the surface, each group was still under the rule of a Hsiung-nu leader chosen from among their nobles. But in reality, it was the Chinese supervising official, bearing the title of *ssu-ma*, who actually had control over their life.[75] As Liu Yuan, the Hsiung-nu rebel leader, later complained, since the end of the Han the *Shan-yü* had become only an empty name without an inch of land whereas the Hsiung-nu nobles, though still bearing the honorary titles of kings and marquises, had been actually degraded to no more than commoners.[76] With the possible exception of the Hsien-pi, all other barbarians including the Wu-huan, Ti, and Ch'iang were equally under the same tightening Chinese control.[77]

At this time it also seems to have been the policy of the Chinese government to treat the surrendered barbarians as much as possible as regular Chinese subjects. According to the *Chin Shu,* the surrendered Hsiung-nu in Han times were treated generally like *pien-hu* or "registered [Chinese] subjects," except that they were not required to pay taxes.[78] Sometime before A.D. 213, for instance, the Hsiung-nu in Ping Chou (in Shansi) actually are reported

---

[74] Ma Ch'ang-shou, *Wu-huan yü Hsien-pi,* pp. 156–158.

[75] *Chin Shu,* 97:17b–18a; *Tzu-chih t'ung-chien,* 5:2146–2147. For modern studies see Ma Ch'ang-shou, *Pei-Ti yü Hsiung-nu,* 85–87; Uchida Gimpū, *Shirin,* 19.2, esp. pp. 275–277.

[76] *Chin Shu,* 101:4a.

[77] T'ang Chang-ju, *Wei-Chin Nan-Pei Ch'ao shih lun-ts'ung,* pp. 134–137.

[78] *Chin Shu,* 97:17b. This situation was probably typical of the third century rather than of the earlier times. Cf. T'ang Chang-ju, *op. cit.,* p. 137.

to have rendered labor services to China just as ordinary Chinese subjects.[79] Their exemption from taxes was probably due not to the leniency on the part of the Chinese government, but to the fact that they were too poverty-stricken and, moreover, had not yet developed agriculture to any significant degree.[80] In the light of the ways in which other surrendered barbarians were treated, however, we even have reason to believe that in some cases the Hsiung-nu people may also have been subject to taxation of some kind. At any rate, the contrast will become very striking when we recall that the surrendered Hsiung-nu in the early days of the Later Han period, instead of paying taxes and rendering corvée to China, received regularly annual food and clothes provisions from the Han court.[81]

Both household levies and land taxes were imposed on the Wu-huan people of Yen-men province, also in Shansi. For instance, Governor Ch'ien Chao requested of Emperor Wen of Wei (220–227) that some five hundred Wu-huan families there be exempted from land taxes and household levies so that they could be made to serve as frontier guards at their own expense.[82] Later under the Western Chin dynasty (265–316) the system of *hu-tiao* or "household levies" formally included barbarians as regular tax-payers, but at lower rates. Even barbarians in remote districts who did not cultivate land at all were required to pay certain amounts of *i-mi* or "voluntarily contributed rice." [83] Since the *hu-tiao* system was first established by Ts'ao Ts'ao in about 204, possibly such levies had already been imposed on many of the surrendered barbarians from about the end of the Later Han dynasty.[84] Thus the third century witnessed the rapidly growing transformation of the surrendered barbarians into Chinese subjects.

---

[79] *SKC, Wei chih,* 15:7a.

[80] Ma Ch'ang-shou, *Pei-Ti yü Hsiung-nu,* pp. 88–89.

[81] Uchida Gimpū, *Shirin,* 19:2, pp. 290–294.

[82] *SKC, Wei chih,* 26:11b. Cf. Ma Ch'ang-shou, *Wu-huan yü Hsien-pi,* pp. 160–161.

[83] Lien-sheng Yang, "Notes on the Economic History of the Chin Dynasty" in *Studies in Chinese Institutional History,* pp. 179–180.

[84] Cf. T'ang Chang-ju, *op. cit.,* pp. 137–139.

In order to fully embrace the surrendered barbarians into the arms of Chinese civilization, it was also the policy of the Later Han government to encourage them to develop a settled economic life. This is clearly shown in the fact that *hsün-li* or "model officials" of the Confucian type were often sent to govern the underdeveloped frontier provinces with a view particularly to civilizing the inner barbarians. It is interesting to note that the *hsün-li* always assumed it to be their immediate duty to teach the barbarians plowing and weaving.[85] On the other hand, Sinicization also led some barbarians to take the initiative to develop agriculture.

Early in the first century B.C., the Hsiung-nu had already begun to plant certain kinds of cereals of their own.[86] In A.D. 10, some two thousand Chinese people are reported to have been kept by the Hsiung-nu in their territory to cultivate land for them.[87] It is quite possible that as the Hsiung-nu became more and more addicted to the grain-eating habit, they found it necessary to engage in agricultural production, either by themselves or with the help of the Chinese.[88] Under the Later Han, the Southern Hsiung-nu inside China underwent a steadier process of economic Sinicization by gradually developing a settled agricultural life of their own.[89] In the early third century the pace of agricultural transformation of the Hsiung-nu was greatly accelerated by the efforts of Chinese local officials. For instance, Liang Hsi, as Circuit-Intendent of Ping-chou, worked hard to encourage the Hsiung-nu under his jurisdiction to develop both agriculture and sericulture.[90] Down to the (Ts'ao) Wei dynasty, the surrendered Hsiung-nu people were already so familiar with agricultural work that the Chinese landlords found it profitable

---

[85] For a brief discussion see Kamada Shigeo "Kandai no Junri to Kokuri," *Shigaku Zasshi*, esp. pp. 330–334; Hisayuki Miyakawa, "The Confucianization of South China," *The Confucian Persuasion*, pp. 29–31.

[86] *HS*, 94A:13a and Yen Shih-ku's commentary.

[87] *HS*, 94B:9b.

[88] Egami Namio, *Yūrashiya kodai hoppō bunka*, pp. 105–112.

[89] *Ibid.*, p. 33.

[90] *SKC, Wei chih*, 13:7a.

to use them to cultivate land. In the T'ai-yüan area alone, some powerful families possessed several thousand such Hsiung-nu and other barbarian serfs.[91]

In our period the Ch'iang barbarians probably adapted themselves to the settled economic life earlier than others. One branch of them in Hsi-hai province (probably Ningsia) was militarily much stronger than other Ch'iang groups because, as we are told, the Ch'iang people there happened to occupy the fertile land of Yü-ku, a region particularly suitable for not only domestication of animals but also agriculture.[92] In Pei-ti province, several thousand surrendered Ch'iang barbarians settled down in a place called Ch'ing-shan, leading a life of farming and herding.[93] Thus in A.D. 231 when the (Ts'ao) Wei troops on the northwestern frontier ran out of food provisions, General Kuo Huai was able to ask every Ch'iang family there to pay grain to the government as a substitute for labor service.[94] This instance fully reveals that the Ch'iang barbarians by then must have been turned into farmers.

The Wu-huan also developed agriculture to some extent, but rather as a sideline.[95] That some of them must have become land-tillers, at least toward the end of our period, is, however, clearly indicated by the fact that they were required to pay land taxes by the Chinese government.[96] By contrast, the Hsien-pi were much less devoted to agricultural development during this period. Theirs was rather a mixed economy of farming, herding, and hunting, and, in the latter part of the second century, fishing was added because of economic insufficiency.[97] Even as late as

---

[91] *Chin Shu*, 93:3b. Cf. T'ang Chang-ju, *op. cit.*, p. 139; Ma Ch'ang-shou, *Pei-Ti yü Hsiung-nu*, p. 90.

[92] *Shui-ching chu*, photolithographic reprint of *Yung-lo ta-tien*, edition, 1:12b. For a general discussion of the agriculturalization of the Ch'iang people in this period, see Hu Chao-hsi, "Lun Han-Chin ti Ti Ch'iang ho Sui-T'ang i-hou ti Ch'iang-tsu," *LSYC*, pp. 168–169.

[93] Hsieh Ch'en's work quoted in *HHS*, 33:4b.

[94] *SKC, Wei*, 26:14b.

[95] Uchida Gimpū, "Wu-huan," pp. 46–47.

[96] Cf. T'ang Chang-ju, *op. cit.*, p. 137.

[97] *HHS*, 120:6b; Wang Shen's *Wei Shu* quoted in *SKC, Wei chih*, 30:5b.

the beginning of the third century, domestication of animals probably still played the leading role in the Hsien-pi economy. This retarded agricultural growth resulted largely from the fact that the Hsien-pi remained outer barbarians beyond the Chinese frontiers throughout the period under review, whereas other peoples, including the Wu-huan, gradually turned into inner barbarians living mostly fact to face with the Chinese within the Han territory.[98]

APPENDIX TO CHAPTER FOUR

A note on H. H. Dubs, *A Roman City in Ancient China,*
London, 1957

In his interesting volume, *A Roman City in Ancient China,* Professor Dubs has tried very hard to show that some 145 Roman legionaries were brought back to China by the Chinese General Ch'en T'ang from Central Asia, sometime after 36 B.C. These Romans, we are told, were allowed to found a city and a *hsien* of their own in a frontier province in today's Kansu with a Chinese name for Rome—Alexandria, namely, Li-hsien or Li-chien in Chang-yeh Province (*HS,* 28B:2a; *HHS,* 33:4b). Since this problem is directly related to our discussion of the treatment of surrendered barbarians in Han China, it is therefore necessary to take a close look at his book. Concerning these "Romans" and the "city" they "founded," Professor Dubs writes in summary, "It was, however, quite probably organized on a Roman model. Its people had not surrendered to the Chinese, but were freemen and consequently would not be expected in every way to submit to Chinese practices. The Chinese government generally left its people alone, as far as practicable, as long as they kept peace, paid the taxes, and rendered due military service. The Chinese almost surely gave these Romans a centrally appointed Chief (*jang*) or Magistrate to oversee the city and county. That they married Chinese women may be taken for granted, since the city continued to exist for centuries" (pp. 22–23). With all my admiration for Professor Dub's solid scholarship and formidable assiduity as shown in this study, I must say that the above statement is but a conjecture without sufficient historical basis. Of course, this is not the place to review extensively Professor Dub's

---

[98] Cf. Ma Ch'ang-shou, *Wu-huan yü Hsien-pi,* pp. 177–178.

book. Nevertheless, I would like to take this opportunity to point out a number of difficulities involved in his theory.

In the light of our analysis in chapter IV, the settlement of the 145 Romans in China, as described by Professor Dubs, seems to run counter to the whole set of institutional devices with which surrendered barbarians were normally handled by the Han government.

First, 145 Romans was too small a number to be allowed to found a city and form a *hsien*. In most cases barbarians were incorporated into the Chinese *chün* and *hsien* administrative system, as we have seen, only when they surrendered to China with their lands. Second, surrendered barbarians in small number, especially if they were good warriors, were usually organized into a special fighting unit and put under the command of a Chinese official in charge of the frontier barbarians. For instance, a group of the Yueh-chih people was thus made into the *I-ts'ung Hu* or "voluntary barbarian followers" by Teng Hsün, the *Hu-Ch'iang Chiao-wei* or Protector-Colonel of the Ch'iang, in about A.D. 89 because the Yueh-chih barbarians were known especially for their fighting ability. (*HHS*, 45:4b–5a; 117:12a–b. Cf., also, G. Haloun, "The Liang-chou Rebellion," p. 119 and note 3.) Since the 145 Romans are described by Dubs as "brave fighters" and "professional soldiers" (p. 15), it is rather difficult to understand why they were, instead of being included in the Chinese army, which was undoubtedly the most logical place for them to go, brought under the control of the *chün-hsien* system as ordinary subjects.

Third, the established practice of the Han government was to organize the surrendered barbarians into either a *shu-kuo* or a *pu* if they were allowed to live according to their own customs, and its transformation to regular *chün* or *hsien* normally took a long time. In case the number of the surrendered barbarians was small, a small scale *shu-kuo* could be established to accommodate them. For instance, in Shang-chün (in northern Shensi and the Ordos), there was a *shu-kuo* bearing the name of Ch'iu-tz'u (Kucha). It was so named under the two Han dynasties because the surrendered Kuchan people were settled there. While all other *shu-kuo* were of the *chün* size, this particular one was only comparable to a *hsien*. (*HS*, 28B:3a; *HHS*, 33:5b. Cf., also, Yen Keng-wang, *Chung-kuo ti-fang hsing-cheng chih-tu shih, shang-pien*, 1:164.) Obviously, such an irregularity can only be understood as having resulted from the fact that the number of the surrendered Kuchans was too small to warrant a regular-sized *shu-kuo*. Now, in the case of Li-chien, it was only a regular *hsien* without any trace of having undergone the process of transformation from a *shu-kuo* or *pu*. It is therefore very unlikely that it was organized on the Roman model by the surrendered Romans.

Fourth, it is even doubtful whether Li-chien ever had foreign settlers at all. In Ch'in and Han China, the name of *hsien* was always changed to *tao* in case it had barbarians under its jurisdiction. For instance, in An-ting (in Kansu) there was a Yueh-chih *tao* (*HS,* 28B:2b). This must be a place in which the Yueh-chih people took their residence since, as we know, in Han times they occasionally came to submit themselves to China. Under the reign of Emperor Ling (A.D. 168–188) several hundred of them are reported to have surrendered to the Han government. (See Yao Wei-yüan, *Pei-ch'ao Hu-hsing k'ao,* p. 378 and note 4 on p. 379.) Had Li-chien been a place with foreign settlers, to say nothing of its being founded by the Romans, it would have been called a *tao* rather than *hsien.*

Last, but not least, the registered population of all the ten *hsien* of Chang-yeh province toward the end of the Former Han period totalled 24,382 households and 88,731 individuals. Unfortunately, we do not know how this population was actually distributed among the ten *hsien.* But it would be by no means unreasonable to assume that each *hsien* had at least several thousand people. This would necessarily mean that the 145 Romans, even if they were settled in Li-chien, were completely submerged in the sea of thousands of native Chinese. Because, we cannot believe, even by the wildest stretch of imagination, that a separate *hsien* government could have been possibly established just to take care of a handful of surrendered barbarians especially in view of the fact that the administrative expenditure involved in the establishment and maintenance of a *hsien* was quite high in Han times. Thus considered, it is impossible to accept Professor Dubs' conclusion that "the place did constitute a Roman settlement and in that sense may be called a Roman colony" (pp. 22–23). I, therefore, quite agree with Professor Schuyler Cammann who, in his review of the book, says "it was never a Roman city in any sense, much less a *colonia.*" (*Journal of Asian Studies,* 21:3 [May, 1962] p. 382.)

Finally, it may be noted that the whole matter seems to have arisen out of the fact that Professor Dubs was misled by the commentary of Wang Hsien-ch'ien (note 3 on p. 24), which was in turn taken from a note made by the Ch'ing scholar, Wu Cho-hsin, in his *Han Shu Ti-li-chih pu-chu* (*Erh-shih-wu shih pu-pien* edition, p. 392). According to Wu, there were surrendered Romans in Li-chien during the Han period, but this is probably all we can say about the case. It still requires evidence to identify the Romans, if any, of Li-chien with the 145 Romans legionaries supposedly found by Professor Dubs.

chapter five

Frontier Trade

Trade, of course, provided a major avenue for Sino-
foreign economic intercourse in Han China, as it did in
other periods in Chinese history. Limited by the highly
scattered and fragmentary nature of our sources, emphasis
will be laid on the various ways in which trade was carried
on rather than in the volume actually involved in it,
which is unfortunately beyond reconstruction. In Han
China there existed three types of foreign trade, namely,
frontier trade, overland trade with western countries, and
overseas trade. As the frontier barbarians often served as
intermediaries in the foreign trade of Han China, it would
be natural to start with frontier trade and then proceed to
discuss the other two.

1 *Frontier Trade and Expansion*

As has been pointed out previously, merchants were
remarkably active in the Han period. Their activities were
especially noticeable along the frontiers and, moreover,
contributed much to the expansion of the Han empire.[1]
In many cases, the profit-seeking adventures of individual
merchants paved the way for the government to extend
Chinese territories by annexing more frontier regions
under the *chün-hsien* administrative system. For instance,
according to a Ch'ing scholar, the trading activities of a
Chinese merchant by the name of P'eng Wu in Korea
eventually led to the establishment of a Chinese province

---

[1] For a general discussion see Ch'ien Mu, *Ch'in-Han shih*, pp. 129–136.

there.[2] At any rate, as both historical and archaeological evidences tend to agree, from the Warring-States period on, the interplay of trade and expansion had been gradually pushing the northeastern frontier of China to as far as northern Korea.[3] Later on under Emperor Wu of Han when Chinese provincial administration was established in Korea, more merchants went there from interior China and their profit-seeking instinct was so strong that they even indulged in theft and thus, gradually corrupted the social customs there.[4]

In the southwestern expansion of the Han empire, a similar role was played by the Chinese merchant. Merchants from Szechwan often illegally crossed the border to trade with Yeh-lang and their trading activities eventually brought the military and political importance of the Yeh-lang area to the attention of the Han government. As a result, the whole southwest (part of Szechwan, Yunnan, and Kweichow) was reopened to China and several of the barbarian states were transformed into Chinese provinces.[5]

On the northern and northwestern frontiers, merchants were also very active in the Ch'in and Chao areas.[6] Moreover, as these areas bordered the lands of the Ch'iang, Jung, Ti, and Hsiung-nu, naturally the Chinese merchants had constant and extensive dealings with the frontier barbarians, which enabled the former to make enormous profits. As early as under the Ch'in dynasty, for instance, a certain Lo of Wu-chih was already able to make great fortunes out of his trade with the king of the Jung barbarians.[7]

---

[2] Ch'ien Ta-hsin, *Nien-erh shih k'ao-i*, 1:49. Cf., also, Ch'ien Mu, *op. cit.*, p. 130 and Nancy Lee Swann, *Food and Money in Ancient China*, p. 243, n. 424; for a different interpretation see, however, Wang Nien-sun, *Tu-shu tsa-chih*, 2:47.

[3] T'ung Chu-ch'en, "K'ao-ku-hsüeh shang Han-tai chi Han-tai i-ch'ien ti tung-pei pien-chiang," *K'ao-ku hsüeh-pao*, pp. 29–42; Wang Yü-ch'üan, *Wo-kuo ku-tai huo-pi ti ch'i-yüan ho fa-chan*, p. 69.

[4] *HS*, 28B:13b–14a.

[5] *SC*, 116:1b–3a; Burton Watson, *Records of the Grand Historian of China*, 2:291–296.

[6] *SC*, 129:4a–b; Watson, 2:485–486.

[7] *SC*, 129:3b; Watson, 2:483.

Not only did the Chinese merchants from the interior often travel all the way to the frontiers to explore new avenues to wealth, but trade between one frontier area and another was also well developed. This situation can be best illustrated by the appearance of the *chü* berry sauce in Canton.[8] The *chü* berry sauce was a native product of Szechwan, which the native merchants exported in large quantities to Yeh-lang. The Yeh-lang people, however, did not consume it all and found it profitable to send the surplus in turn to the markets of Yueh, via the Tsang-ko River. Thus, the two important frontier areas—then known as the Southwest and Southern Yueh respectively— were economically linked up by the water route. This situation made it possible for the king of Southern Yueh even to contemplate the control of Yeh-lang by economic means.[9]

The fact that the exploratory activities of the Chinese merchants along the frontiers often led to political and military expansion of the Han empire was already noticed by a keen contemporary observer, Ssu-ma Ch'ien, who remarked in the case of the Southwestern barbarians, thus: "The whole affair of Han relations with the southwestern barbarians came about because someone saw some *chü* berry sauce in P'an-yü and because the people of Ta-hsia (Bactria) carried canes made of Ch'iung bamboo! Later the western barbarians were split up into two groups and their lands made into seven provinces." [10]

Apart from the merchants, stationed military forces also helped the growth of trade on the frontiers. From the Chan-kuo period on, there had been established camp markets (*chün-shih*) where military forces were stationed especially in the frontier regions. For instance, in the third century B.C., when Li Mu, the famous general of Chao, was entrusted with the task of guarding against the Hsiung-nu

---

[8] On the *chü* berry sauce see Fujita Toyohachi, *Tōzai kōshō-shi no kenkyū, Nankai hen,* p. 647. According to Yü Ching-jang, *chü* is probably a kind of pepper. See *Ta-lu tsa-chih,* pp. 20–24.

[9] *SC,* 116:2a; Watson, 2:291–292.

[10] *SC,* 116:3b; translation from Watson, 2:296. Cf., also, Fujita Toyohachi, pp. 645–648.

invasions in the Yen-men area (in modern Shansi) he set
up markets in the army camp, the taxes from which all
went to secure provisions for his soldiers.[11] Similar camp
markets are occasionally found in use through much of the
Han period. Under Emperor Wen's reign, Wei Shang,
Governor of Yün-chung (modern Suiyuan), established
camp markets on the border, modelled closely on those of
Li Mu.[12] In Emperor Wu's time, one military officer even
went so far as to transform the camp of the Northern
Palace Guards in the capital into a market place to trade
with the soldiers.[13] The *chün-shih* later not only was extended to the interior but also tended to become institu-
tionalized within the Han military system. Thus, for each
camp market normally a military officer, under the title of
chün-shih ling, would be appointed to take charge, presumably, of its management.[14] Down to the age of the
Three Kingdoms, the same institution was still very much
alive. Both Wei and Wu established camp markets for the
convenience of the stationed soldiers.[15] Unfortunately,
due to lack of detailed information we do not know how
regular an institution the *chün-shih* was, or what types of
goods were on sale there.

It was the soldiers stationed in the frontier regions that
played, however, a particularly active role in the development of frontier trade. Generally speaking, we can distinguish three different categories in which Han stationed
soldiers participated in the frontier trade. The first was the
camp market just discussed above. The second was the
border market, known as *kuan-shih* (barrier market) or
Hu-shih (barbarian market), which will be further in-
vestigated later in this chapter. Right now it is sufficient to
keep in mind that when peace prevailed on the border,
stationed Chinese soldiers, like Chinese merchants, also

[11] *SC*, 81:5b, 102:3b; Watson, 1:540.
[12] *SC*, 102:4a; *HS*, 50:3a; Watson, 1:541.
[13] *HS*, 67:1b–2a.
[14] *HS*, 74:4a; *HHS*, 50:3b. Cf., also, Sun Yü-t'ang, "Hsi-Han ti ping-chih,"
Chung-kuo she-hui ching-chi shih chi-k'an, p. 55.
[15] T'ao Yüan-chen, *San-kuo shih-huo chih*, pp. 113–114.

traded with the barbarians in such places.[16] The third was the ordinary market in various frontier cities. A picture of the commercial activities of the frontier soldiers can be reconstructed from the newly-discovered Han documents on wood. In the famous Chü-yen documents, we often encounter the term *ssu-shih,* or "to do private shopping," and *wei-chia ssu-shih,* or "to do private shopping for the family." This was so because many of the soldiers brought their families to the frontier garrisons with them. They not only went to the nearby city of Chü-yen district, but sometimes also travelled as far as to the capital city of Chang-yeh Province, or even to that of the neighboring frontier province of Chiu-ch'üan.[17]

These documents also reveal a number of other interesting facts about the trading activities of the Han military forces on the frontiers. First, although there is no clear and direct reference to the existence of the camp market in these documents, we do find several instances in which the soldiers traded between themselves. In one case, a garrison soldier sold a piece of silk worth 1,000 cash in the market to a chief of a beacon station at the official price of 600.[18] In another case, a soldier of one station sold a suit of clothes he received from the government to a soldier of another station.[19] Quite a number of documents show that the soldiers sometimes were involved in debts with each other, resulting mostly from trade of this kind.[20]

Second, frontier soldiers also had direct commercial relations with the common people in the neighborhood of their stations. For instance, one document records that both the garrison and farming soldiers sold clothes and other goods that they received from the government to the

---

[16] Sun Yü-t'ang, *op. cit.,* p. 55.

[17] For instances see Lao Kan, *Chü-yen Han-chien, shih-wen,* no. 691, p. 15; no. 1281, p. 26; no. 2080, p. 42; no. 2294, p. 46; no. 2301, p. 47; no. 5534, p. 115; no. 6828, p. 141. Cf. also Lao Kan, "Han-chien chung ti Ho-hsi ching-chi sheng-huo," *CYYY,* 11, pp. 72–73.

[18] Lao Kan, *Chü-yen Han-chien, shih-wen,* no. 3909, p. 78.

[19] *Ibid.,* no. 6211, p. 129.

[20] *Ibid.,* no. 3742, p. 75; no. 4475, p. 92; no. 4916, p. 101; no. 5703, p. 119. Cf., also, Lao Kan's remarks in *k'ao-cheng,* p. 6.

frontier people at high prices for profit.[21] In another case a soldier sold three pieces of cloth to a local resident for 1,000 cash.[22] It seems that officials and soldiers on the frontiers, unlike those in the interior provinces, were allowed by the government to engage in trade,[23] probably out of the consideration that their meager income was far from sufficient to support their families. Thus, it is not surprising to find an officer reporting, presumably to his superior, his business transactions with an ordinary market man (shih-jen).[24]

Third, traces of intercourse between stationed military forces and barbarians on the frontiers are also clearly shown in these documents. One fragmentary document from Chü-yen records some person or persons of barbarian origin as from the Small Yüeh-chih.[25] This fits very well with similar documents discovered at Tun-huang.[26] It may be noted that the so-called Small Yüeh-chih barbarians had long surrendered to Han China and lived inside the Chinese territory. Moreover, since they were good warriors, many of them were incorporated into the Han army under the policy of "using barbarians to attack barbarians." [27] It would then seem that this barbarian in question may well have been such a soldier. Another piece of evidence gives three strange names with two bearing the character Hu, which highly suggests that they are barbarians. Of the three, the first one seems to have been a cavalry man and

---

[21] Ibid., no. 5995, p. 126.

[22] Ibid., no. 4587, p. 94.

[23] Cf. Ch'en Chih, Liang-Han ching-chi shih-liao lun-ts'ung, p. 32; Michael Loewe, "Some Notes on Han-time Documents from Chüyen," TP, p. 301.

[24] Lao Kan, Chü-yen Han-chien, shih-wen, no. 7394, p. 152. One document from Tun-huang also reports that a commoner, presumably a travelling merchant, from interior China sold a suit of clothes to a chief of a beacon station for 1,300 cash. See Lo Chen-yü and Wang Kuo-wei, Liu-sha chui-chien, 2:47a.

[25] Lao Kan, Chü-yen Han-chien, shih-wen, no. 866, p. 18.

[26] Lo Chen-yü and Wang Kuo-wei, Liu-sha chui-chien, pu-i, 7a.

[27] See Yao Wei-yüan, Pei-ch'ao Hu-hsing k'ao, pp. 366–368. On the Yüeh-chih people, see Gustav Haloun, "Zur Ue-tsi-Frage," Zeitschrift der Deutschen Morgenländischen Gesellschaft, pp. 243–318.

the second one a female servant.[28] One Tun-huang document also reports a surrendered barbarian woman from
Wu-sun, a small state in the Western Regions.[29] A most
interesting bit of information is provided by a Chü-yen
document, which bears importantly on the economic relations between the Han military forces and the surrendered
barbarian troops on the border. It states that on *chi-wei*
day, eighth month, third year of Cheng-ho (90 B.C.), a
Chinese officer handed 43 *shih* and 2 *tou* of grain to two
commanding officers of a barbarian *shu-kuo* or subject
state.[30] The *shu-kuo* in this instance probably can be
identified as one of the five *shu-kuo* established in 121 or
120 B.C. to accommodate the surrendered Hsiung-nu, as
discussed in the preceding chapter. The transaction shown
in this document looks like an official one rather than
private, although it is not altogether clear whether the *shu-
kuo* barbarians normally received their food provisions
from the Han government in this way.

In the light of these newly-discovered documents discussed above, it would seem that the Han military forces
on the frontiers at least had some dealings of general economic nature with the barbarians. Against this historical
background it is probably legitimate to interpret the term
wai-shih in both the *Shih Chi*[31] and the *Han Shu*[32]
differently. The whole sentence says something rather
vaguely to the effect that the generals and officers would
feel uneasy and start to have "dealings with outsiders"
(*wai-shih*). Traditional understanding takes it to mean
that they would bargain with the outside enemy, which of
course makes sense.[33] Recently, however, it has been suggested that *wai-shih*, in this instance, could be taken literally as referring to the fact that the Han frontier soldiers
would sell prohibited goods, especially iron weapons, to

---

[28] Lao Kan, *Chü-yen Han-chien, shih-wen*, no. 2361, p. 48.
[29] Lo Cheng-yü and Wang Kuo-wei, *Liu-sha chui-chien*, 2:50b.
[30] Lao Kan, *Chü-yen Han-chien, shih-wen*, no. 7293, p. 150.
[31] *SC*, 112:4a.
[32] *HS*, 64A:8b.
[33] Watson, 2:228.

the Hsiung-nu.[34] It seems that this modern interpretation is made even more likely by our foregoing analysis, in which it has been shown that the Han frontier soldiers did have opportunities to deal with the barbarians.

Thus, we see that economic activities of both the Han merchants and stationed military forces on the frontiers may be conveniently taken to illustrate the two closely interwoven aspects of Sino-barbarian economic intercourse, that is, trade and expansion. On the one hand, it was the merchants that helped to bring about expansion of the empire by way of trade, and, on the other hand, it was the soldiers that widened the range of trade through expansion.

2 Trade with the Hsiung-nu

As has been noted, economic insufficiency made it necessary for the Hsiung-nu to trade with others to increase their income. The Hsiung-nu had developed such a strong interest in trade that even their women are reported to have occasionally taken an active part in it. According to the *Han Shu*, "When the Hsiung-nu, as usual, sent an envoy to collect the Wu-huan tributes, such as the Hsiung-nu men and women as were desirous of trading all followed the deputation." [35] The Hsiung-nu were so much accustomed to commercial transactions that, it is quite amusing to note, even in his insulting letter to Empress Lü, *Shan-yü* Mo-tun still displayed such a sense of humor as to talk in terms of trade. The last part of the letter says that since he is a widower and the empress a widow, both must be equally unhappy. "Let us exchange with each other," he concludes the letter with a malicious suggestion, "what we have for what we do not have." [36]

We have seen in chapter III that official trade between China and the Hsiung-nu began with the establishment of

---

[34] See the discussion in Egami Namio, *Yūrashiya kodai hoppō bunka*, pp. 309–310.

[35] *HS*, 94A:8a–9b. English translation is adapted from A. Wylie, "History of Heung-noo in Their Relation with China," *The Journal of the Royal Anthropological Institute*, 5:1, p. 66.

[36] *HS*, 94A:4a.

border markets under Emperor Wen. A similar policy of allowing the Hsiung-nu to trade on the border was followed by Emperor Ching, and it proved very effective in keeping them quiet. As Ssu-ma Ch'ien says: "Emperor Ching once more renewed the peace alliance with the Hsiung-nu, allowing them to buy goods in the markets along the Han border and sending them supplies. . . . Thus throughout Emperor Ching's reign, although the Hsiung-nu from time to time made small plundering raids across the border, they did not carry out any major invasions." [37] This seems a sufficient proof that the Hsiung-nu invasion was primarily motivated by their greed for Chinese goods, and, war probably could have been avoided if such goods were obtainable through peaceful channels, that is, trade. The same situation continued well into the early years of Emperor Wu, and the frontier trade won for China such a firm relationship with the Hsiung-nu that from the *Shan-yü* on down, they all became friendly with the Han, coming and going along the Great Wall.[38]

Even after the breakout of war between the Chinese and the Hsiung-nu, trade between the two belligerent peoples was still continued in the border markets. This was possible because the Hsiung-nu were badly in need of Han goods, while the Chinese government found the border trade useful as a method of dissipating some of the Hsiung-nu energy, as well as a way of satiating part of their rapaciousness, which might otherwise have become sources of military aggression. Also, the border markets had become such a haunt of the Hsiung-nu that the Han forces sometimes could make surprise attacks on them there.[39] As late as 98 B.C. the Hsiung-nu, in a peace proposal, still asked China, among other things, to open large border markets.[40] At this juncture one may be tempted to ask why the border market was such an attraction to the Hsiung-nu? Neither the *Shih Chi* nor the *Han Shu* give a description

---

[37] SC, 110:10a; English translation by Watson, 2:176.
[38] SC, 110:10a; Watson, 2:176. Cf., also, *Yen-t'ieh lun*, p. 48.
[39] SC, 110:10b; Watson, 2:177–178.
[40] HS, 94A:12b.

of it. However, in the writings of Chia I, we find a passage which throws much light on the problem. According to him, the border market was something that the Hsiung-nu needed. It was then called *kuan-shih*, or barrier market, because the market was, in most cases, established near a well-guarded barrier, which was normally located in a spot of strategical importance to border defense. Moreover, the fact that the border market often swarmed with the Hsiung-nu was not only because it was a place for the exchange of commodities, but also because it was a place where fine Chinese food and wine could always be obtained.[41] This probably explains why the Chinese forces could have taken them there by surprise.

Under the Later Han dynasty, as has been previously noted, the Hsiung-nu were split permanently into two groups. We have treated the economic relations of the Southern Hsiung-nu with China under the general category of the surrendered barbarians. But what happened to the Northern Hsiung-nu? Generally speaking, while the Southern Hsiung-nu gradually turned to a settled life as a result of continuing Sinicization, the Northern Hsiung-nu remained nomadic and moved step by step westward until they finally reached Europe.[42] As the Northern Hsiung-nu, unlike their southern brothers, did not receive regular aid from the Han court, they suffered at least as much economic insufficiency as in the Former Han period. Trade and plundering thus became their two main sources for the increase of income. In the first few years following the split between the Southern and Northern Hsiung-nu in A.D. 48, the Northern Hsiung-nu repeatedly sent envoys to China to negotiate peace.[43] Under the "divide and rule" barbarian policy, the Later Han government, however, had to turn down all such proposals from the latter in order to retain the allegiance of their southern brothers.

---

[41] Chia I, *Hsin shu*, 4:5a.

[42] For a general account see Uchida Gimpū, *Tōyōshi kenkyū*, 2:1, pp. 15–35. Cf., also, Egami Namio, *op. cit.*, pp. 33–35, 319–402.

[43] For instance, in A.D. 51, 52 (*HHS*, 1B:9a) and 55 (*HHS*, 119:4a) the Northern Hsiung-nu sent envoys either to the frontier province or to the court, together with tribute, asking for the reestablishment of peace.

For instance, in the year A.D. 51, a court conference was held to discuss whether the Northern Hsiung-nu's request for resumption of peace relations should be granted. The conference went on undecided until the heir-apparent finally pointed out that to reach a peace agreement with the Northern Hsiung-nu would inevitably alienate the newly-surrendered Southern Hsiung-nu.[44] The same opinion was actually shared by many Later Han officials.[45] On the other hand, the Southern Hsiung-nu, in many instances, also deliberately made attempts to bar their northern brothers from concluding any long-term peace with China, presumably because they wanted to monopolize the imperial favor.[46]

Even under such unfavorable circumstances, however, the Northern Hsiung-nu still sought every possible opportunity either to trade with China or to obain "gifts" from the court. According to a memorial of Pan Piao dated A.D. 52, the Northern Hsiung-nu had several times brought cattle to the Chinese markets.[47] In 63, when they were still very powerful, they repeatedly invaded the border. Emperor Ming granted their request for trade in the hope

---

[44] *HHS*, 119:3b. According to Yüan Hung, *Hou Han Chi, SPTK* edition, 8:3b, the conference was held four years earlier in A.D. 47. It is interesting to add that the heir-apparent's (later Emperor Ming) fear later proved well-grounded. See *HHS*, 119:4b.

[45] For instance, Cheng Chung, during the reign of Emperor Ming, was against the idea of resuming diplomatic relations with the Northern Hsiung-nu. He even declined the appointment to serve as an envoy to the latter. (*HHS*, 66:3a–b; Yüan Hung, *Hou Han Chi*, 10:1a–b.) Under Emperor Chang (76–88), when the Northern Hsiung-nu again sent envoys with tribute to the court requesting peace, most officials opposed it on the ground that it might incur the displeasure of the Southern Hsiung-nu (*HHS*, 70B:5b). In the year A.D. 91, Yüan An pointed out in his memorial that the basic policy of the Later Han had been such from its very beginning that China should cultivate the friendship of the Southern Hsiung-nu on the one hand and suppress the Northern Hsiung-nu on the other hand. Under such a policy the court, in the periods of Emperors Chang and Ho (76–105), refused to settle some hundred thousand surrendered Northern Hsiung-nu along the frontiers for fear that in so doing the Southern Hsiung-nu might lose confidence in China (*HHS*, 75:2a–b).

[46] For instance see *HHS*, 75:1b and 119:5a–b.

[47] *HHS*, 119:3b.

that they might thus be more or less appeased.[48] The last report on the Northern Hsiung-nu trading with China came in the year 84. This time they notified the governor of Wu-wei that they wanted to trade with both the Chinese government and people. The governor then reported it to the court, in response to which an imperial edict was issued, allowing the governor to dispatch envoys to welcome them. Thereupon, the Northern *Shan-yü* sent several of his princes, together with more than ten thousand head of cattle, to trade with the Chinese merchants. Many other Hsiung-nu nobles also joined the trip. They were all well accommodated by the Chinese government wherever they stopped and, moreover, were generously rewarded with gifts.[49] In addition to trade, the Northern Hsiung-nu also occasionally received gifts from the Chinese court, although they had never been formally admitted to the Chinese tributary system. For instance, in A.D. 52 the Northern Hsiung-nu presented to the Emperor, in the name of tribute, horses and furs. To return the favor, the Emperor conferred on their *Shan-yü* and nobles a considerable amount of silken fabrics. As, according to Pan Piao, the imperial gift was approximately equal to the Hsiung-nu tribute in value, such an exchange may very well be understood as a form of trade.[50] In dealing with the Northern Hsiung-nu, it seems that the Later Han government recognized them more as a de facto economic and military force than as a de jure political entity. Thus, the former did not fail to reciprocate the latter's tribute with gifts, mostly silks, but was very reluctant to send envoys to return their calls.[51] In A.D. 105, the economic state of the Northern Hsiung-nu had so deteriorated that they could not even afford to present tribute to the Chinese court. They, nevertheless, expressed their willingness to send a hostage prince to China only if China should be kind enough to favor them with an imperial envoy. Even such a

---

[48] *HHS*, 119:4b.

[49] *HHS*, 119:5a.

[50] *HHS*, 119:3b–4a. Cf. Frederick J. Teggart, *Rome and China*, pp. 214–215.

[51] This point is shown in the cases of A.D. 55 and 104 (*HHS*, 119:4a, 8a).

humble request was not complied with. Instead, however, they were generously rewarded with imperial gifts.[52]

Traces of trade between the Hsiung-nu and Han China can also be detected in archaeological discoveries. The famous finds of Noin-ula include not only silk and lacquer, which, as has been shown earlier, may have been originally imperial gifts from the Han court, but also other Chinese goods of Han date such as jade ornaments and bronze mirrors and vessels. The latter group could fall into the Hsiung-nu's possession through private channels, especially trade.[53] Similar discoveries have also been made in other areas, notably the well-known Altai district where the Russian archaeologists have found many tombs of the Hsiung-nu, or other nomads closely associated with the Hsiung-nu.[54] From Schibe come pieces of typical Han lacquer as well as other ornaments of Han design.[55] From Pazirik come Chinese silk embroideries, which, according to Dagny Carter, were obtained by the owners of these tombs either through trade or by way of diplomatic exchanges.[56] In the Talas area the necropolis of Kenkol was excavated. Here, rich imported Chinese goods, together with the Hsiung-nu bows, are reported to have been unearthed. Some archaeologists even consider these remains to be a mark left by the Northern Hsiung-nu during their western adventure in the period of 43–36 B.C. At any rate, it seems beyond doubt that Kenkol is at least a memento of an eastern people who came from the east and established

---

[52] *HHS,* 119:8a.

[53] Umehara Sueji, *Mōko Noin-Ura hakken no ibutsu,* pp. 34–42; Perceval Yetts, "Discoveries of the Kozlov Expedition," *Burlington Magazine,* pp. 168–173; S. I. Rudenko, *Kul'tura khunnov i noinulinskie kurgany,* pp. 38–48.

[54] For a general account of the Altai district, see Karl Jettmar, "The Altai before the Turcs," *BMFEA,* pp. 135–223; for the connections between China and the Altai region in ancient times see Lu-chin-k'o (Rudenko), "Lun Chung-kuo yü Ah-erh-t'ai pu-lo ti ku-tai kuan-hsi," *K'ao-ku hsüeh-pao,* pp. 37–48.

[55] Umehara Sueji, *Kodai hoppō kei bumbutsu no kenkyū,* p. 178; H. Kuhn, "Zur Chronologie der Sino-Sibirischen Bronzen," *Ipek,* pp. 165–168.

[56] Dagny Carter, *The Symbol of the Beast,* pp. 72, 75; Edith Dittrich, "Das Motiv des Tierkampfes in der Altchinesischen Kunst," *Asiatische Forschungen,* 13 (1963), p. 24.

rule over a European tribe.[57] The most interesting archaeological evidence of trade is, however, provided by the
discovery of two *wu-shu* coins of Han date from the Hsiung-
nu tombs in the Minussinsk area. Although the coins alone
probably cannot be relied upon to date the finds,[58] in this
case, in light of the entire Minussinsk and other Transbaikal archaeological discoveries, we have good reason to
believe that these coins came originally from Han China.[59]

3 Trade with Other Frontier Barbarians

On the northwestern frontiers, the Chinese probably
had begun to trade with the Ch'iang people at a very early
date. From the beginning of our period, it was already
known to the Chinese that there were profits to be gained
from among the Ch'iang barbarians.[60] According to the
Han Shu, the whole frontier region known as Liang-chou,
or popularly Ho-hsi, where the Ch'iang population spread
all over, was especially famous for producing the best kind
of domestic animals.[61] The economic prosperity of this
region is further attested elsewhere. For instance, toward
the end of Wang Mang's reign, the Ho-hsi region was so
wealthy and stable that Tou Jung tried to seek an appointment as *shu-kuo tu-wei,* the Chinese official supervising the
Ch'iang and other barbarians there.[62] Moreover, a large
part of the wealth of Ho-hsi derived from international
trade, and it remained a center for merchants from various
countries at least down to the T'ang dynasty.[63]

However, as the Ch'iang people mostly lived face to face
with the Chinese as "inner barbarians," very little is men-

---

[57] K. Jettmar, "Hunnen und Hiung-nu—ein archäologisches Problem,"
Archiv fur Volkerkunde, pp. 166–180.

[58] Yetts, p. 182.

[59] H. Kuhn; Jettmar, "Hunnen and Hiung-nu"; Ellis H. Minns, "The
Art of the Northern Nomads," *Proceedings of the British Academy,* p. 74.

[60] *SC,* 129:4a; Watson, 2:485.

[61] *HS,* 28B:10a.

[62] *HHS,* 53:1a–b.

[63] For a general account see Matsuda Hisao, *Tōa ronsō,* pp. 55–90. For
aspects of economic life of the area as revealed in the newly-discovered
Han documents on wood see Lao Kan, "Han-chien chung ti Ho-hsi
ching-chi sheng-huo," *CYYY,* 11:1–2, pp. 61–75.

tioned of their trading activities in the dynastic histories.[64] Fortunately, the following story preserved in the *Hou Han Shu* throws much light on the prosperity of trade between the Ch'iang people and the Chinese. In the early years of Emperor Kuang-wu's reign, K'ung Fen was appointed the magistrate of Ku-tsang, the capital city of Wu-wei province in Ho-hsi. Being the wealthiest city of the area, its prosperity came almost entirely from trade with the Ch'iang and other barbarians. There the barbarian markets opened four times a day and the city was so prosperous that many of K'ung Fen's predecessors, it is reported, had been able to make a fortune within a few months, presumably through illegal exactions from both Chinese and Ch'iang merchants. As K'ung Fen was an official of incorruptible integrity, when he left Ku-tsang, after having served four years as magistrate, he did not acccumulate any personal property. The people of Ku-tsang, including both Chinese and Ch'iang, however, in order to express their appreciation for what he had done for them, presented to him, of their own accord, gifts worth several millions cash, which K'ung declined.[65] The importance of this story, short and simple as it is, lies in the fact that it fully indicates the extent to which the Chinese-Ch'iang trade flourished in the Ho-hsi area during the Han period. As the commentator has rightly pointed out, in ancient China it is believed that at most three times each day people gathered in the market for trade. Since the barbarian markets in Ku-tsang opened four times a day, this can only mean that there was a greater need for commercial transactions in terms of both people and commodities.[66]

In contrast to the Ch'iang, the Wu-huan and Hsien-pi, the two Eastern Barbarian peoples,[67] seem to have estab-

---

[64] For example, the entire chapter devoted to the Ch'iang people in the *Hou Han Shu* (*Chüan* 117) says nothing of the kind.

[65] *HHS*, 61:3a–b.

[66] Cf. the discussion in Matsuda Hisao, *op. cit.*, pp. 88–89.

[67] According to the Later Han scholar Fu Ch'ien, the name Eastern Barbarians (Tung Hu) derived from the fact that they were located to the east of the Hsiung-nu (Hu). Quoted in *So-yin, SC*, 110–3a. Whether they can be identified with Tungus as held by some of the western

lished more regular trade relations with the Chinese. As
early as in Emperor Wu's time, the office of *Hu Wu-huan
chiao-wei* was set up somewhere in Yu-chou (near modern
Peking) to take care of the Wu-huan people.[68] A similar
office was reestablished under the Later Han, in Ning
Ch'eng of Shang-ku (probably in modern Kalgan, Chahar).
Part of the function of this office was to regulate trade
between the Chinese on the one hand and both the
Wu-huan and Hsien-pi on the other. The barbarian
market proved so satisfactory to the Wu-huan that they
remained quiet on the frontiers for about half a century
(58–103).[69] Because of their close contact with the Chinese, their economic life, as compared with other barbarians, reached a relatively advanced stage in the Later Han
period. In addition to domestication of animals, they also
developed agriculture to a limited extent, as well as iron,
woolen and silk industries. In some aspects, however, they
still needed Chinese technical assistance. For instance, in
making wine they did not yet know how to produce yeast
and therefore always relied on China for some kind of fer-
menting rice.[70] It may be legitimate to infer that this kind
of need must have accounted much for their trading with
the Chinese. Toward the end of the Later Han dynasty,
the barbarian market in Shang-ku, where both Wu-huan
and Hsien-pi peoples came to trade, turned out to be
extremely prosperous, owing very much to the encouragement of Liu Yü, who was appointed Governor-General of
Yu-chou in the year 188. Later on when the Yellow
Turban rebels threw the central region of China into great

Sinologists is still a matter of controversy. Cf. Ma Ch'ang-shou, *Wu-huan
yü Hsien-pi*, p. 113, especially nn. 2 and 3. For a general account of both
Wu-huan and Hsien-pi peoples in English, see Edward Harper Parker,
"The History of the Wu-wan or Wu-huan Tunguses of the First Century;
Followed by That of Their Kinsmen the Sien-pi," *China Review*, pp.
71–100.

[68] Ying Shao, *Han Kuan-i* in Sun Hsing-yen, *Han-kuan ch'i-chung,
shang*, 39a.

[69] *HHS*, 120: 2a–b and 3b. Cf., also, Ying Shao, *Han Kuan-i*, 39a; *Wei
Shu* quoted in *SKC*, *Wei*, 5b.

[70] *Wei Shu* quoted in *SKC*, *Wei*, 30:2b. Cf. Uchida Gimpū, "Wu-huan"
pp. 46–47.

turmoil, more than a million people are reported to have
fled northward to seek refuge in Yu-chou, and the wealth
gained from the barbarian market proved of tremendous
help in the accommodation of so many refugees.[71] In case
the Wu-huan's economic need could not be met through
normal means such as trade, they also resorted to force as
did other barbarians. For instance, in the winter of A.D.
135 they invaded Yün-chung Province (in modern
Suiyuan) and robbed a Chinese caravan of over a thousand ox-drawn carriages.[72] This instance, however, also
shows with how much enthusiasm and to what extent the
Chinese merchants took part in the frontier trade.

Of all the barbarian peoples in the Han period, the
Hsien-pi were probably most interested in trade. In A.D.
185, Ying Shao characterized them in the following fashion:

> The Hsien-pi people, who live north of the desert, group together
> like dogs and sheep. They have neither king to lead them nor houses
> to shelter them. Born greedy and cruel by nature they observe no
> promise. Therefore, they have repeatedly invaded the borderland of
> China and caused her uninterrupted trouble. Only on occasions of
> trade do they lay down their weapons to assume friendly intercourse
> with the Chinese. But by doing so they have neither respect for
> Chinese power nor gratitude for Chinese leniency. They are only
> bent on gaining Chinese precious goods. As soon as they have
> enough of what they want, they would start anew plundering the
> frontier people. It is exactly on account of this that our government
> keeps them outside instead of taking them inside.[73]

This statement not only shows how much trade meant to
the Hsien-pi,[74] but also bears on our previous discussion
of the inner-outer division of barbarians in Han China.
Ying Shao went on to tell us how the Hsien-pi could make
so much trouble on the border. According to him, much of
it resulted from the fact that the Chinese frontier generals

---

[71] *HHS*, 103:1b. It may be further noted that Liu Yü was especially
known for his lenient policy toward the barbarians, on whom he often
bestowed money and other valuable articles. *HHS*, 103:2a and *Wei-shih
ch'un-ch'iu* quoted in *SKC, Wei*, 8:5a.

[72] *HHS*, 120:2b.

[73] *HHS*, 78:5a–b.

[74] Cf. Ma Ch'ang-shou, *Wu-huan yü Hsien-pi*, pp. 183–184.

often hired them as mercenaries to fight against the Ch'iang rebels, which, in turn, was a result of the Later Han policy of "using barbarians to attack barbarians." As mercenaries, however, strict military discipline would cause them to revolt on the one hand, while loosening of control would encourage them to engage in looting, on the other. They sacked the residents, robbed the caravans, ate up people's cattle as well as captured Chinese soldiers and horses. In one case, for instance, they refused to leave after having received large payments for the military services they rendered China unless they were granted the right to exchange such payments for iron. When the frontier generals denied their demand, on the ground of government regulations, they threatened to set fire to the Chinese silk storage there. Being very much afraid of these barbarian mercenaries' open revolt, the frontier generals eventually yielded.[75] As a matter of fact, to force a trade on others was quite typical of the Hsien-pi economic behavior, as shown in their intercourse with the Chinese. To illustrate this point further, the following instance may be cited. Toward the very end of our period when Liang Hsi served as the Circuit Intendent of Ping-chou, the chieftain of a powerful Hsien-pi tribe, by the name of Yu Yen, was much feared by people of that region. One day Yu Yen came to Liang Hsi with his five thousand cavalrymen asking for exchange of trade. After careful consideration Liang eventually gave his consent but made arrangements to have the trade carried out in a deserted city on the border in order to prevent the Hsien-pi from plundering the frontier residents immediately following the completion of the transactions.[76] This report fully confirms the words of Ying Shao that the Hsien-pi would start looting as soon as they obtained what they needed from the frontier market.

Official trade existed between the Chinese and most, if not all, the Hsien-pi tribes. During the Chien-an period (196–220), for instance, one tribe that lived far beyond

---

[75] HHS, 78:5b.
[76] Wei Lüeh quoted in SKC, Wei, 15:7a–b.

the northeastern frontier in Manchuria presented tribute to the court to request trade.[77] Demand for trade, however, sometimes came also from the Chinese side at the government level. The horse trade was exactly a case in point. Throughout the Han period the Chinese government was badly in need of horses.[78] The need became even greater toward the end of the dynasty, and especially in the age of the Three Kingdoms when war was characteristic of the political scene. Thus, the trade developed to such a large scale that in 222 the Hsien-pi escorted, with 3,000 cavalrymen, some 70,000 head of cattle and horses to trade with the Wei government on the northern border.[79] The Hsien-pi, interestingly enough, even knew how to use trade as a weapon to invalidate the Chinese control of barbarians. Toward the end of the period, for example, all the Hsien-pi tribes once united in a firm alliance against China and took a common oath to stop horse trade with the latter. It took the great efforts of an able Chinese frontier official to break up their united front by inducing one of them to sell a large number of horses to the Chinese government.[80]

In 1959 and 1960 more than 300 tombs belonging to some nomadic people were excavated in Inner Mongolia.[81] It has been suggested that the owners are probably the Hsien-pi of the Later Han.[82] Among the burial objects are typical Later Han mirrors, lacquerware, pottery, and silk embroideries bearing Chinese characters.[83] In

---

[77] SKC, Wei, 30:9b.

[78] For the efforts made by Emperor Wu of the Former Han to seek horses see Yü Chia-hsi, Yü Chia-hsi lun-hsüeh tsa-chu, 1:175–180. Cf., also, a recent study by H. G. Creel, "The Role of the Horse in Chinese History," The American Historical Review, esp. pp. 657–664.

[79] SKC, Wei, 30:8a.

[80] SKC, Wei, 26:7a.

[81] Cheng Lung, "Nei Meng-ku Cha-lai-no-erh ku-mu ch'ün tiao-ch'a chi," Wen wu, pp. 16–18; K'ao ku, 1961:12, pp. 673–680; Tseng Yung, "Liao-ning Hsi-ch'a-kou ku-mu ch'ün wei Wu-huan wen-hua i-chi lun," K'ao ku, 1961:6, p. 335. For a different view, see An Chih-min, "Kuan-yü Nei-Meng-ku Cha-lai-no-erh ku-mu ch'ün ti tsu-shu wen-t'i," Wen wu, pp. 41–45.

[82] Tseng Yung, p. 335; K'ao ku, 1961:12, p. 679.

[83] Cheng Lung, p. 18; An Chih-min, p. 42.

view of the fact that the Hsien-pi were extremely enthusiastic about trade, it seems quite possible that these Han goods were obtained by them from the frontier markets.

Earlier in this chapter mention has been made of how the trade between the Chinese and the Southwestern barbarians had eventually brought the Southwest under the administrative control of the Han empire. Since, however, trade with the Southwestern barbarians also formed an important link in the Sino-barbarian economic intercourse in Han China as a whole, it is necessary that we pursue the matter a little further.

Through the Szechwan traders, economic relations between the Chinese and Southwestern barbarians had been established long before Emperor Wu made attempts to open the southwestern passage. Probably as early as under the Ch'in dynasty, the Szechwan traders already brought from the Southwest such famous living commodities as horses and long-haired oxen (yaks?) from Tso and slave boys from P'o to interior China. And it was the prosperity of this kind of trade, as we are further told, that made the entire Szechwan area especially wealthy.[84] The slave trade between the Chinese and Southwestern barbarians is a highly interesting subject; however, detailed discussion of it lies beyond the scope of this book. Suffice it to say here that it had its beginning at least as early as under the Ch'in dynasty and continued well into the Later Han period. For instance, the slave boys from P'o had already been famous in the Ch'in times [85] and during the Later Han even the use of women from P'o as slaves became fashionable among the Chinese. As a Later Han scholar has noted, "Formerly there were female slaves from P'o in the capital (i.e., Loyang)." This last item of information, simple as it is, clearly shows the extent to which the P'o barbarians were exposed to enslavement in our period.[86]

---

[84] *SC,* 116:1b–2b; 129:4a; *HS,* 95:1b. Cf., also, Watson, 2:291 and Swann, pp. 438–439.

[85] *Hua-yang Kuo chih,* 3:15a.

[86] Fu Ch'ien's words as quoted in *SC,* 116, *so-yin,* 1b–2a. On the P'o barbarians see Cheng Te-k'un, "P'o-jen k'ao," *Shuo-wen yüeh-k'an,* pp. 297–320; Jui I-fu, "P'o-jen k'ao," *CYYY,* pp. 245–278.

The Southwestern barbarians also played a role of considerable importance in the development of trade between China and the western countries such as India and Bactria. According to the famous report of Chang Ch'ien of 122 B.C., the Szechwan traders went all the way to India (Shentu) where they sold, among other commodities, bamboo canes from Ch'iung and cloths of Shu. And from India some of these were further brought to Bactria (Ta-hsia), as witnessed by Chang Ch'ien when he was sent as the Chinese delegate there.[87] It may be noted that this report also bears out the existence of the well-known overland India-Burma-Yunnan trade route in Han times.[88] What remains now to be discussed of this trade is the role of the Southwestern barbarians in it. Chang Ch'ien's report seems to give a general impression that it was the Szechwan traders who took initiative in the business and it was Chinese commodities that were exported to India since both bamboo canes and cloths are said to have been produced in Szechwan. Actually very little, if any, is mentioned of the Southwestern barbarians in the report. Recently, a reasonable doubt has been cast on the reliability of Chang Ch'ien's report as far as the Chinese origin of bamboo canes and cloths is concerned. It has been pointed out that various kinds of bamboo grow wild in Northeastern India and the cloth (pu), if it was of cotton, could also have been made in India since India had cotton long before China did.[89] However, in spite of, as much as because of, the fact that the extant source materials are too scanty to warrant any final judgment, the possibility of the existence of the India-Burma-Yunnan trade route in Han China cannot be completely ruled out.[90] Take the so-called Shu-

---

[87] SC, 116:2b; 123:4b. Cf. Watson, 2:269; 293-294.

[88] Yu Chung, "Han-Chin shih-ch'i ti Hsi-nan I," p. 25; Berthold Laufer, Sino-Iranica, p. 535. On the India-Burma-Yunnan route, see a recent article by L. Carrington Goodrich, "Trade Routes to China," Highways in Our National Life.

[89] See Schuyler Cammann's review of P. C. Bagchi's "India and China: A Thousand Years of Cultural Relations," The Far Eastern Quarterly, p. 58.

[90] Professor Cammann further writes: "If there were any early contacts between India and China over a southern route, Chang Ch'ien's de-

pu or Szechwan cloth for example. While the word *pu* definitely does not refer to silk materials,[91] it probably cannot be identified with ordinary cotton either. Very recently a Chinese writer offers the new interpretation that the *Shu-pu* was made of *mu-mien* or tree-cotton, rather than ordinary cotton. Furthermore, it was produced abundantly, not in Szechwan, but in Ai-lao (later known as Yung-ch'ang) in Yunnan, then under the control of the Southwestern barbarian tribes.[92] The *Hou Han Shu* relates that the Ai-lao barbarians made cloth out of the tree-cotton,[93] which is further confirmed by the *Hua-yang Kuo-chih* of the fourth century.[94] Instead of referring to the place of origin, the name *Shu-pu* therefore most likely may have derived from the Shu traders, through whom the cloth eventually passed into the hands of foreign consumers. If this was the case, the Southwestern barbarians must also have taken a direct interest in the trade. Whether the Southwestern barbarians ever went to India for commercial pursuits, we do not know, since on this point evidence remains silent. Nevertheless, it seems certain that some of them at least had some knowledge of the India-Burma-Yunnan trade route. Although it is emphatically stated in the *Shih Chi* that Emperor Wu failed in his attempt at the opening of the southwestern passage, a

ductions certainly are not reliable as evidence that these contacts existed in the second century B.C., and it is high time that people stopped quoting them as such" (p. 58). This actually amounts to a complete denial of the existence of the route since Chang Ch'ien's report is the only literary evidence we have concerning the use of the route in the Former Han period. Recent archaeological finds in mainland China, as we shall see shortly, however, seem to indicate that this route may have been used by the merchants.

[91] See S. Cammann, "Archaeological Evidence for Chinese Contacts with India During the Han Dynasty," *Sinologica*, p. 6 and n. 24. Cf. also Laufer, *Sino-Iranica*, p. 535, and n. 2

[92] Yu Chung, p. 25, and n. 1. Laufer, in discussing the history of cotton in China, also says something to the effect that the tree-cotton or *Bombax malabaricum*, which originated among the Southern barbarians, was known in China from very ancient times, and its product was used in the manufacture of cloth before the introduction of the cotton plant or *Gossypium herbaceum* (*Sino-Iranica*, p. 491, n. 4).

[93] *HHS*, 116:8b.

[94] *Hua-yang Kuo chih*, 4:16a.

careful reader would find, however, that this failure cannot be simply taken to mean that there was no such route
at all.[95] As a matter of fact, the Grand Historian has told
us very clearly why Emperor Wu's attempt ended in
failure:

> The emperor was therefore delighted, and approved Chang
> Ch'ien's suggestion. He ordered Chang Ch'ien to start out from
> Chien-wei in Shu on a secret mission to search for Ta-hsia. The party
> broke up into four groups proceeding out of the regions of Mang,
> Jan, Hsi, and Ch'iung and P'o. All the groups managed to advance
> one or two thousand *li,* but they were blocked on the north by the
> Ti and Tso tribes and on the south by the Sui and K'un-ming tribes.
> The K'un-ming tribes have no rulers but devote themselves to
> plunder and robbery, and as soon as they seized any of the Han
> envoys they immediately murdered them. Thus none of the parties
> were ever able to get through to their destination. They did learn,
> however, that some one thousand or more *li* to the west there was a
> state called Tien-yueh whose people rode elephants and that the
> merchants from Shu sometimes went there with their goods on un-
> official trading missions.[96]

In this interesting passage two points bearing on our discussion may be emphasized. First, the Han envoys could
not reach their destination, not because of the non-
existence of the route, but due to the fact that they were
blocked by various groups of the Southwestern barbarians
from all directions.[97] Second, in spite of their inability to
fulfill their missions, the Han envoys nevertheless found
out something about the India-Burma-Yunnan trade
route.[98] Unfortunately, it is not known why it was so important for the barbarians to prevent the Han envoys from
using this route. Judged by both its effectiveness and

---

[95] This seems to be exactly the opinion of S. Cammann, "Archaeological
Evidence for Chinese Contacts with India," p. 6.

[96] *SC,* 123:4b–5a; *HS,* 61:2a. Translation by Watson, 2:270.

[97] In another place the Grand Historian gives the same story in slightly
different detail, where we are told that the Han envoys were detained by
the King of Tien for about a year and on the former's account the latter
sent people to search the way to India who returned only with the
report that all roads to the west had been closed off by the barbarians
of K'un-ming (*SC,* 116:2b; Watson, 2:294).

[98] The so-called elephant-riding state Tien-yueh, according to Yu Chung
(p. 25), probably refers to the area around the Yunnan-Burma border.

ubiquity, the blockade certainly looks like something pre-
meditated and well organized and can hardly be understood as sporadic actions simply resulting from the primitive cruelty of the barbarians. In the light of the foregoing
discussion, however, I am very much tempted to venture
the conjecture that the Southwestern barbarians inten-
tionally blocked the Han envoys, probably because they
feared that the interference and control of the trade route
by the Han government would inevitably deprive them of
the privileged position they enjoyed in their lucrative
foreign trade. Thus the blockade may very well be understood against the same psychological background that led
merchants of An-hsi (Parthia) to prevent Han envoys, by
way of deception, from establishing direct contact with the
Roman Empire, a story to which we shall return in the
next chapter.

The existence of the India-Burma-Yunnan trade route
in Han times can further be proved by the following two
instances: First, barbarians and the king of the state of
Shan in modern Burma sent tributes to the Han court via
Yunnan in A.D. 94, 97, and 120 respectively.[99] Second,
later in the third and fourth centuries, it is even reported
that the Indians (people of Shen-tu) migrated to, and
settled down in, Yung-ch'ang, the Chinese province on the
Yunnan and Burma border.[100] Taking all these facts together, it seems beyond doubt that the Southwestern barbarians must have developed increasingly close economic
relations with some of the natives of Burma and India and,
through them, Han China also gradually but steadily came
into economic intercourse with both Burma and India
along this famous trade route.

Recent archaeological finds also throw much light on
trade relations between the Chinese and Southwestern
barbarians. Important data have been brought to light by

---

[99] *HHS*, 4:4a, 5b and 5:7b; cf., also, 116:9a. For a brief English account
of the state of Shan based on Chinese sources see E. H. Parker, "The
Old Thai or Shan Empire of Western Yunnan," *China Review*, pp. 337–
346.

[100] *Hua-yang Kuo chih*, 4:16a. Cf. Chi Hsien-lin, *Chung-Yin wen-hua
kuan-hsi shih lun-ts'ung*, pp. 176–177.

three large-scale excavations, made between 1955 and 1958 at Shih-chai Mountain in Chin-ning, Yunnan of a group of tombs, which reveal much of the life of the Southwestern barbarians in the Han period. Most of the tombs have been dated as of the Former Han dynasty.[101] It is reported that among some thirty-four tombs, three types may be distinguished, each representing a different stage of development. Accordingly, burial remains unearthed from these tombs also differ from one type or stage to another. In the last stage, which probably covered a period from toward the end of the Former Han to the early years of the Later Han, it is vessels of pure Han Chinese style that seem to have occupied the leading place in the burial remains. Copper seals, mirrors, lamps, buckles and lacquer wares, for instance, are considered as products of central China in Han times, and, moreover, some of the cooking and drinking utensils are similar to those unearthed from tombs of late Former Han date excavated in Ch'angsha, Hunan. It may therefore be assumed that at least a large part of these Han style remains must have been brought to the Southwestern barbarians from central China through trade.[102]

Traces of trade along the Burma-Yunnan route are also reflected in Han burial remains. Here we may take the amber trade as an illustration. Amber beads have been found in many of the Han tombs in interior China such as at Ch'angsha, Hunan[103] and Kuei-hsien, Kwangsi.[104] Archaeologists tend to believe that one of the possible sources of amber supply might have been the Burma-

---

[101] The discovery of a gold seal of the King of Tien in one of the tombs provides us with sufficient evidence that most, if not all, of the tombs are datable to the Former Han period. See Yünnan po-wu Kuan, *Yünnan Chin-ning Shih-chai Shan ku-mu ch'ün fa-chüeh pao-kao,* p. 113. Cf. also, pp. 132–134 for a brief discussion on the dating of these tombs. A concise summary of the Shih-chai Shan culture in English may be found in Kwang-chih Chang, *The Archaeology of Ancient China,* pp. 290–292.

[102] *HCKTKKSH,* pp. 89–90.

[103] Chung-kuo K'o-hsüeh Yuan K'ao-ku Yen-chiu So, ed., *Ch'ang-sha fa-chüeh pao-kao,* p. 129.

[104] *K'ao-ku hsüeh-pao,* 1957:1, p. 161. Here it is reported that altogether 57 amber beads have been found in the Former Han tombs and 141 from the Later Han tombs.

Yunnan area.[105] Both the *Hou Han Shu* and *Hua-yang Kuo chih* say that amber was produced in the province of Yung-ch'ang.[106] As Yung-ch'ang borders on Burma, it is also possible that amber in Han times was originally imported from northern Burma to Yunnan and then, from there, distributed to the rest of China. More than half a century ago Barthold Laufer, in an interesting article on amber based on both early Chinese sources and modern mineralogical researches, emphatically pointed out that:

> The first acquaintance of the Chinese with this amber may date from the first century of our era, when their relations with Yunnan and its manifold tribes become more intimate. During the following centuries the reference in Chinese literature to the amber of this region became more frequent, and we see that the amber utilized in China was actually supplied from the region named [Ai-lao], and is located in such places of southern Yunnan as are near the Burmese frontier, along the ancient trade-route leading from Burma to southwestern China.[107]

On the whole, it would seem that this general statement is rather confirmed than invalidated by recent advances in the historical archaeology of Han China.

4 Contraband Trade

With a borderline as long as that of China, it is by no means surprising that contraband trade was active on the frontiers under almost every dynasty, no matter how strict and severe the legal restrictions may have been. By contraband trade is meant the smuggling of prohibited goods both to and from China. Throughout the period of two Han dynasties, contraband trade thrived in several frontier areas where there were strong demands for Chinese goods from the outer barbarians. Limited by the meagerness as well as the highly fragmentary nature of source materials, however, no detailed study can be fruitfully attempted. What is given below does no more than outline a general picture.

Contraband trade seems to have been carried out on a

---

[105] *HCKTKKSH*, p. 82.
[106] *HHS*, 116:8b; *Hua-yang Kuo chih*, 4:16a.
[107] Berthold Laufer, "Historical Jottings on Amber in Asia," p. 234.

comparatively large scale on the northern frontier, especially between the Chinese and Hsiung-nu in the early
years of the Former Han. This situation may be well illustrated by the case of Nieh Weng-i's [108] secret dealings
with the Hsiung-nu. Nieh was a rich man of Ma-i (in
modern Shansi), who through trade, both legal and illicit,
won the trust of the barbarians. In 134 B.C., Nieh offered
his service to the Han government by agreeing to trap the
Hsiung-nu in a Chinese ambush. Thereupon, Emperor
Wu ordered him to cross the border secretly in the disguise
of a smuggler carrying contraband goods to the Hsiung-nu.
Nieh was not only well received by the Hsiung-nu but also
succeeded in deceiving the *Shan-yü* by offering to sell to
him illegally all the goods in the city of Ma-i only if the
Shan-yü would come with his people to take them. Needless to say, all these arrangements were but a plot intended
to lure the Hsiung-nu into the area.[109] This story reveals,
however, at least two important things as far as the contraband trade is concerned. In the first place, we can see from
it the profitability of the contraband trade to Chinese
traders. Undoubtedly, Nieh's wealth must have come
largely, if not entirely, out of it. The way in which he went
to the Hsiung-nu in order to strengthen their trust further
explains how he originally established friendly relations
with them. In the second place, it also shows the extent to
which the contraband trade had been developed. The fact
that Nieh could promise to hand over to the Hsiung-nu
the wealth and goods of a city without even arousing their
suspicion seems to be a sufficient indication that selling
contraband goods to the Hsiung-nu on a similar scale must
have been previously handled by Chinese merchants. Obviously, Nieh can by no means be taken as the only one
who accumulated an enormous personal fortune out of the
profits from the contraband trade.[110]

---

[108] The name Nieh Weng-i is given as Nieh I in *HS*, 52:7a and Yen
Shih-ku suggests in his commentary (*HS*, 94A:7b) that this man's surname
was Nieh and his name I while *weng* was only used to indicate his being
an "old man."

[109] For details see *SC*, 108:2b–3a, 110:10a–b (Watson, 2:136–137, 176–177);
HS, 52:8b–9a; 94A:7b–8a.

[110] On this point see the discussion in Ch'ien Mu, *Ch'in-Han shih*, p. 132.

In order to find out the true nature of contraband trade in Han China it is necessary to know the general scope of Chinese goods, the exportation of which was prohibited by law. Although source materials bearing on this matter are extremely scarce and highly fragmentary, they nevertheless can be pieced together to provide a rough outline. Under Empress Lü for instance, when the Kingdom of Southern Yueh was considered a hostile barbarian state by the Han court, an imperial edict was issued to prohibit Chinese trade with all the barbarians, including Southern Yueh, in metal, especially iron; vessels; and agricultural implements; as well as such livestock as horses, oxen, and sheep. It is even more interesting to note that the edict further specified that in cases of absolute necessity only the male animals, not the female ones, should be given to them. According to a commentator, this restriction was made with a view to preventing the propagation of animals.[111] Such trade prohibitions against Southern Yueh were not removed until Emperor Wen succeeded to the throne.[112] Similar prohibitions are also recorded in other connections. In 146 B.C., Emperor Ching approved a memorial from Wei Wan which proposed that horses below the age of ten should not be allowed to go out through the frontier

---

[111] *HS*, 95:5a. This edict is not fully reproduced in the *SC*, 113:1b; Watson, 2:240.

[112] *HS*, 95:4b–5b. The unfriendly relations between Han China under Empress Lü and Southern Yueh under King Chao T'o, which according to the latter, originally grew out of some unfortunate misunderstanding due to the slanders of the King of Ch'ang-sha, were greatly aggravated by the trade prohibitions of the former (cf. Watson, 2:240–242). With Emperor Wen, the Han court adopted a new and friendly policy toward Southern Yueh. It was this change in policy that eventually brought Chao T'o to terms. Emperor Wen's letter to Chao T'o (*HS*, 95:4b–5a) which has been considered as one of the great pieces of Chinese literature, (Dubs, *History of the Former Han Dynasty*, 1:273, n. 2) must be understood in this light. In the very beginning the emperor wrote: "I am a son of the late Emperor Kao-tsu by his concubine." Traditionally scholars have taken this sentence as evidence of Emperor Wen's unusual frankness toward Chao T'o as if the latter were his old friend, which, it is believed, must have touched the latter deeply. In my opinion, this opening sentence, which has undoubtedly the literary merit of being terse and to the point, is but an ingenious way of conveying the idea that he was not Empress Lü's son and therefore would not continue her wrong policy toward Southern Yueh.

barriers.[113] In 82 B.C., under Emperor Chao, however, an imperial decree was issued which abolished the barriers throughout the empire for prohibiting the exportation of both horses and cross-bows.[114] We are not sure for how long a period the prohibition was removed, nor do we know when it was reintroduced. As we shall see below, however, at least prohibitive regulations to some extent are found to have been imposed upon Sino-barbarian trade during the Later Han period. The relaxation under the reign of Emperor Chao was probably due to the fact that the Hsiung-nu threat was no longer as serious as in the early years of the Former Han.

From the above instances it seems clear that the Chinese goods which were then prohibited from falling into the hands of the outer barbarians consisted mainly of two kinds: weapons and strategic materials such as cross-bows and iron, which would directly strengthen the military power of the barbarians; and means of production such as agricultural implements, metal vessels, and domestic animals which would help to enrich their economic resources. In other words, the prohibitions were made primarily out of political and military considerations rather than on economic grounds. This point would become even more obvious if we take into consideration the fact that contraband trade in Han China was for the most part a one-way traffic. Legal restrictions seem to have been laid primarily on exportation of certain Chinese goods to the barbarians, but very rarely on importation of foreign commodities to China. On one occasion, and probably the only one, however, we do have the information that in 150 B.C. one nobleman was deprived of his inherited feudal title on account of having sent a messenger to buy certain pro-

---

[113] *HS*, 5:3b; Dubs, *op. cit.*, 1:321. The original edict reads: "horses five feet and nine inches and more in height whose teeth are not yet smooth should not be allowed to go out through the barriers." According to Fu Ch'ien's commentary, this means horses of ten years old. Elsewhere, however, another commentator, Meng K'ang (ca. 180–260), gives the height of horses as "five feet and six inches" (*HS*, 7:2a).

[114] *HS*, 7:2a; Dubs, *op. cit.*, 2:159 and n. 4.1.

hibited goods from the Hsiung-nu outside the frontier.[115] Since the nature of the "prohibited goods" for import is not revealed at all, we are not allowed even to guess why such prohibitions were made. And moreover, so far as we can tell from the extant source materials, exportation of Chinese goods of purely consumptive nature, such as silk, suffered no prohibition of the kind under the Han dynasty.

If the law regulating Sino-barbarian trade somewhat relaxed under Emperor Chao as a result of the lessening of tension in the Han and Hsiung-nu relations, severity of the law probably reached its apex during the reign of Emperor Wu when the Hsiung-nu threat was most keenly felt by the Chinese. The well-known instance of the execution of some five hundred merchants at Ch'ang-an, the capital, on account of contraband trade may be cited here to serve the purpose of illustration.[116] In 121 B.C., King Hun-yeh of the Hsiung-nu surrendered to China and in his subsequent homage-paying visit to the court at Ch'ang-an he brought with him a large number of followers. Naturally, many of the Chinese merchants in the capital came to trade with the Hsiung-nu people in the markets. But quite unexpectedly, some five hundred among these merchants were soon found guilty of selling contraband goods to the barbarians and were, therefore, condemned to death. Upon learning of this, Chi An, an upright official, made a strong protest to Emperor Wu. In his words: ". . . how are the common people in their ignorance to know that goods which are sold in the markets of Ch'ang-an will be regarded as contraband by law when they are transported to the border and traded to the barbarians? Now, . . . do you intend to execute the five hundred or more ignorant men simply because of some petty law?" [117]

The protest, it may be noted, came virtually to nothing. The text gives no information as to what contraband goods were involved in this case. Ying Shao, in the commentary,

---

[115] *HS,* 16:38b.
[116] *SC,* 120:2b–3a; *HS,* 50:4b–5a. Cf. Watson, 2:349–350.
[117] Translated by Watson, 2:350.

however, quotes an article of Han law saying: "In the bar-barian market officials as well as common people are not allowed to carry weapons and iron out of the [frontier] barriers. The same regulation applies also to the market in the capital." [118] We may, therefore, assume that the con-traband goods probably consisted mostly of iron vessels, since it is rather unlikely that the Chinese merchants would openly sell weapons to the barbarians in the capital. This instance not only best illustrates the severity of Han law concerning contraband trade, it also raises the ques-tion of how the trade was exactly defined in the period under review.

Let us first introduce and discuss the technical legal term for this trade. In Han law, contraband trade was known as *kan-lan ch'u-wu*[119] or *lan-ch'u ts'ai wu.*[120] In the first instance, the commentator says that *kan-lan* means "secretly send goods out [of the border] in defiance of the prohibitions" and, in the second, as another commentator explains, *lan* means "cross the border from either side without *fu* or *chuan* (i.e., passports)." Taking all these to-gether, it seems obvious that contraband trade consisted of two different, but practically inseparable parts: Chinese goods that were prohibited to be exported to the outer barbarians and the Chinese merchants who crossed the border or went to the frontier market to trade with bar-barians without government-issued travel documents. We have discussed in the foregoing the problem of prohibited goods. Let us now take this opportunity to briefly examine the problem of travel documents or passports in Han China, because more knowledge of this aspect of contra-

---

[118] *HS*, 50:5a. The *chi-chieh* by P'ei Yin in *SC*, 120:3a quotes the same law which omits the word "iron." It may further be noted that the last sentence—"the same regulation applies also to the market in the capital" —instead of being part of the article, may have been an explanation offered by the commentator. Cf., also, Martin C. Wilbur, *Slavery in China During the Former Han Dynasty*, pp. 110–111.

[119] *SC*, 110:10a. According to P'ei Yin, *chien* should read *kan*.

[120] *SC*, 120:3a; *HS*, 50:5a. Cf. Ch'eng Shu-teh, *Chiu-ch'ao lü k'ao*, 1:146–147. Unfortunately, I have not been able to find any discussion concerning this point in A. F. P. Hulsewé's excellent study, *Remnants of Han Law*.

band trade will not only deepen our understanding of the trade itself but also shed light on the travelling life of the merchants in this period as a whole.

Issuing of passports by the government for the purpose of travel both at home and abroad had an early origin in Chinese institutional history. In the Warring-States period (450?–221 B.C.), it had already developed into a highly complicated system, largely as a result of the hostilities between the various contending states. *Chou-li,* a work probably composed in the late Warring-States period,[121] contains much information about this system. According to it, there were all kinds of passports—then generally known as *chieh.* For instance, to state envoys in various official trips, metal passports of different kinds were to be issued, whereas the merchants were required to obtain bamboo passports from the government for the transportation of goods.[122] It is even emphatically stated that "those who travel everywhere under heaven must possess *chieh,* together with the supporting [travel document of] *chuan.* Without *chieh* one cannot reach [one's destination]." According to Cheng Hsüan (A.D. 127–200), the great Han commentator, *chieh* was but a certificate identifying its holder, while *chuan* gave details as to what the holder was carrying on his trip and where he was going.[123] It may be noted that in Cheng's commentary, as we shall further see below, the system of the Han period is also more or less reflected. The use of a passport was closely related to the establishment of border barriers (*kuan*) by various states of the time. At its beginning, the barriers probably were only used as check-points to check all the passengers for the sake of border defense, but governments of various states soon found it profitable to collect transit dues from the merchants at such points. Thus the *kuan* became really a barrier to the travelling merchants in the sense of an ob-

---

[121] Cf. Ch'ien Mu, "Chou-kuan chu-tso shih-tai k'ao, *Yen-ching hsüeh-pao,* pp. 2191–2300; reprinted in *Liang-Han ching-hsüeh chin-ku wen p'ing-i,* pp. 285–434.

[122] *Chou-li, shih-san ching chu-shu* edition, 15:10b–12a.

[123] *Ibid.,* 15:13b.

stacle.[124] For instance, toward the end of the Warring-States period, one minister suggested to the king of Wei that, in order to enrich the state, Wei should make a joint effort with the state of Han to establish barriers on the border for the purpose of collecting taxes from the passengers.[125] Under such circumstances, passports therefore were required of all merchants, to be shown at the barriers when they were passing with goods.[126]

The passport system of the Warring-States period, as it is described in the *Chou-li* and other works of the time, has been confirmed by recent archaeological discoveries. In 1957, four metal pieces of *chieh*, with inscriptions, were unearthed in Shou Hsien, Anhui. They were all issued by the famous King Huai of Ch'u in 323 B.C. to a member of his royal house. The *chieh* are of two different kinds: one for travel along the water route and another the land route. According to the inscriptions the water-route passport, which was valid for a year, allowed its holder to pass all the barriers without taxation in places of today's Hupei and Hunan. It further specified, that the holder should use no more than 150 boats and carry no livestock such as ox, sheep, and horses. The land-route passport, also of one year's validity, permitted its holder to pass barriers free in places of today's Hupei, Hunan, Anhwei, and Honan. His carriages were limited to the number of fifty. In case animals or coolies were used instead to carry things, ten animals or twenty coolies were to be counted as one carriage. Carrying weapons, however, was strictly prohibited.[127]

---

[124] Mencius already made the criticism that "Anciently, the establishment of the frontier-gates (i.e. *kuan*) was to guard against violence. Nowadays, it is to exercise violence" (James Legge, tr., *The Chinese Classics*, 2:481). Cf. Lü Ssu-mien, *Hsien-Ch'in shih*, p. 369; Kuo Pao-chün, *Chung-kuo ch'ing-t'ung ch'i shih-tai*, pp. 154–155.

[125] *Chan-kuo ts'e*, WYWK edition, 24 (*Wei*), 3:15.

[126] *Chou-li*, 14:22b; 15:9a–b.

[127] See *Wen-wu ts'an-k'ao tzu-liao*, 1958:4, pp. 3–11; T'an Ch'i-hsiang's article in *Chung-hua wen-shih lun-ts'ung*, 2 (1962), pp. 169–190; further discussions by T'an Ch'i-hsiang and Huang Sheng-chang, *ibid.*, 5 (1964), pp. 143–193 and Shang Ch'eng-tsu, "O-chün Ch'i chieh k'ao," *Wen-wu ching-hua*, pp. 49–55.

There are a few interesting points to be observed in these *chieh* passports of Ch'u. First, the listing of so many place names along both water and land routes seems to indicate that barriers were established not only on the frontiers but also on many spots within the Ch'u territory. Second, the barriers, especially those inside the state, must not be simply taken as military fortifications in the nature of defense. It seems beyond doubt that they must also have functioned as custom stations. This point is amply borne out by the fact that taxation is actually mentioned in both kinds of passports.[128] Third, it is very significant that the contraband goods mentioned in the passports, such as the livestock and weapons, are almost identical with those prohibited under the Han dynasty. In the light of this fact both the barrier system as well as the trade regulations of Han China may legitimately be understood as very much in the institutional tradition of the preceding Warring-States period. In both cases, similar prohibitions were also made for similar purposes: to prevent the outside enemy from strengthening its economic and military power, although, of course, the enemy was by no means the same. It must also be pointed out that these passports were issued to a nobleman of Ch'u and therefore may have differed considerably from those used by the commoners, including the merchants. In the latter case, prohibitions may have been much more strict. Either prohibitions imposed on commodities or transit taxes levied at the barriers, or a combination of both, could stimulate the growth of contraband trade. Thus even in the Warring-States period, contraband trade had already presented itself as a serious problem. A strong evidence may be found in the *Chou-li* in which it is stated: "All the commodities that do not pass through the barriers are to be taken away [from the

---

[128] According to Kuo Mo-jo, however, transit taxes were not directly collected at the barriers. Barrier officials were probably only responsible for making tax assessment and reporting it to the financial authorities in the central government. It was the latter that would do the actual work of tax-collection (*Wen-wu ts'an-k'ao tzu-liao*, 1958:4, p. 5). This may well have been the case with O-chün Ch'i who was a royal clansman, but does not seem applicable to ordinary merchants or the common people.

owners] and persons [who are involved in such cases] are
to be punished." According to Cheng Hsüan, this means:
"[commodities] that are smuggled out in order to avoid
taxes are to be confiscated and persons [who are thus in-
volved] are to receive beatings." [129] Here again we may
take Cheng's interpretation as a reflection of trade regulations of his own time—the Han dynasty.

Under the Han dynasty, the barrier system continued to
exist to some extent but with more emphasis on the northern and northwestern frontiers. At home, however, the
number of barriers probably was considerably reduced,
though they were no less important for garrisoning the
central government, especially in the early part of the
Former Han when there were still a number of powerful
and semi-independent feudal kingdoms within the empire.
This was particularly true for the capital area which was
well guarded within four barriers, the Kuan-chung. To
pass the barrier, people were required to show their *chuan*
passports. In 168 B.C., Emperor Wen once relaxed the
barrier and passport system,[130] but it probably affected
only the Kuan-chung area and may not have been applicable to the frontiers. In 153 B.C., however, the whole system was reestablished by Emperor Ching as a result of the
rebellion of the Seven Kingdoms, an important event that
marked his reign.[131]

Whether barriers were also used in the Han period as
customs stations is still a matter open to question. Although records of transit dues collected at barriers are extremely scarce, complete discontinuation of the practice is
rather unlikely. At least, in 101 B.C., it is recorded that at
Wu Kuan, one of the four barriers that guarded the
capital, people going out and in were to be taxed.[132]

---

[129] *Chou-li*, 15:9a.

[130] *HS*, 4:6a: Dubs, *op. cit.*, 1:252, especially the long note, 252–253, which
is based on Wang Hsien-ch'ien, *Han-shu pu-chu*, Hsü-shou t'ang edition,
4:14a. Cf., also, Ch'eng Shu-teh, *Chiu-chao lü k'ao*, 1:147–148.

[131] *HS*, 15:2b; Dubs, *op. cit.*, 1:315 and n. 4.5. For an account of the
rebellion, see Dubs, 1:292–297.

[132] *HS*, 6:13a; Dubs, *op. cit.*, 2:103. In spite of this fact, Li Chien-nung
still thinks that there were no transit taxes at the barriers throughout the

There is another instance which bears on the problem. In 70 B.C., because of the grain shortage in the capital, Emperor Hsüan issued an edict permitting the common people to transport grain by cart or by boat through the barriers without using passports.[133] According to a Ch'ing scholar, this actually means that the transportation of grain was tax free.[134] That the barrier was more or less related to the collection of transit taxes can further be seen from the way in which the common people obtained their passports. As a recent study, based on the Han documents on wood, shows, people of the time applied for passports almost invariably through the village functionary known as *se-fu* and the power of approval or disapproval rested, in most cases, with one of the assistant magistrates of the *hsien* or district.[135] It is interesting to note that one of the assigned duties of the *se-fu* was to take care of both tax collection and tax appraisal.[136] The fact that the *se-fu* was also made responsible for passport application for the people makes one wonder whether this was because he knew better than anyone else how to assess and rate taxes on goods carried by people during their travel.

Apart from the *chuan*, there arose, probably under Emperor Wu's reign, another form of passport by the name of *kuo-so*. Many of the *kuo-so* have been found among the Han documents on wood.[137] *Kuo-so*, as passports carried by travelling people in order to be shown

---

Han period (*Hsien-Ch'in Liang-Han*, p. 199). It may be noted that the *HS* has given only *kuan* or barriers whereas the *SC*, 11:2a, has both *kuan* and *chin*, barriers and fords. (Cf. Watson, 1:369.)

[133] *HS*, 8:3b; Dubs, *op. cit.*, 2:213.

[134] Wang Hsien-ch'ien, *Han-shu pu-chu*, 8:6b. Translated in Dubs, *op. cit.*, 2:213, n. 6.5.

[135] Ch'en Chih, "Han-Chin kuo-so t'ung-k'ao," *LSYC*, p. 147.

[136] *HS*, 19A:8a; *HHS*, 38:3b. On *se-fu* see Yen Keng-wang, *Chung-kuo ti-fang*, 1:237–239; Ōba Osamu, "Kan no shoku-fu," *Tōyōshi kenkyū*, pp. 61–80.

[137] For examples see Lao Kan, *Chü-yen Han-chien, shih-wen*, no. 23, p. 1; nos. 460, 461, p. 10; no. 715, p. 15; no. 985, p. 20; no. 2063, p. 42; no. 2240, p. 45; no. 2991, p. 60; no. 6658, p. 138. For other forms of passport such as *chuan* and *fu*, see those collected together and discussed by Lao Kan, *ibid.*, *k'ao-cheng*, pp. 3–5.

while passing barriers or fords,[138] were used by both officials on official tours as well as by commoners on private trips. Usually, the purpose of the trip, places of destination, and, in some cases, things carried by the passenger were all clearly indicated in the *kuo-so* passport. We are not altogether sure about the differences and relations between the *kuo-so* and *chuan*. Evidence tends to show that they were somehow used jointly in the Former Han period when the *kuo-so* was just introduced into the passport system.[139] From the Later Han dynasty on, however, *kuo-so* seems to have been used alone as a passport without necessarily being supplemented by *chuan*. This probably explains why Cheng Hsüan interpreted *chuan* in terms of *kuo-so* of his own day.[140]

Now we must return to contraband trade iself. In the Former Han dynasty, the law against contraband trade seems to have been strictly enforced along the frontiers. The word *lan,* meaning "unlawful crossing" as in the case of *kan-lan ch'u-wu,* for instance, appears in a number of places in the Han documents on wood discovered at Edsin Gol.[141] In one place we even find the term *lan ch'u sai* which possibly indicates that someone, presumably a Chinese soldier, had crossed the border illegally.[142] In another case, one fragmentary document says something like "Chü-yen being a border barrier, how could one bring ox

[138] This is a definition given to the term *kuo-so* in a Later Han dictionary, *Shih Ming* by Liu Hsi, *SPTK* edition, p. 46a. (Cf. translation by Dubs, *op. cit.,* 1:253.) According to Nicholas Cleveland Bodman, *A Linguistic Study of the Shih Ming, Initials and Consonant Clusters,* Harvard, 1954, pp. 3–5, this dictionary was compiled probably toward the end of the second century A.D. For a general study of the Han passport system see Ōba Osamu, "Kandai no sekisho to pasupōto," in *Kansai Daigaku Tōzai gakujutsu kenkyū ronsō.* Professor M. Loewe is preparing a study of the *kuo-so* based on the Han documents from Chü-yen. See his "Some Military Despatches of the Han Period," *TP,* p. 350, n. 2.

[139] Ch'en Chih, "Han-Chin kuo-so," pp. 145–147. Cf., also, Lo Chen-yü and Wang Kuo-wei, *Liu-sha chui-chien, pu-i,* 5a–6a.

[140] *Chou-li,* 15:9a.

[141] Lao Kan, *Chü-yen Han-chien, shih-wen,* no. 2691, p. 54; no. 4067, p. 82; no. 4144, p. 84; no. 4382, p. 90; no. 8293, p. 171. For the meaning of *lan* used in these documents see *ibid.,* *k'ao-cheng,* pp. 42–43.

[142] *Ibid.,* no. 6768, p. 140.

out of it?" [143] This last instance probably has a direct bearing on our discussion. The most interesting piece of evidence, however, is provided by a Han document unearthed at Tun-huang, which may be translated as follows: "[According to] the prohibition, it is not allowed to export weapons, grain, horses, oxen, and sheep." [144] With the exception of grain, as we have seen previously, all the items agree exactly with the prohibited goods several times mentioned in the Han imperial edicts. It seems quite safe to take this document as a sure indication of the actual enforcement of the regulations concerning contraband trade by the frontier local government. Strict observation of trade law in the frontier area is also borne out by the fact that all economic activities of the individuals there were put under careful government control. For example, border people including garrison soldiers, were required to report to and, in some cases, apply for passports from, their local authorities whether they wanted to do shopping in the nearby trading centers or to collect debts in other beacon-fire stations. Items like places of destination, purposes of the trip, persons to be met, means of transportation to be used, or goods to be sold or bought, probably all had to be listed in their reports to the local authorities concerned, for official approval.[145]

In spite of the constant vigilance maintained on the border, smuggling activities probably could not be thus put completely to an end, especially in areas where the frontier situation was not tense enough to be so vigilantly guarded. Traces of contraband trade may still be detected in archaeological finds. For instance, in 1956 a group of tombs of Han date were discovered at Hsi-ch'a-kou, Hsi-feng hsien, Liaoning—a place beyond the northern frontier of Liao-tung Province under the Han dynasty. These tombs are believed to have belonged to either the Hsiung-nu or to the Wu-huan, and are dated at around the time of

---

[143] *Ibid.*, nos. 7560 and 7568, p. 157.
[144] Lo Chen-yü and Wang Kuo-wei, *Liu-sha chui-chien*, 2:49a.
[145] Lao Kan, *CYYY*, 11:72–73.

Emperor Wu's reign.[146] Among the remains unearthed there are a large number of iron weapons and implements, which have been identified as of Han origin. These include swords, double-edged swords, axes, spades, knives, etc., some of which even bear Chinese inscriptions.[147] Since the barbarians, whether they be Hsiung-nu or Wu-huan, could obtain weapons and iron vessels neither from the Han government as "gifts" nor from the barbarian markets as exchanged goods, the most likely channel through which such things went all the way from interior China and got out of the border was probably contraband trade.

In Inner Mongolia, similar Han products have also been excavated at various sites along the Great Walls of Han China, which possibly also indicates the existence of contraband trade in that area in the latter part of the Former Han period.[148] The Szechwan traders, as has been shown above, were particularly famous for smuggling Chinese goods to the Southwestern barbarians, which is described in history precisely as *kan ch'u-wu*. This description, of course, is to be understood as *kan-lan ch'u-wu*, the legal term for contraband trade.[149] In this case, it is not mentioned whether weapons and iron vessels were also among their contraband commodities. However, recent discovery of various kinds of Han metal (such as iron) works, including weapons and agricultural tools, in Yunnan [150] seems to show that the Szechwan smugglers may also have had a hand in the bringing of these prohibited goods to their barbarian neighbors. It has been suggested that some of them, especially the iron vessels, very possibly came from Han China through trade.[151] If so, the trade could only be of the illicit kind. It is also interesting to note that

---

[146] *HCKTKKSH*, p. 86.

[147] Sun Shou-tao, *Wen wu*, esp. pp. 26–28.

[148] *HCKTKKSH*, p. 88; *Wen-wu ts'an-k'ao tzu-liao*, 1955:10.

[149] *SC*, 123:5a; *HS*, 61:2a.

[150] *Yünnan Chin-ning Shih-chai Shan ku-mu ch'ün fa-chüeh pao-kao*, p. 133.

[151] Chien Po-tsan, *Li-shih wen-t'i lun-ts'ung*, p. 322. Li Chia-jui, "Liang-Han shih-tai Yünnan ti t'ieh-ch'i," *Wen-wu*, 1962:3, pp. 33–34.

three 4-*shu pan-liang* coins of Emperor Wen's time are also found in the Yunnan site together with several hundred *wu-shu* coins of later date. Since the 4-*shu pan-liang* circulated only for a short period and certainly before the full opening of the southwestern passage under the reign of Emperor Wu, it is quite possible that they had been brought there by the Szechwan smugglers as a result of *kan-lan ch'u-wu*.[152]

Under the Later Han dynasty, garrisoning of the frontier seems to have been more or less relaxed, resulting from the fact that the Hsiung-nu were no longer an enemy as dangerous as their Former Han ancestors. Consequently, contraband trade on the border became so active that even Chinese weapons in large quantities fell into the possession of outer barbarians. In order to bring this long discussion of the illicit frontier trade to an end, I would like first to indicate some possible archaeological evidence to support my general observation, and then conclude with a testimony given by a Later Han scholar. Recently, a Chinese crossbow mechanism has been recognized from among the collection of excavated objects at the museum in Taxila (now in the Pakistan territory). It was discovered in 1915 in the ruins of the second Parthian palace at Sirkap which was rebuilt sometime after A.D. 30. This Chinese crossbow, therefore, may very well be dated as a product from the beginning of the Later Han period. Conjecture has been made as to how this piece had gotten there. One reasonable guess would be that it was captured from a Chinese garrison soldier and then brought to Taxila. But the possibility of its having been among the contraband commodities sold to some outer barbarians cannot be completely ruled out.[153]

It must be emphatically pointed out that this archaeological piece of evidence alone can by no means claim to

---

[152] *Yünnan Chin-ning Shih-chai Shan ku-mu ch'ün fa-chüeh pao-kao,* pp. 102–103. On the 4-*shu pan-liang* coins see Lien-sheng Yang, *Money and Credit in China,* pp. 21–22.

[153] S. Cammann, "Archaeological Evidence," esp. pp. 8–15. Professor Cammann does not consider the crossbow as a trade piece because its export from Chinese territory was then forbidden (p. 14).

bear directly on the contraband trade. But when we read the following words from a memorial of Ts'ai Yung, presented to the emperor probably in A.D. 177, it becomes much less surprising if the crossbow mechanism should prove to be a trace left by Chinese frontier smugglers of the Later Han period:

> Ever since the Hsiung-nu ran away, the Hsien-pi have become powerful and prosperous. [The Hsien-pi] took over [much of] the former lands [of the Hsiung-nu] and claim that they have 100,000 soldiers. . . . Moreover, [the Chinese] frontier barriers have not been strict and the legal net of prohibitions have many loopholes. Therefore, refined metal (bronze?) and iron were smuggled out without [our] notice, and fell into the possession of the [Hsien-pi] rebels. . . . . Now, their weapons are even sharper and horses faster than those of the [previous] Hsiung-nu.[154]

Previously we have seen that the Hsien-pi were not only very eager to trade with China, but also had a particularly strong interest in Chinese iron. Owing, probably, to both the relaxation of law and the localization of iron monopolies, the Hsien-pi must have been able to obtain large amounts of metalworks, especially iron, from Later Han China through frontier trade of both the legal as well as the illegal kinds. And Chinese crossbows and other ready-made weapons may very well have been among the "sharp weapons" here referred to in Ts'ai Yung's memorial.

---

[154] Here I follow the collated text in *CHHW*, 73:1b, which is primarily based on *HHS*, 120:5b and *Ts'ai Chung-lang wen chi, SPTK so-pen* edition, p. 37.

chapter six

Economic Relations Between China and the Western Countries

In the last chapter we have examined in considerable detail the frontier trade of Han China. With the western expansion of the Han Empire economic relations of one kind or another were also established between China and many of the "Western countries." By "Western countries" I mean not only the so called "thirty-six" countries in the Western Regions,[1] but also countries lying farther west such as India, Parthia and Rome. As generally known, the Han western expansion was an historical event of singular importance with far-reaching political, military, and eco-

---

[1] Here the number "36" is a matter of much controversy. The crux of the problem lies in our inability to identify all the original 36 countries of the Western Regions as reported in many Han texts. The German Sinologist, A. Hermann, for instance, is puzzled by the fact that out of the 36, only 25 could be identified. On the whole, however, he takes it as a real number. (*Die alten Seidenstrassen zurischen China und Syria,* Berlin, 1910, S.59 as qouted in Ise Sentarō, *Seiiki keiei-shi no kenkyū,* pp. 30–31.) Now some Japanese scholars have advanced a new theory, according to which the number "36" in ancient China was used not as a real number, but as a pseudo-number meaning "many" or "countless," because it had long acquired a special astrological significance. (Ise Sentarō, pp. 30–37; Matsuda Hisao, *Kodai Tenzan no rekishi chirigaku teki kenkyū,* pp. 36–38. Moreover, the latter considers the number "36" possibly a corruption of "26," p. 36.)

In view of the fact that it is clearly stated in the *Han Shu* that there were altogether 36 countries in the Western Regions, which were later split into more than 50 (*HS,* 96A:1a), I am not too sure whether the number "36" in this case should be taken as a pseudo one. That "36" may have been among the pseudo numbers in ancient Chinese texts has been already suggested by Chinese scholars. See Lien-sheng Yang, "Numbers and Units in Chinese Economic History," *HJAS* 12:1/2 (June, 1949), esp. p. 218. Reprinted in his *Studies in Chinese Institutional History,* p. 77.

nomic consequences not only in China but in Central Asia as well. It becomes therefore at once natural and necessary for us to follow, in this chapter, the story of how trade and other forms of Sino-barbarian economic intercourse gradually developed farther and farther beyond the Chinese frontier.

The period stretching from the latter part of the past century to the early years of the present witnessed tremendous progress in the study of the history of the Western Regions (Chinese Turkestan) and Central Asia. More importantly, during this period a number of large-scale archaeological excavations were made in Central Asia, as well as along the northwestern frontiers of China.[2] These excavations have brought to light numerous remains datable to Han and later dynasties, which have in many ways enriched our historical knowledge of Sino-barbarian relations in that direction. Thus in writing the present chapter, our problem concerning source material is rather one of selection and emphasis than that of paucity, as in the case of contraband trade. It must be pointed out, however, that most modern studies of the Han expansion, especially those by Chinese and Japanese scholars, lay stress either on the broad line of cultural contacts in general, or on the location of places recorded in ancient Chinese texts in particular. With the exception of the silk trade and silk routes, which have been examined time and again by experts, the economic aspect of Sino-foreign relations in Han China is comparatively little known. Needless to say, in what follows it is impossible to cover the whole ground of economic relations between Han China and the western countries. Instead, I shall deal with the subject with a view to finding out the basic structure, or pattern, behind such relations, which is the central purpose set for this book.

---

[2] For a brief account of these excavations conducted by Western and Japanese scholars, see Ho Ch'ang-ch'ün's Foreword in his Chinese translation of Hatani Ryotai's *Hsi-yü chih Fo-chiao*. See also Jack A. Dabbs, *History of the Discovery and Exploration of Chinese Turkestan*, for more details.

1 *The Western Regions Under the Tributary System*

Han China's expansion to the Western Regions was a direct result of the change of her policy toward the Hsiung-nu. Like the Ch'iang and Wu-huan, barbarian states of the Western Regions had also been conquered by the Hsiung-nu and were subject to the Hsiung-nu's exploitation. The Hsiung-nu's exploitation of the Western Regions probably took two forms: extortion of their wealth and enslavement of their people. For collection of tax and exaction of labor services, the Hsiung-nu even established there an office known as *T'ung-p'u tu-wei*, presumably a Chinese translation of an original Hsiung-nu title.[3] Since the term *T'ung-p'u* had the meaning of "slaves" in Han China, it has been suggested that this office seems to indicate the enslavement of the peoples in the Western Regions by the Hsiung-nu.[4] According to a contemporary report, "The lands from that of Wu-sun (in the Ili Valley north of the Tarim Basin) on west to An-hsi (i.e., Parthia) were situated nearer to the Hsiung-nu than to China, and it was well known that the Hsiung-nu had earlier caused the Yüeh-chih people great suffering. Therefore, whenever a Hsiung-nu envoy appeared in the region carrying credentials from the *Shan-yü,* he was escorted from state to state and provided with food, and no one dared to detain him or cause him any difficulty."[5] This report fully reveals the extent to which the Western Region states were dominated by the Hsiung-nu.

In order to separate the Hsiung-nu from their military and economic base in the Western Regions, the Han court found it imperative to seek allies from among Hsiung-nu's enemies there. It was because of this urgent need that the famous diplomatic mission headed by Chang Ch'ien was sent to the Western Regions in 139 B.C. According to the

---

[3] *HS,* 96A:1a–b.
[4] Chang Wei-hua, *Lun Han Wu-ti,* p. 166.
[5] *SC,* 123:7b. Translation by Burton Watson, *Records of the Grand Historian of China,* 2:279.

information furnished by the surrendered Hsiung-nu, a
people in Central Asia, known as the Great Yüeh-chih
(Indo-Scythians), hated the Hsiung-nu most. The Han
court therefore contemplated a plan of establishing military alliance with the Yüeh-chih in order to attack the
Hsiung-nu from both sides. As the Yüeh-chih people had
been driven far away to the west from their original residence in the area between the Ch'i-lien or Heavenly
Mountains and Tun-huang (in Kansu), it was therefore
necessary to first track down their whereabouts. To reach
them, however, an envoy would have to pass through the
Hsiung-nu territory. When the court was looking for people capable of undertaking such a difficult mission, Chang
Ch'ien, who then served as a *lang* or a Court Gentleman,
volunteered and was appointed as envoy. Unfortunately,
Chang Ch'ien's mission was a failure. He was first captured, with his men, by the Hsiung-nu and was detained
there for more than ten years. He and his party, nevertheless, went westward in search of the Yüeh-chih after their
escape. With the help of the King of Ta-yuan (Ferghana),
they eventually reached the Yüeh-chih territory in what
was later the Kushan Empire, but only to find the Yüeh-
chih people too well settled there to be interested in fighting a revenge war against the Hsiung-nu. Chang Ch'ien
returned to Ch'ang-an in 126 B.C. Although he accom-
plished nothing as far as the immediate objective of his
mission was concerned, he nevertheless brought home first-
hand information about the Western Regions as well as
second-hand knowledge of the lands beyond, which
aroused the keen interest of the Emperor. In 115 B.C.,
Chang Ch'ien was again sent to the Western Regions as a
Han envoy, this time to explore the possibility of establishing diplomatic relations with the Wu-sun in the Ili Valley,
a former subject state of the Hsiung-nu. Once again Chang
Ch'ien failed to fulfill his mission because of the Wu-sun's
hesitation to enter into an alliance with Han China. On
the other hand, Chang Ch'ien's second embassy did make
tremendous progress in establishing relations with many
other Central Asian states such as Ta-yuan (Ferghana)

and K'ang-chü (Sogdiana) and thus paved the way for the subsequent expansion.[6]

What made Chang Ch'ien believe that friendly relations with the Western Regions could be eventually established was the simple fact that he had found during his visits to the Western Regions, that the peoples there were all greedy for Han goods. Therefore, it was possible for China to win them over by using her immense economic influence. Chang Ch'ien further proposed to the throne that countries in the Western Regions like Wu-sun, and those lying further west like Ta-hsia (Bactria), should all be brought into the Chinese tributary system as "outer vassals." [7] Thus, he set the basic policy line toward the Western Regions for the Han court to follow practically throughout the period.

From the point of view of the Han court, it is obvious that the western expansion was primarily motivated by political and military considerations, but when we examine the individual envoys who were sent to the Western Regions after Chang Ch'ien it would become at once clear that economic motivation certainly played a no less important role. As it is reported by the Grand Historian,

After Chang Ch'ien achieved honor and position by opening up communications with the lands of the west, all the officials and soldiers who had accompanied him vied with one another in submitting reports to the emperor telling of the wonders and profits to be gained in foreign lands and requesting to become envoys. When the envoys returned from a mission, it invariably happened that they had plundered or stolen goods on their way or their reports failed to meet with the approval of the emperor . . . the envoys were all sons of poor families who handled the government gifts and goods that were entrusted to them as though they were private property and looked for opportunities to buy goods at a cheap price in the foreign countries and make a profit on their return to China.[8]

---

[6] On Chang Ch'ien and his diplomatic missions see Kuwabara Jitsuzō, *Tōzai kōtsūshi ronsō*, Tokyo, 1933, 1–117; Friedrich Hirth, "The Story of Chang K'ien, China's Pioneer in Western Asia," *JAOS*, 89–152. G. Haloun, however, believes that Chang Ch'ien did not set out for the Far West until 133 B.C. at the earliest. ("Zur Ue-tsi-Frage," pp. 249–250 and notes.)

[7] *HS*, 61:2b.

[8] *SC*, 123:8b; translation by Watson, 2:276–277.

This situation not only continued but also intensified in the Later Han period. For instance, in A.D. 94, when General Pan Ch'ao launched a military expedition against a small state known as Yen-ch'i (Karashahr) in the Western Regions, several hundred Chinese merchants joined him in the fighting.[9] On the other hand, it is interesting to note that tribute-bearers from countries of the Western Regions also came to China with the same profit-making purpose in mind. As Tu Ch'in pointed out sometime during the reign of Emperor Ch'eng (32–7 B.C.), countries in the Western Regions like Chi-pin (Kashmir) never sent nobles or high officials to pay homage to the Han court. Instead their merchants always came to China in the name of tribute-bearers with the obvious purpose of seeking trading opportunities with the Chinese.[10] And, as we shall see later, foreign merchants from the Western Regions visited China in rapidly growing number during the Later Han period.

Let us now turn to glance at how the Western Region countries were eventually brought under the tributary system of Han China. The inclusion of these countries into the tributary system was a gradual process. At the beginning, the Han court, following Chang Ch'ien's advice, tried to use its wealth to win them over. For instance, in Chang Ch'ien's second diplomatic trip to Central Asia, his party "took along tens of thousands of cattle and sheep and carried gold and silk goods worth a hundred billion cash." [11] But as time went on, money alone proved insufficient to hold the friendship of these distant countries. Moreover, because the court later sent too many envoys to the Western Regions, some of the countries even became surfeited with Han goods and no longer regarded them with any esteem.[12] At this early stage when Han China had yet to demonstrate its military superiority, the court even found it necessary to extend the *ho-ch'in* policy to the Western

---

[9] *HHS*, 77:4b.
[10] *HS*, 96A:5b; cf., also, Ise Sentarō, p. 84.
[11] Watson, 2:272.
[12] *Ibid.*, 2:276.

Regions. Emperor Wu thus approved the request of the King of Wu-sun to marry a Han princess as well as to conclude an alliance of brotherhood in the hope that the latter could be estranged from the Hsiung-nu.[13] But other countries did not submit themselves to the Han rule until China defeated the Hsiung-nu in battlefield and fought wars of conquest successfully in the Western Regions. Therefore, the conquest of Ferghana in 101 B.C., particularly, marks the beginning of Han domination in Central Asia. Although the immediate cause of the war of expedition against Ferghana was the latter's refusal to present fine horses to the Emperor, it was at least an equally important concern for the throne that failure to subdue a small state like Ferghana would inevitably lead the Western Regions peoples to slight the Chinese power.[14] It is interesting to note that many states in the area participated in the Chinese tributary system of their own accord immediately after the Han victory over Ferghana. When the Han forces were on their triumphant returning trip, as the Grand Historian reports, "the rulers of all the small states they passed through, having heard of the defeat of Ta-yuan (Ferghana), sent their sons or brothers to accompany the army to China, where they presented gifts, were received by the emperor, and remained at the Han court as hostages." [15] Pan Ku also makes the following remark: "After the Erh-shih General (i.e., Li Kuang-li) conquered Ta-yuan, the entire Western Regions were shocked and frightened. Most [states] sent envoys to present tribute [to China]." [16]

Another important event that directly strengthened the Chinese tributary system in the Western Regions was the surrender of the Hsiung-nu group under *Shan-yü* Hu-han-yeh to the Han in 53 B.C. Prior to this date, peoples of the Western Regions were still more fearful of the Hsiung-

---

[13] *HS*, 96B:1b–2b. For more details about Wu-sun see Shiratori Kurakichi, *Seiiki shi kenkyū*, 1:1–68.

[14] *SC*, 123:8b; Watson, 2:283.

[15] *SC*, 123:9b; Watson, 2:287.

[16] *HS*, 96A:1b.

nu and therefore, as we have seen, treated the Hsiung-nu envoys well. But as the *Han Shu* says, "As for the Han envoys, if they did not use money or silks they would not be able to obtain food, and if they did not go to market for animals they would have no mounts for riders. This was so because peoples there considered that the Han was too far away [to be a threat] and, moreover, that China was wealthy. Thus, whenever [the Han envoys] wanted anything they had to pay for it. However, coming down to the time when Hu-han-yeh paid homage at the Han court, [these peoples] all turned their respect [from the Hsiung-nu] to China." [17]

Thus the full establishment of tributary relations between Han China and the various countries in the Western Regions took a period of more than half century. Moreover, since the tributary system was in a highly delicate equilibrium, such relations between China and the Western Regions by no means remained stable through the rest of the Han period. As a matter of fact, all the states of the area revolted against, and eventually severed their relations with, China during Wang Mang's time when turmoil characterized the political scene of the empire. Not until some sixty-five years later, under the reign of Emperor Ming of the Later Han (58–75), did they return to the Chinese tributary system. Furthermore, during the first century of the Later Han dynasty alone, to about A.D. 125, tributary relations with the Western Regions were maintained with three intervening severances. And only after General Pan Ch'ao's reconquest of the area toward the end of the first century did the tributary system give its full swing for a very short period. In A.D. 94, more than fifty states of the Western Regions all sent hostages to the Han court together with tribute.[18]

Under the Later Han dynasty, especially in the early

---

[17] *HS*, 96A:8b. Cf., also, *SC*, 123:7b; Watson, 2:279.

[18] *HHS*, 118:1a–2b; 77:5a. For more details on Pan Ch'ao's activities in Central Asia see Edouard Chavannes, "Trois généraux chinois de la dynastie des Han Orientaux," *TP*, pp. 210–269 and more recently, Inoue Yasushi and Iwamura Shinobu, *Seiiki*, pp. 24–38.

years, the Northern Hsiung-nu were still very active. They never failed to avail themselves of an opportunity to compete with the Han for the domination of the Western Regions. Each time when tributary relations between China and the Western Region states broke off, the Hsiung-nu moved in to establish their political and economic control there. As in the former Han period, the Hsiung-nu imposed heavy economic exploitations on the peoples of the Western Regions including taxes and labor services. In several cases the exploitation became so unbearable for some of the small states there that they even requested to return to the Han tributary system for protection.[19]

Let us now further examine how the tributary relations between China and the Western Regions were maintained under normal circumstances. Hostage was, of course, an ever-present feature of the tributary system. From 108 B.C. to A.D. 175 numerous hostages had been sent to the Han court from all the tributary states in the Western Regions.[20] Hostages from the Western Regions, unlike those from minor barbarians such as the Wu-huan and Hsien-pi who normally were kept on the frontiers, lived in the capital.[21] They received Chinese education and were subject to Chinese laws and punishments.[22] On many occasions they were also invited to important imperial gatherings. For instance, in A.D. 172 when Emperor Ling made sacrificial offerings to the imperial ancestral tombs outside the capital he was found in the company of not only the nobility and high-ranking officials but also the *Shan-yü* of the Southern Hsiung-nu as well as hostage princes from thirty-six states of the Western Regions.[23]

---

[19] For instance, see *HHS*, 77:7a and 118:1a.

[20] See the table in Ise Sentarō, pp. 57–58.

[21] In the capital there were living quarters built to accommodate the barbarians from all places, bearing the name of *Man-i ti* (residences for barbarians). See *HHS*, 118:8a and commentary.

[22] Ise Sentarō, pp. 59–60; Lien-sheng Yang, *Studies in Chinese Institutional History*, p. 45.

[23] Yuan Hung, *Hou Han Chi*, 23:16a. In this case, however, the number 36 probably means "many" or "all" (or rather the "previous 36"), since

Apart from the hostage, the Han also tried to control the Western Regions through generously conferring Chinese official titles on the leaders of the tributary states. According to the *Han Shu*, toward the end of the Former Han dynasty, no less than 376 official titles, ranging from interpreters to generals and marquises, were made to the fifty states of that region together with official seals.[24] Of this number at least 237 can be identified.[25] The Later Han dynasty followed the same policy in this regard and it is possible that these tributary officials even received regular salaries from the Chinese government.[26]

The Han, of course, also adopted direct methods for the control of the tributary states in the Western Regions. By direct methods, I mean the establishment of such Chinese officials as the *Hsi-yü Tu-hu* or Protector-General of the Western Regions and the *Wu-chi Chiao-wei*. The office of the *Tu-hu* was first created in 59 or 60 B.C. under the reign of Emperor Hsüan.[27] Though primarily a military official, the *Tu-hu* also functioned as the political representative of the emperor, not only to keep the Western Regions under the control of the tributary system, but to regulate relations between all the tributary states as well. From this time on, the *Tu-hu* became an inseperable part of the tributary system in the Western Regions. Therefore, in the Later Han times, revival and severance of tributary relations with the Western Region states was invariably marked by the reestablishment and abolition of the office of *Tu-hu*.[28]

Next in importance was the office of *Wu-chi Chiao-wei* or *Wu-chi* Colonel, which was established by Emperor

the Western Regions were split into more than 50 states during the Later Han period.

[24] *HS*, 96B:10a.
[25] Ise Sentarō, pp. 75–77.
[26] *HHS*, 38:6a–b; Ise Sentarō, p. 80.
[27] *HS*, 96A:1b; cf., also, Ying Shao, *Han Kuan-i* (*Han-Kuan Ch'i-chung* edition), *shang*, 39b. For the *Tu-hu* or Protector General see also E. Chavannes, "Les pays d'Occident d'après le Heou Han Chou," *TP*, p. 154, n. 1; A. Stein, *Innermost Asia*, pp. 790–797; Huang Wen-pi, *Lo-pu-nao-erh k'ao-ku chi*, pp. 180–183.
[28] For instance see *HHS*, 118:1b; 77:8b.

Yüan in 48 B.C.[29] Under the Later Han dynasty, however, this office was split up into two branches entrusted to two officials known as *Wu Chiao-wei* and *Chi Chiao-wei* respectively.[30] Like the *Tu-hu*, the *Wu-chi Chiao–wei* was also more than an office of pure military nature. For instance, it was not only in charge of the *t'un-t'ien*, or military agricultural colonies, but also responsible for general food supplies for the Han soldiers in the Western Regions.[31] On the whole it seems certain that the *Tu-hu* and *Wu-chi Chiao-wei* were jointly entrusted with the task of setting the tributary system to work in the entire Western Regions. Their functions are best described by Fan Yeh, the author of the *Hou Han Shu* as follows:

> Records of the customs and lands of the Western Regions were unheard of in the ancient times. During the Han period, however, Chang Ch'ien . . . and Pan Ch'ao . . . eventually succeeded in carrying out expansion to the far west and bringing foreign territories into submission. Overawed by military strength and attracted by wealth, none [of the rulers of the states in the Western Regions] did not present strange local products as tribute and his beloved sons as hostages. They bared their heads and kneeled down toward the east to pay homage to the Son of Heaven. Thereupon, the offices of *Wu-chi* [*Chiao-wei*] were instituted separately to take care of their affairs and the command of the *Tu-hu* was established to exercise general authority. Those who were submissive from the very beginning received money and official seals as imperial gifts, but those who surrendered later were taken to the capital to receive punishment. Military agricultural colonies were set up in fertile fields and post stations built along the main highways. Messengers and interpreters travelled without cessation and barbarian merchants and peddlers came to the border [for trade] everyday.[32]

The above description clearly indicates that the power of the *Tu-hu* and *Wu-chi Chiao-wei* was very broad in scope, including even the handling of the tribute-gift

[29] *HS*, 19A:6b. Or Mou-and-Chi Colonel, as translated in H. H. Dubs, *The History of the Former Han Dynasty*, 2:331.

[30] On both the *Tu-hu* and the *Wu-chi Chiao-wei* see Lao Kan, "Han-tai ti Hsi-yü Tu-hu yü Wu-chi Chiao-wei," *CYYY*, pp. 485–496. Huang Wen-pi, pp. 184–185, believes that there were already two *chiao-wei* offices under the Former Han.

[31] *HS*, 96A:2a. Cf. Ise Sentarō, pp. 9–14.

[32] *HHS*, 118:9b.

transactions. In this connection it is necessary to examine further the economic significance of the tributary relations between China and the Western Regions.

From the economic point of view there were many reasons for most states of the area to join the Chinese tributary system. In the first place, as tributary states they normally received, at least at the beginning, generous gifts from the Han court. We have seen how Chang Ch'ien tried to buy an alliance from the Wu-sun. The same method was used repeatedly in later times, especially under the reigns of Emperors Hsüan (73–49 B.C.) and Ch'eng (32–7 B.C.). Moreover, it is interesting to note that these gifts, which consisted of gold and silk, were distributed among the pro-Han nobility of the Wu-sun either by the *Wu-chi Chiao-wei* or by the *Tu-hu*.[33] To send gold and silk to the Western Regions as imperial gifts for the rulers of the various states had become such an established general practice that in 77 B.C. the famous Han envoy, Fu Chieh-tzu, even used it as a pretext to trap the king of Lou-lan and thus killed him.[34] During the Later Han period, too, gold and silk together with official titles were often given to the rulers of those states who expressed the intention of becoming participants of the tributary system, such as in the case of Sha-ch'a (Yarkand) and the two Chü-shih states (Turfan and Jimsa).[35]

In the second place, trade was no less an attraction to these tributary states. In fact, not a few of them used tribute as a cloak for trade. For instance, in spite of the cold reception of the Han court, Chi-pin sent envoys to China every several years because of the gains from both imperial gifts and trade.[36] The same was also true with

---

[33] *HS*, 96B:2b–3b.

[34] *HS*, 70:1a–b. This famous event is also borne out by the newly-discovered Han documents on wood. See Lao Kan, *Chü-yen Han-chien, k'ao-cheng*, p. 23.

[35] *HHS*, 118:6b and 8b–9a. Pan Ch'ao also successfully used imperial gifts to attract kings of several states to attend a meeting called by him, *HHS*, 77:5a. I owe the reading of Sha-ch'a (popularly Sha-chü) to Professor Lao Kan.

[36] *HS*, 96A:6a.

K'ang-chü (Sogdiana). According to the memorial of Kuo Shun, *Tu-hu* of the Western Regions during the reign of Emperor Ch'eng, K'ang-chü sent their hostage prince to China not because they respected the Han power but because only through participation in the tributary system could they be entitled to trade with the Chinese.[37]

On the other hand, it must also be pointed out that the sincerity of many of the small states in seeking protection from Han China should not be unreasonably doubted. They preferred the Chinese rule simply on account of the fact that they suffered least economic exploitation under the Chinese tributary system. We have already indicated how the Hsiung-nu enslaved peoples of the Western Regions. Apart from the Hsiung-nu, small states of the region sometimes were also subject to the oppression of the large and powerful ones. For instance, in the first few decades of the Later Han dynasty when China had not yet restored the tributary system in the Western Regions, the powerful state of Sha-ch'a usurped the title and power of the Han *Tu-hu* and imposed heavy levies as well as regular tribute on no less than eighteen small states. Failure or refusal to render payments on the part of such small states as Ch'iu-t'zu (Kucha) and Ta-yuan (Ferghana) often resulted in being conquered by Sha-ch'a. It was exactly this kind of exploitation that caused the eighteen states to request restoration of the tributary system from the Later Han court.[38]

Under the Chinese tributary system, however, in addition to the regular tribute, peoples of the Western Regions still had certain other obligations to fulfill. These obligations constituted no small economic burden on some of the small states, even though they were probably light when compared to the exactions of the Hsiung-nu and other powerful states. Of these obligations, two may be particularly worth mentioning: to provide food and other supplies for Chinese soldiers and envoys and to contribute

---

[37] *HS*, 96A:7b.
[38] *HHS*, 118:6b–7a.

fertile lands for the purpose of *t'un-t'ien* or military agricultural colonies. According to an edict of Emperor Wu, formerly when China was about to make a military expedition against Chü-shih (Turfan), hostage sons of six tributary states including Yü-li (Kalmagan) and Lou-lan were all sent back to prepare animals and food supplies for the Chinese army.[39] In A.D. 16, when Wang Mang dispatched an army to the Western Regions to attack the rebellious Hsiung-nu, many states sent not only grain but also soldiers to assist the Chinese forces.[40]

Instances of their supplying Han envoys with food and other necessities are even more numerous. It seems that such supplies had long become regular duties imposed on all the tributary states. In A.D. 10, for example, Wang Mang decided to send a diplomatic mission to the Western Regions. Upon learning this, the King of Hou Chü-shih (in Jimsa) was so upset that he even contemplated running to the Hsiung-nu in order to evade the heavy financial burden. According to him, it had been an established practice (*ku-shih* or precedent) that the tributary states must provide the Han envoys with ox, sheep, grain, and hay, as well as guides and interpreters, and in his case, he had not yet even gotten over the effects of furnishing supplies for a previous recent mission. Another such mission would inevitably bankrupt the finances of his state.[41] As a matter of fact, almost from the very beginning of the Han western expansion, small states of the region already complained about the tremendous expenditure they had to bear on behalf of the Han envoys. Early in Emperor Wu's time, states lying right across the path that envoys travelled like Lou Lan and Ku-shih (or Chü-shih) were much impoverished in this way.[42] Moreover, food supplies were furnished not only to the Chinese envoys sent to the Western Regions but to the tributary missions coming to the Han court from various states as well. As a Han official

[39] *HS*, 96B:5a.
[40] *HS*, 96B:10a.
[41] *HS*, 96B:9b.
[42] *HS*, 96A:2b.

memorialized to Emperor Ch'eng, two small frontier provinces and eight states of the Western Regions on the Southern Route were dreadfully distressed by the fact that they had to feed people, horses, donkeys and camels of foreign embassies on their trips, both going and returning.[43] In the case of the Han diplomatic mission, however, it was probably its size and frequency that particularly annoyed the tributary states. During Emperor Wu's reign, the largest of the Han missions to the Western Regions numbered several hundred people, while the smaller ones included over a hundred members. Within one year the Han court would normally send from five or six, to over ten, such missions to the west. In the case of distant places, it would even take them eight or nine years to complete the journey.[44]

Lastly, a few words may be said about the *t'un-t'ien* lands. The whole *t'un-t'ien* system is too complicated to be fully discussed here.[45] What will be touched upon below is only a small point, namely, the contribution of lands by the tributary states of the Western Regions to the Han *t'un-t'ien* system. As early as after the conquest of Ferghana, *t'un-t'ien* were already established in many of the western states. At the beginning, however, it seems that the *t'un-t'ien* experiments were carried out on a small scale, and, moreover, their purpose was to produce grain to supply the Han envoys rather than soldiers. According to the *Han Shu*: "In both Lun-t'ai (Bugur) and Ch'ü-li (Kurla) a force of several hundred farming soldiers was set up, each under the direction and protection of a *shih-che Chiao-wei*.[46] [The grains they produced] were to be used

---

[43] *HS*, 96A:7b.

[44] *SC*, 123;6a; Watson, 2:275.

[45] For a general discussion see Ise Sentarō, pp. 37-47; for more detailed studies based on the Han documents on wood see Ch'en Chih, *Liang-Han ching-chi shih-liao lun-ts'ung*, pp. 1-75 and Ch'un-shu Chang, "The Colonization of the Ho-hsi Region—A Study of the Han Frontier System."

[46] I have not been able to find the office of *shih-che Chiao-wei* elsewhere in the *Han Shu*. Presumably it existed only for a short time and its main function was to take charge of all the envoys sent to the Western Regions. *SC*, 123:10a gives *shih-che* as its title which is probably incorrect.

to supply the Han envoys who passed through on their way to foreign countries." [47]

Later on, however, the size of *t'un-t'ien* in these places was considerably enlarged so as to be capable of supporting large numbers of soldiers. For instance, under the reign of Emperor Hsüan, the farming soldiers in Kurla increased to 1,500 persons; [48] the grains stored there were used by a Han general to feed thousands of foreign soldiers in a military expedition against Turfan. [49] In the case of Lun-t'ai (Bugur), during the Chen-ho period (92–89 B.C.), several ministers at the court jointly presented to Emperor Wu a proposal of expansion of the *t'un-t'ien* establishments there. The proposal was not accepted by Emperor Wu because of the cost, but was adopted, though only to a limited extent, by Emperor Chao (86–74 B.C.). This time, it is also interesting to note, the important *t'un-t'ien* task was assigned, not to a Chinese official, but to a hostage prince from a small tributary state. [50] Sometimes the tributary states even of their own accord offered lands to the Han for *t'un-t'ien* cultivation. For instance, in 77 B.C. the Han-supported King of Lou-lan requested the emperor to establish *t'un-t'ien* in the fertile land of I-hsün (Miran) so that his own position in Lou-lan could also be strengthened. [51] Thus *t'un-t'ien*, at least as this particular case shows, also performed the political function of extending the Han recognition and support to the government of a tributary state.

Under the prudent, but conservative, foreign policy of the Later Han, only occasionally was the *t'un-t'ien* system reestablished in some areas of the Western Regions. Take the *t'un-t'ien* establishment in I-wu (Hami), for example. *T'un-t'ien* was first introduced there in A.D. 73 but was abolished four years later in 77. In 119, *t'un-t'ien* was revived in I-wu with a group of over one thousand farming

[47] *HS*, 96A:1b. Cf. *SC*, 123:10a. (Watson, 2:288.)

[48] *HS*, 96B:8b.

[49] *HS*, 70:2b.

[50] *HS*, 96B:4b–6a. Cf. also Lao Kan, *CYYY*, 28, Part 1, pp. 485–488.

[51] *HS*, 96A:3a. On the place I-hsün see Fujita Toyohachi, *Tōzai kōshō-shi no kenkyū, Seiiki hen*, pp. 253–263.

soldiers, which, probably the largest establishment in the Western Regions during this period, was unfortunately cut short by an invasion of the Northern Hsiung-nu only a few months later. In 131, considering the fertility of the lands in I-wu, Emperor Shun again ordered the restoration of *t'un-t'ien* and created the office of *I-wu Ssu-ma* to take charge of it. But this time the end of the Han domination in the entire Western Regions was already drawing near.[52] The size of the *t'un-t'ien* settlement was also smaller than that of the preceding age. The average number of farming soldiers for each *t'un-t'ien* unit was probably 500.[53]

On the whole, it seems that the application of the *t'un-t'ien* policy to the Western Regions was quite effective as far as the establishment of the Chinese tributary system in that area was concerned. That the *t'un-t'ien* settlements formed a basis of vital economic and military importance for the Han control over Central Asia was keenly understood by the Hsiung-nu, as well as the tributary western states. It was probably out of this very understanding that the Hsiung-nu and a few other defiant peoples in the Western Regions repeatedly attacked the Han *t'un-t'ien* settlements in their open conflicts with China.[54] As a matter of fact, the nobles of both Kucha and the Hsiung-nu actually said something to the effect that the Han *t'un-t'ien* establishments were extremely harmful to them and therefore must be destroyed in one way or another.[55]

On the other hand, however, it must also be pointed out that the maintenance of the tributary system in general, and that of the *t'un-t'ien* establishments in particular, in the Western Regions altogether formed a far from small burden on the Han state finance. They were maintained by the Han government mainly out of consideration for the political and military necessity, rather than economic desirability. We have seen that toward the end of his reign,

---

[52] *HHS*, 118:1a–2b.

[53] *HHS*, 49:7a; 77:7a–b; 118:2a and 2b.

[54] For instances, see *HS*, 96B:8b; *HHS*, 118:2b, 3a, 9b.

[55] *HS*, 96B:6a and 8b.

Emperor Wu turned down a proposal to establish *t'un-t'ien* in Lun-t'ai (Bugur). Later under the reign of Emperor Hsüan when Cheng Chi, the first Chinese *Tu-hu* of the Western Regions, requested that more farming soldiers be sent to Chü-shih (Turfan) to strengthen the *t'un-t'ien* there, the request however, was denied by a court conference on the ground of the enormous costs involved.[56] Under the Later Han, Emperor Kuang-wu's refusal to accept tribute and hostages from the western states must also have been partly motivated by economic considerations. The complete withdrawal of Han China from the Western Regions during the period A.D. 107–119, as the heated debate in the court conference of 119 reveals, was a direct result of the fact that the court considered it could not afford the expenditure for the *t'un-t'ien* nor meet the demand for financial aid from the tributary states.[57] Earlier in 91, one memorialist already pointed out that the fixed annual amount of money used in the Western Regions was 74,800,000 cash.[58] This amount, it may be noted, probably does not include the *t'un-t'ien* expenses because it apparently refers only to the regular aid extended to the various tributary states. It seems, then, obvious that at least on the state finance level, the inclusion of the vast Western Regions into the Chinese tributary system, together with the *t'un-t'ien* establishments there, was definitely not economically desirable.

2 Non-Tributary Trade with the Western Countries

In the above section we have seen that trade played a very important role in the intercourse between the Chinese and peoples of the Western Regions. Chinese merchants made adventures to the Western Regions in search of commercial wealth as often as their barbarian counterpart visited the Han empire to explore trading opportunities. And, in both cases, it was a common practice for the merchants either to be appointed envoys representing

---

[56] *HS*, 96B:8b.
[57] *HHS*, 77:7a–b. Cf., also, 118:2a–b.
[58] *HHS*, 75:2b.

their own governments or simply to style themselves so, which must undoubtedly have facilitated their trading activities. Of the barbarian merchants in China during the Han period, further discussion will be made later at another juncture. In this section what will be attempted is to draw a general picture of the commercial intercourse between China and three western countries which remained beyond the reach of the Han tributary system, namely, India, Parthia and Rome. As historical material bearing on this problem is rather scanty in the Han records, the following discussion is based primarily on archaeological finds and studies of modern scholars.

Of all the goods exported from Han China, silk was the single commodity that was by far most cherished by foreign peoples. The great value of silk, coupled with its small bulk and light weight, must have made it a particularly favorite object, as we shall see later, among both Chinese and barbarian merchants and envoys during their journeys from and to the Han empire. Silk was so highly valued by peoples of the Western Regions that in some places the Chinese had to use it, along with gold, to trade for food.[59] It is therefore necessary that we begin our discussion with the silk trade between China and the western countries. It hardly needs mention that there existed between Han China and Rome the famous Silk Road, which has been often described and mapped with amazing accuracy in modern studies.[60] Leaving out all its various detailed ramifications, the main line of the Silk Road may be briefly described as follows: it began at its eastern end at Ch'ang-an, went westward along the Kansu Corridor, crossed the Tarim Basin and Pamirs, then passed through what is now Russian Turkestan (especially Samarkand), Iran, Iraq and Syria, and eventually reached the Mediterranean.[61]

---

[59] HS, 96B:4b. Cf., also, Yen Shih-ku's commentary.

[60] See G. F. Hudson, *Europe and China*, pp. 77–90; an interesting map may be found in A. Hermann, *Die Verkehrswege zwischen China, Indien und Rom um 100 nach Chr*, Leipzig, 1922.

[61] See Hsia Nai, *K'ao-ku hsüeh-pao*, pp. 45–46.

In spite of the existence of the Silk Road as a link between China and Rome, direct commercial intercourse had hardly been established between the two great empires during the Han period, although attempts had been made by both sides. Han-Roman silk trade was carried out mainly through the intermediation of a number of countries in between, of which India and Parthia were by far the most important and therefore deserve closer examination.

Let us first turn to India. In an excellent chapter on the traffic of silk in his *Europe and China*, G. F. Hudson says: "Trade between the Mediterranean, Iran and India had existed for centuries before the imperialism of Wu Ti brought China to this circle of economic intercourse, and though exact figures are lacking, it is certain that throughout Roman imperial times the trade with India was far larger than that with China. The silk trade had its own peculiar problem for the historian, but in many ways it is inseparable from the Roman-Indian trade, which by its pre-existence and permanently greater importance determined the principal channels of commercial intercourse and the structure of the market in western Asia." [62]

This is of course a true characterization, but we must remember that Sino-Indian silk trade also had a history earlier than the opening of the Western Regions by Emperor Wu. The earliest evidence of the trade is to be found, however, not in Chinese history but in ancient Indian literature. In Kautiliya's *Artha'sastra*, which is generally believed to be a product of the fourth century B.C.,[63] we already find the Sanskrit compound *Cinapatta* meaning "a bunch of Chinese silk." [64] This would indicate that silk had been brought to India even long before the unification of China. In later Indian works, silk is even more frequently mentioned, notably the *Manusmrti*, a

---

[62] Hudson, p. 68.
[63] R. C. Majumdar, *An Advanced History of India*, p. 126.
[64] Chi Hsien-lin, *Chung-Yin wen-hua kuan-hsi shih lun-ts'ung*, pp. 163-164; Chang Hsing-lang, *Chung-hsi chiao-t'ung shih-liao hui-pien*, 6:26.

well-known code compiled during the period from about the second century B.C. to the second century A.D.[65]

That private commercial intercourse between the Chinese and Indians had already begun at least in early Han times before the opening of the Western Regions is also well attested by the famous story of Chang Ch'ien's having seen in Bactria certain Szechwan commodities which were imported there through India. As has been pointed out previously, there had existed a trade route leading from Szechwan via Yunnan to Burma from probably the beginning of the Han period. Moreover, at a very early date, Szechwan already produced silk.[66] Therefore, it would be by no means impossible that Chinese silk may have first found its way to India through this Yunnan-Burma land route as well as along a more readily available sea route, which will be discussed in the next chapter.

With the opening of the Western Regions there came into existence a more important land route along which Chinese silk was brought to India. This point has been amply borne out by modern archaeological finds unearthed in the Western Regions. For instance, the discovery of a strip of silk with Brahmi inscript on it in a watch-station in the Han site of Yü-men Kuan may be taken as an unmistakable trace of the Han-Indian silk trade. According to Sir M. Aurel Stein, this piece of silk was made in interior China toward the end of the Former Han dynasty.[67] A coin of Hermaeu's, the last Greek king in India (ca. 50–30 B.C.), found in Chinese Turkestan,[68] together with another one from Khotan bearing his name, further indicates that commercial intercourse may have existed between Hermaeu's kingdom and Han China during this period.[69] Moreover, it should also be noted that Khotan seems to

[65] Chi Hsien-lin, pp. 164–165; Ho Ch'ang-ch'ün, *Ku-tai Hsi-yü chiao-t'ung yü Fa-hsien Yin-tu hsün-li*, p. 2.

[66] Cf. Chi Hsien-lin, pp. 158–159; Fang Hao, *Chung-Hsi chiao-t'ung shih*, 1:133–134.

[67] Sir M. Aurel Stein, *Serindia*, 2:701–704. Cf., also, Stein's article, "Central-Asian Relics of China's Ancient Silk Trade," pp. 370–372.

[68] Stein, *Serindia*, 3:1340.

[69] W. W. Tarn, *The Greeks in Bactria and India*, p. 338.

have played a very important role in the Sino-Indian silk trade along this route. Archaeological discoveries tend to show that close contact existed between Khotan and north-western India in the Han times. It may therefore be inferred that silk from interior China must have been first exported to Khotan and then forwarded to India, as was normally the case of Han China's silk trade with other western countries.[70] The inference is by no means unreasonable and, as a matter of fact, can be justified by the recent discovery of a large amount of Later Han remains of silk fabrics in Niya, east of Khotan.[71]

Under the Later Han dynasty, direct official intercourse is reported to have been established between India and China. During the reign of Emperor Ho (A.D. 89–105) Indian envoys several times visited the Chinese court with tribute. They all came by way of the Western Regions.[72] At this time, it may further be noted, the Chinese had already learned a great deal about India. For instance, the Han record about the prosperity of the Indian-Roman sea trade has been fully borne out by modern studies of the subject.[73] That Sino-Indian silk trade in Later Han times must have been more flourishing than in the preceding period is clearly indicated by the fact that even a first century A.D. Western writer knew exactly how Chinese silk was brought to India via the Western Regions. In the *Periplus*

---

[70] Chi Hsien-lin, pp. 173–175.

[71] Hsia Nai, *K'ao-ku hsüeh-pao*, pp. 45–76 and *Wen-wu ching-hua*. Both works contain excellent color reproductions of Han silks. An earlier short English version of Hsia's article may be found in *China Reconstructs*, 11:1 (January, 1962), pp. 40–42. The bits of delicately woven silk fabrics discovered in Khotan by Aurel Stein, which could only have come from Han China, also throw light on the importance of Khotan as a link of the silk trade between China and the western countries including, of course, India. See Stein, *Sand-Buried Ruins of Khotan*, p. 405.

[72] *HHS*, 118:5b.

[73] *HHS*, 118:5a and 5b; F. Hirth, *China and the Roman Orient*, p. 42. For an account of the sea trade route between India and Rome, see M. P. Charlesworth, *Trade-Routes and Commerce of the Roman Empire*, pp. 57–74 and his more recent article, "Roman Trade with India: A Resurvey," pp. 131–143. For more recent studies see a review article by Takeshima Atsuo, "Roman Trade with India," (in Japanese) *Kodaigaku*, 3:3 (September, 1954), pp. 305–315.

of the Erythraean Sea,[74] we find the following interesting passage: "After this region under the very north, the sea outside ending in a land called This, there is a very great inland city called Thinae, from which raw silk and silk yarn and silk cloth are brought on foot through Bactria to Barygaza, and also exported to Damirica by way of the river Ganges. But the land of This is not easy of access; few men come from thence, and seldom." [75] According to the excellent study of W. H. Schoff, 'a land of This' is but another name for Ch'in,[76] Barygaza the modern Broach,[77] and Damirica which does not appear in India means the "country of the Tamils," that is, the Southern Dravidians of the first century, including the Chera, Pandya and Chola Kingdoms.[78] With these key names being identified, the routes from Bactria to Barygaza and "to Damirica by way of the Ganges" all become clearly traceable.[79] It is certainly justifiable to classify this Sino-Indian silk trade in the category of "transit trade" because large quantities of Chinese silk must have been further transported westward to Rome from India.[80] But, on the other hand, as Warmington has long pointed out, the Indians, both men and

---

[74] The date of this important work has been a subject of much controversy. W. H. Schoff first proposed A.D. 60 (in his annotated translation, *The Periplus of the Erythraean Sea*, pp. 7–15) and then revised it to between 70 and 89 ("As to the date of the Periplus," *Journal of the Royal Asiatic Society of Great Britain and Ireland*, 1917, p. 827). M. P. Charlesworth favored an earlier date by putting it in the middle of the first century A.D. ("Some Notes on the Periplus Maris Erythaei," *The Classical Quarterly*, 22, 1928, p. 93). In 1947, J. A. B. Palmer suggested the date between 110 and 115 for certain portions of the work by using Indian datings. ("Periplus Maris Erythraei: The Indian Evidence as to the Date," *The Classical Quarterly*, 41, pp. 136–140.) This dating, however, is considered too late by Charlesworth in his "Roman Trade with India: A Resurvey," p. 132, where he also gives his definitive date as between A.D. 40 and 75. More recently Jacqueline Pirenne has ably shown that, in view of the Ethiopian data, this work was probably written as late as the third century A.D. ("Un probleme-clef pour la chronologie de l'Orient: la date du 'Périple de la Mer Erythrée'," *Journal Asiatique*, pp. 441–459).
[75] Schoff, *The Periplus of the Erythraean Sea*, p. 48.
[76] *Ibid.*, p. 261.
[77] *Ibid.*, p. 180.
[78] *Ibid.*, p. 205.
[79] *Ibid.*, pp. 268–270, 272–273.
[80] Sir Mortimer Wheeler, *Rome Beyond the Imperial Frontiers*, p. 137.

women, may have also consumed part of the silk imported from China, since they cherished silk no less than the Romans did.[81]

Now we must turn to Parthia. Silk trade between the Chinese and Parthians is clearly recorded in the *Hou Han Shu* as follows: "The Kings of Ta Ch'in (Roman Empire) always desired to send embassies to China, but the Parthians wished to carry trade with Ta Ch'in in Chinese silks and therefore cut them off from communication."[82] Elsewhere we are further informed that, "In the 9th year of Yung-yuan of Ho-ti [A.D. 97] the *Tu-hu* Pan Ch'ao sent Kan Ying as an envoy to Ta Ch'in, who arrived in T'iao-chih,[83] on the coast of the great sea. When about to take his passage across the sea, the sailors of the western frontier of An-hsi [Parthia] told Kan Ying: 'The sea is vast and great; with favorable winds it is possible to cross within three months; but if you meet slow winds, it may also take you two years. It is for this reason that those who go to sea take on board a supply of three years' provisions. There is something in the sea which is apt to make men homesick, and several have thus lost their lives.' When Kan Ying heard this, he stopped."[84]

Obviously, the second instance is a full account of what is referred to in the first quotation as the Parthians having purposely cut off Han China and Rome from communication. The story about the difficulties of crossing the sea has long been considered as but an ingenious deception fabricated by the Parthians.[85] Modern studies of the trading

---

[81] E. H. Warmington, *The Commerce Between the Roman Empire and India*, pp. 176–177.

[82] *HHS*, 118:5b; translated in Hirth, *China and the Roman Orient*, p. 42.

[83] The identification of the place name T'iao-chih has been a highly controversial one. For examples, Hirth (*op. cit.*, esp. pp. 144–152) takes it to be Chaldaea; Fujita Toyohachi (*Tōzai kōshō shi no kenkyū, Seiiki hen*, pp. 211–252) identifies it with Fars in modern southern Iran; for Shiratori Kurakichi (*Seiiki shi kenkyū*, 2:273–313) it designates an ancient state Mesena-kharacene in the lower valley of the Euphrates near the Persian Gulf. Another Japanese scholar, Miyazaki Ichisada argues that it is originally a transliteration of Seleucia in Syria (*Ajiashi kenkyū*, 1:151–184).

[84] *HHS*, 118:4b; Hirth, *op. cit.*, p. 37.

[85] Hirth, *op. cit.*, pp. 164–165 and p. 165, n. 1, citing Wei Yuan's *Hai-kuo t'u-chih*.

position of Parthia have established beyond doubt that the Parthians did have a strong motive to invent such a story. Generally speaking, Parthia played a role more of an intermediary in the silk trade between China and Rome than of a consumer. The trade in silk between the east and west had enriched her tremendously.[86] As Schoff has once remarked, "Between the two (i.e., China and Rome), astride every avenue of trade, lay the Parthian Empire, imposing its tariffs on the caravans and enriching itself without adding anything of value to the trade that passed through its boundaries." [87]

Although it is true that Parthia had profited greatly by serving as intermediary for the silk trade, problems such as how long and to what extent the Parthians had enjoyed the monopoly of this precious merchandise through their geographical advantage are still open to discussion. We have just seen that the Indian merchants had not only tried but succeeded considerably in diverting the silk trade from Parthia. Similar efforts were also made on the part of the Romans. Since Rome had especially suffered from the Parthian intervention in her trade with the east, it was her policy during the two centuries following the Christian era "to encourage direct sea trade with India, cutting out all overland routes through Parthia and thus avoiding the annoyance of fiscal dependence on that consistent enemy of Rome." [88] Evidence tends to show that from the second century A.D. on, especially after the Parthian War of A.D. 162–165, Chinese silk was brought to Rome more and more by the Indians through the sea-route. The expensive land-route via Parthia was thus gradually avoided.[89]

---

[86] Schoff, *The Periplus of the Erythraean Sea*, p. 172.
[87] Schoff, "The Transcontinental Silk Trade at the Christian Era," p. 56.
[88] Schoff, *Parthian Stations by Isidore of Charox*, p. 19.
[89] Warmington, pp. 175–177; Hirth, *op. cit.*, pp. 173–178; A. Stein, *On Ancient Central Asian Tracks*, p. 27; H. G. Rawlinson, *Intercourse between India and the Western World*, pp. 129–130. This interruption of silk trade between Rome and Parthia and its historical consequences have been most thoroughly examined, but perhaps over-emphasized, by Professor Frederick J. Teggart in his interesting book entitled *Rome and China, A Study of Correlations in Historical Events*. See esp. Preface, vii–

The Parthian empire, however, was a loose conglomeration of discordant races including Greeks, Chaldaeans, Nabataeans, Arabs, as well as Persians. Obviously, not all these peoples could equally share the profit of the silk trade between China and Rome. According to Schoff, it was the Nabataeans that actually played the role of the silk-trade intermediaries and were, therefore, the real profiteers. With its capital in Rekam or Petra, the Nabataean kingdom had a firm control over the Sino-Roman silk trade, on which a duty of as high as 25 percent was normally levied, as was the case with all transit trade. It was probably also the Nabataeans who had craftily prevented Kan Ying from travelling further west to reach the Roman Empire.[90]

Having examined the main routes through which Chinese silk was indirectly carried to the Roman Empire, a brief discussion of the introduction of silk to Rome must be made. It has been suggested that Chinese silk fabrics were known in Egypt probably as early as the first century, B.C., and Cleopatra's silks, as described by Lucan, were possibly of Chinese origin.[91] Silk reached Rome at still a later date. The concensus of historians seems to date it in the reign of Augustus (27 B.C.–A.D. 14).[92] Before silk appeared in the Roman market, however, the Chinese silk textures had to undergo the process of dyeing at Tyre or Sidon, or that of being woven or rewoven at Berytus or Tyre.[93] Thus Chinese silk became an important raw material for the weaving industry in the Roman Orient.[94] Almost immediately after its introduction, it was widely accepted by the wealthy Romans, men and women alike. Many references to the use of silk for clothing, pillows,

ix. For a brief criticism of the book see M. Wheeler, *Rome Beyond the Imperial Frontiers*, pp. 180–181.

[90] Schoff, "The Transcontinental Silk Trade at the Christian Era," pp. 56–58.

[91] W. W. Tarn, *Hellenistic Civilization*, pp. 256–257.

[92] Warmington, p. 175; Charlesworth, *Trade-Routes and Commerce of the Roman Empire*, p. 109.

[93] Hirth, *op. cit.*, p. 158.

[94] Hudson, pp. 73, 91; Yao Pao-yu, *Chung-kuo ssu-chüan hsi-ch'uan shih*, Chungking, 1944, p. 59.

cushions, and so forth may be found in Augustan writers.[95] Writing in the second half of the first century A.D., Pliny includes silk among his list of the most expensive and precious products, and deplores that the Seres, together with India and Arabia, drained away from Roman Empire at least 100 million sesterces every year. "That is," he remarks, "the price that our luxuries and our womankind cost us!" [96] It was even rumored in Rome that one pound of silk was equal in value to as much weight in gold—a fantastic statement which, interestingly enough, even has its counterpart in ancient China.[97] Needless to say, Pliny's charge of China having taken large amounts of money from Rome is as unfair as it is ignorant of the true situation along the silk routes. Most of the money went into the pockets of the intermediaries. Nevertheless, his statement gives us a clear notion as to how much the Romans squandered annually in this merchandise from China.[98]

On the whole it seems justifiable to say that the Chinese had a smaller interest in the Roman trade than vice versa.[99] No mention can be found in literary sources of any serious attempt ever made by the Chinese merchants to reach the Roman Empire. Kan Ying's quest of Ta-ch'in, in all likelihood, was motivated by diplomatic rather than commercial considerations. The report by a western writer that in the time of Augustus, envoys from the Seres arrived in Rome, however, cannot be verified. Its very authenticity is very much subject to doubt.[100] But, on the other hand, the Roman merchants did show considerable enthusiasm in the establishment of direct commercial intercourse with Han China. In A.D. 166, as the *Hou Han Shu* reports, a so-called "Roman embassy sent by Marcus Aurelius Anton-

---

[95] Warmington, p. 175; Charlesworth, *op. cit.,* p. 262.

[96] Sir Henry Yule, *Cathay and the Way Thither,* 1:200.

[97] Hirth, *op. cit.,* p. 225 and n. 2.

[98] Cf. Kung Chün, "Liang-Han yü Lo-ma ti ssu mao-i k'ao" *Wen-shih tsa-chih,* esp. pp. 26–27.

[99] Schoff, "The Transcontinental Silk Trade at the Christian Era," p. 60.

[100] Yule, 1:18.

ius" appeared in the Han court.[101] Modern scholars, however, generally do not believe this as a considered imperial mission. Rather the episode seems to indicate "the opportunism of some private merchant" as well as "the adventurous spirit in which Roman trade was conducted *in partibus*." [102] This may well have been the case because, later in A.D. 226, a Roman merchant is actually reported to have arrived in South China.[103]

In his *Natural History,* Pliny gives his impression of the Chinese as follows: "The Seres are inoffensive in their manners indeed; . . . though ready to engage in trade, [they] wait for it to come to them instead of seeking

---

[101] *HHS,* 118:5a; Hirth, *op. cit.,* p. 42.

[102] Wheeler, pp. 174–175.

[103] *Liang shu,* 54:17a–b. In the light of this instance I am inclined to believe that the so-called "embassy from Rome" of A.D. 166 most probably resulted from the fact that the Roman merchant in question professed to represent Marcus Aurelius Antonius. Otherwise the Chinese court would have no way of knowing the name of the "King of Ta-Ch'in." It is unlikely that the Chinese officials falsely presented a private Roman merchant to the court as an imperial envoy from Rome. Moreover, as we have seen previously in the case of some tributary states of the Western Regions, the Han officials were realistic enough to distinguish an envoy from a merchant as far as his knowledge went. In his classical work *Trade-Routes and Commerce of the Roman Empire,* M. Charlesworth, however, has the following remarks concerning the "Roman embassy" of 166: "It is only natural that national pride should have transformed the visit of an adventurous merchant into a formal embassy, and the presents offered to the King into a tribute. The same thing was done to Western nations not so many years ago" (p. 72). In offering this explanation, obviously, Mr. Charlesworth must have had in mind particularly such famous embassies as that of Lord Macartnay in 1793, of which the transformation into a tributary mission by the Chinese greatly hurt the national pride of England. Nevertheless, Mr. Charlesworth seems to have over-modernized the case. In pre-modern China it was rather a general practice on the part of the western merchants to style themselves as "envoys" in the hope of facilitating their trading activities in China. As has been shown by Fairbank and Teng, as late as 1604 we still find the description, by Benedict de Goez, of the "sham embassies" of merchants from the western kingdoms who "forge public letters in the names of the kings whom they profess to represent" and "under pretense of being ambassadors go and offer tribute to the Emperor." ("On the Ch'ing Tributary System," *HJAS,* 6:2 (June, 1941), p. 139 and n. 7.) Therefore, I prefer G. H. Stevenson's explanation that this "Roman embassy" was probably a band of merchants masquarading as representatives of the emperor (C. Bailey, ed., *The Legacy of Rome,* p. 165).

it." [104] Needless to say, this statement was true only as far
as Pliny's knowledge went because no single Chinese
merchant of the period under discussion is known to have
ever set his foot on Roman soil. But this does not mean
that the Han merchants remained inactive in silk trade. In
the above section we have seen many cases in which Chinese merchants are reported to have gone to the Western
Regions in great number for trade. We have also pointed
out that most of the so-called "Han envoys," who made
trips to Central Asia following in Chang Ch'ien's tracks,
were actually merchants in search of commercial wealth. [105]
There can be no doubt that they must have carried silk
with them. The Han merchants thus have shown a spirit
which is by no means less adventurous than their Roman
counterparts. On this very aspect, fortunately, considerable
light has been shed by the archaeological excavations of
our times.

In one of the refuse heaps adjoining a post on the old
Chinese *limes* west of Tun-huang, Stein discovered, among
other things, two strips of undyed cream coloured silk,
datable between A.D. 84 and 137. One of the two strips,
which bears a Chinese inscription, is translated by M.
Chavannes as follows: "A roll of silk from K'ang-fu in the
Kingdom of Jen-Ch'eng; width two feet and 2 inches,
length 40 feet; weight 25 ounces; value 618 pieces of
money." [106]

As Chavannes further points out, the historical importance of this text lies in the fact that it indicates precisely
the origin, the dimensions, the weight and the price of silk
at the close of the first century or at the beginning of the
second century A.D. Moreover, since this find dates precisely from the period to which relates the famous classical

---

[104] Yule, 1:18.

[105] On this point see also Chu Chieh-ch'in, "Hua-ssu ch'uan-ju Ou-chou
k'ao," in this *Chung-Hsi wen-hua chiao-t'ung shih i-ts'ui,* pp. 293–294 and
Fang Hao, 1:134.

[106] For the Chinese inscription and a study of its historical significance
see also Lo Chen-yü and Wang Kuo-wei, *Liu-sha chui-chien, k'ao-shih,*
2:43b. Cf. the original plate in E. Chavannes, *Les documents chinois
découverts par Aurel Stein dans les sables du Turkestan oriental,* no. 539.

record about the direct trade of the West with the land of the Seres as learned by Marius of Tyre and preserved by Ptolemy, Stein is even led to believe that "the roll of silk specified in the inscription had found its way there in connection with China's silk export to Central Asia and the distant West as carried on about the close of the first century A.D." [107] Whether such a small piece of evidence can bear out the whole statement of Marius about the direct trade between the West and China is of course another matter. Nevertheless, it seems reasonable to take it as a clear trace of Han China's silk trade with the Central Asian peoples, especially when it is considered against the historical background of the frequency with which Chinese merchants visited the Western Regions during this period. As one author puts it, this discovery by Stein "enables us to appreciate how thoroughly the trade was organized on the Chinese side." [108]

The important discoveries of silk fabrics in the site of the ancient Lou-lan (Lop Nor) also have bearings on China's silk export. In *Serindia,* Stein reports that the silk relics he discovered in this site can be classified as of two categories: the miscellaneous fragments of silk fabrics that are local products; and the numerous small pieces of silk in a variety of rich colors that are certainly Chinese imports. In Stein's opinion, "The ancient silk trade of China with Central Asia and beyond must have moved for centuries along the very route marched by this ruined settlement, and that to it the latter owed its *raison d'être.*" [109]

Many more relics of the trade have been found along the Silk Road since Sir Aurel Stein made his third journey of exploration in Central Asia.[110] Of these recent discoveries two particularly bear on our discussion. One is the above-

---

[107] Stein, "Central Asian Relics of China's Ancient Silk Trade," pp. 368–369.

[108] C. G. Seligman, "The Roman Orient and the Far East," p. 554.

[109] Stein, *Serindia,* 1:373; cf., also, his *Ruins of Desert Cathay,* 1:381. The importance of this site to silk trade is further emphasized in his *Innermost Asia,* 1:232.

[110] See literature cited in Hsia Nai, "Hsin-chiang fa-hsien ti ku-tai ssu-chih p'in," *K'ao-ku hsüeh-pao,* p. 45, n. 4.

mentioned silk fabrics of Later Han date unearthed in 1959 at a burial place near the ancient city of Niya, which was abandoned sometime in the third century. The Niya finds include figured silk fabrics as well as several beautiful pieces of the Han embroidery.[111] Another one is the Chinese silks found during the thirties in several tombs datable between 83 and 273 in Palmyra in Syria, a trading center near the western end of the ancient Silk Road. Many western experts believe that these silks are of Han origin and therefore call them "damasks in Han weave." [112] In an excellent technical study, Hsia Nai, a leading Chinese archaeologist, has ably shown that the newly-discovered silk remains of Niya bear certain striking resemblances to those of Palmyra. For instance, from among silk fabrics of both places it is found that several pieces were woven by the same particular method of the so-called "Han-weave." In decorative design as well as in motifs, common elements are also present in both cases. Thus, in the light of the Niya finds we are now more assured than ever that the Palmyra silks must have been brought by silk merchants all the way from Later Han China.[113] As Palmyra was known in ancient times for its close trade connections with the Orient to which it largely owed its prosperity, possibly it also played an important role in the silk trade between China and Rome.[114] Although it is unlikely that the Han merchants ever set foot in Syria, the very fact that Han damasks have been found not only at Palmyra, but also in many other places including Lop-nor,

---

[111] Reported in *Wen wu*, 1960:6; 1962:7–8; *K'ao ku*, 1961:3.

[112] R. Pfister, "Les Soieries Han de Palmyre," *Revue des Arts asiatiques*, pp. 67–77; O. Mänchen-Helfen, "From China to Palmyra," *The Art Bulletin*, pp. 358–362; R. J. Charleston, "Han Damasks," *Oriental Art*, pp. 63–81. For a different view see, however, P. Ackerman, "Textiles through the Sassanian Period," *A Survey of Persian Art*, vol. 1, esp. pp. 685–691.

[113] Hsia Nai, "Hsin-chiang fa-hsien," esp. pp. 50–54. For a general study of the technological innovations in the textile industry in Han China see Sun Yü-t'ang, "Chan-kuo Ch'in-Han shih-tai fang-chih-yeh chi-shu ti chin-pu," *LSYC*, pp. 143–173.

[114] For the importance of Palmyra in the eastern trade of the Roman Empire see Charlesworth, *Trade Routes and Commerce of the Roman Empire*, pp. 48–50 and Wheeler, p. 170.

Edsin Gol, Noin-ula, Kerch in Crimea and Ilmova Pad in Buryat-Mongolia [115] is sufficient indication of the existence of a wide market abroad for Chinese silk, which in turn points to a well organized silk trade with foreign peoples on the part of the Han merchants.

Apart from trade, it may be noted, there were also other channels through which Chinese silk was brought to the western countries. One important channel was the imperial gifts made to various barbarian chiefs as well as nobles, especially those of the tributary states. Of such gifts many examples have been given above.[116] Another channel was the possible use of silk as currency, especially during the Later Han period. Early in the Former Han times, when the Han envoys and merchants went to the Western Regions, they already were using silk to cover their travel expenses.[117] In one of the Han documents discovered by Stein, it is recorded that the chief of a certain watchtower (*sui-chang*) received "32 feet of silk fabrics," which Chavannes takes to be an indication of the use of silk as currency. He is even of the opinion that "the use of silk as a sort of currency is likely to have been resorted to in China long before the Later Han times." [118] It was, however, under the Later Han dynasty that silk was more widely used as a medium of exchange. For instance, in the Former Han period, in some cases, instead of receiving legal punishment one could pay a total sum of fine either in gold or in copper coins. But down to the Later Han such fines were normally paid in silk. Several imperial

[115] Hsia Nai, "Hsin-chiang fa-hsien," p. 75.

[116] See also those given in Yao Pao-yu, pp. 20–21.

[117] Cf. Fang Hao, p. 134 and Teggart, *Rome and China*, pp. 213–215.

[118] Stein, *Serindia*, 2:758, n. 39 and 701, n. 6B. It may be noted that mistaking *sui* (watchtower) for *tui* (company) Chavannes wrongly interprets the title *sui-chang* as "captain of a certain company." Similar mistakes may often be found in Chavannes', *Les documents chinois découverts par Aurel Stein dans les sables du Turkestan oriental*, as well as in the famous *Liu-sha chui-chien*. See Ho Ch'ang-ch'ün, "Feng-sui k'ao" in *Kuo-hsüeh chi-k'an*, p. 77. The occasional use of silk (*po*) as money in ancient China is also mentioned in Lien-sheng Yang, *Money and Credit in China: a Short History*, p. 12.

edicts were actually issued to this effect.[119] Moreover, evidence both historical[120] and archaeological,[121] tends to show that during the period under review silk in considerable quantity was stored in many places along the northern and northwestern frontier. Possibly it was used by the Han government to pay the soldiers as a form of money, as revealed in the above-mentioned case of a watchtower chief.[122] And it was probably also in the same capacity that some of the Han silk fabrics eventually went beyond the imperial boundaries as a result of frontier trade.

Finally, a word may be said about the origin of silk trade between the east and west. Hudson has made a keen observation as follows: "Silk . . . . was probably introduced into Western Asia by the Parthians when they had been made familiar with it *by the presents of Chinese embassies;* after a while the Parthians bought it not only for their own consumption but also to sell further west. Silk thus first reached the Mediterranean by an overland route. . . ." [123] A similar conclusion has also been reached by Owen Lattimore, according to whom, "It may even be that the primary export of silk arose out of gifts and subsidies, that bolts of silk thus became a standard of luxury value,

[119] See P'eng Hsin-wei, *Chung-kuo huo-pi shih,* p. 75 and p. 78 (nn. 16 and 17).

[120] It is reported in the *Hou Han Shu* (78:5b) that the Hsien-pi people once threatened the Han frontier general by trying to set fire to all the silk fabrics (*ch'ien-po*) stored there.

[121] More instances of silk mentioned in the Han documents on wood may be found in Lao Kan, *Chü-yen Han-chien, k'ao-cheng,* pp. 64–65.

[122] Sometime during the Yung-ch'u period (107–114), Prince Su of Tung-hai contributed 10,000 pieces of silk to the government to cover part of the expenses for the northwestern frontier (*HHS,* 72:2a). In Emperor Shun's time (126–144), Prince Ch'ung of Jen-ch'eng also made contributions in coins as well as in silk to subsidize the northwestern frontier expenses because of the Ch'iang rebellions (*HHS,* 72:8a). In both cases, it may be pointed out, silk is mentioned together with coins as a sort of currency. The latter case, as Wang Kuo-wei rightfully suggests, is archaeologically verified by the discovery of the above-mentioned "a roll of silk from K'ang-fu in the Kingdom of Jen-ch'eng. . . ." (Lo Chen-yü and Wang Kuo-wei, *Liu-sha chui-chien, k'ao-shih,* 2:43b).

[123] Hudson, p. 77. Italics are mine.

that the rulers of little states who received silk as gifts and
subsidary acquired an actual surplus, and that trade thus
arose at a secondary level in order to dispose of the silk in
more distant markets." [124]

This theory is further confirmed by studies by Chinese
scholars based on Chinese sources.[125] Here, however, we
can still add another interesting piece of evidence in its
support. According to Schoff, "The trade in silk yarn and
silk cloth existed in Northern India soon after the Aryan
invasion. Silk is mentioned several times, *as gifts from
foreign countries,* in *The Mahabharata, the Ramayana,*
and *The Institutes of Manu;* and it may be assumed that
some trade at least went farther west." [126] Although
names of "foreign countries" are not given, it seems,
nevertheless, safe to identify one of them with Han China.
Even if these silks did not come directly from China, they
may well have been originally Han imperial gifts conferred on the various tributary states of the Western Regions. The weight of evidence has at least led Schoff to
speculate that silk mentioned in these sources was imported to India from China by way of the Brahmaputra
valley, Assam and Eastern Bengal.[127] Moreover, the silk
sold to the Romans by the Indians possibly also included
part of such "gifts from foreign countries," especially when
we consider the words of Pliny that "more recently again
they (i.e. silks) have been imported from India, or from
nations beyond the countries of India." [128] It is certainly
tantalizing to think that the "foreign countries" in the
former case are somehow related to the "nations beyond"
in the latter one. Thus the "gift theory" is also attested in
ancient Indian sources. It applies not only to the Parthian-
Roman silk trade but to the Indian-Roman one as well. As
shown above, "gifts" or "subsidies" figured centrally in the
Chinese tributary system. Should the "gift theory" be ac-

---

[124] Lattimore, *Inner Asian Frontiers of China,* p. 493.
[125] Yao Pao-yu, pp. 12, 14; Chi Hsien-lin, esp. pp. 142–145.
[126] Schoff, *The Periplus of the Erythraean Sea,* p. 142. Italics are mine.
[127] *Ibid.,* p. 264.
[128] Quoted and discussed in *ibid.,* p. 265.

cepted as valid, then even the non-tributary trade in Han China also had a tributary origin.

Apart from silk, Han iron is also spoken of as having reached the Roman Empire. It all starts with a statement of Pliny that "of all the different kinds of iron, the palm of excellence is awarded to that which is made by the Seres."[129] Both Hirth[130] and Yule[131] agree that the "Seres" in this case also refers to the Chinese. Yule even further speculates that Pliny's iron "was probably that fine cast-iron, otherwise unknown to the ancients." [132] On the other hand, however, doubt has been cast on such an interpretation. The fact that *The Periplus of the Erythraean Sea* does not indicate the importation of silk and steel together at the same marts has led Schoff to believe that the "Seres" in this particular case rather points to the Cheras of the Malabar coast.[133] In spite of this objection, scholars like Hudson,[134] Tarn,[135] and more recently Miyazaki Ichisada [136] still think that Chinese iron was introduced to Rome in view of the existence of a large and highly skilled iron industry in Han China.

In this connection both old Chinese sources as well as new archaeological discoveries throw some light, though only indirectly, on the problem. History has shown that under the Former Han dynasty the iron industry was a centralized government monopoly, and moreover, the severe and prohibitive law against exportation of iron implements was strictly enforced. It is, therefore, very unlikely that iron could have been brought to the western countries in any significant volume, even through contra-

---

[129] *Ibid.*, p. 171.

[130] Hirth, *China and the Roman Orient*, pp. 225–226, n. 2.

[131] Yule, pp. 17–18, n. 3.

[132] That cast iron was developed in China earlier than elsewhere in the ancient world is now a well-established archaeological fact. See Kwang-chih Chang, *The Archaeology of Ancient China*, p. 197.

[133] Schoff, "The Eastern Iron Trade of the Roman Empire," pp. 7–8, 14–15. Cf., also, Warmington, pp. 157–158, 257–258.

[134] Hudson, p. 93.

[135] Tarn, *The Greeks in Bactria and India*, p. 364 and n. 4; and his *Hellenistic Civilization*, p. 253 and n. 13.

[136] Miyazaki Ichisada, "Shina no tetsu ni tsuite," *Shirin*, esp. pp. 2–5.

band trade. But in Later Han times, due to the relaxation and localization of the iron monopoly, along with the loosening of law, refined iron is actually reported to have been smuggled out of the frontier and to have fallen into the possession of the barbarians, especially the Hsien-pi. Thus, the possibility, no matter how slight, cannot be entirely ruled out that in the first two centuries of the Christian era, Chinese iron was brought farther west through the Central Asian intermediaries.

Archaeology tends to confirm such a conjecture. Iron articles of Han date have been unearthed from many tombs of the nomads in such places as Noin-ula [137] and the Transbaikal region.[138] Since, however, as the Russian archaeologist Rudenko has pointed out, the Hsiung-nu not only obtained iron from China but also knew how to smelt iron and forge iron implements,[139] it is rather difficult to distinguish among such finds the Han imports from the native products. According to Egami, the iron culture of the Hsiung-nu, especially their use of iron weapons, was developed under the direct influence of Han China from about the first quarter of the first century B.C.[140] This direct influence includes probably both the importation, through contraband trade, of Chinese iron implements and the introduction of metal casting techniques to the Hsiung-nu. It is actually reported in Chinese sources that such techniques spread from Han China to the neighboring barbarians. For instance, in General Ch'en T'ang's memorial to Emperor Ch'eng (32–7 B.C.), he mentioned that the Wu-sun barbarians had recently learned much about the Han techniques of making sharp (presumably iron) weapons.[141]

---

[137] For instance, see C. Trevor, *Excavations in Northern Mongolia*, p. 58; Umehara Sueji, *Mōko Noin-Ura hakken no ibutsu*, pp. 98–99.

[138] H. Kuhn, "Zur Chronologie der Sino-Sibirischen Bronzen," *Ipek*, pp. 165–168.

[139] S. I. Rudenko, *Kul'tura khunnov i noinulinskie kurgany*, p. 60; *Seikai kōkogaku taikei*, vol. 9, pp. 70–71.

[140] Egami Namio, *Yūrashiya kodai hoppō bunka*, pp. 307–318.

[141] *HS*, 70:7b. Egami Namio is in error in taking these barbarians (*Hu*) to be the Hsiung-nu (p. 315).

In another case we are told that both Han envoys and surrendered soldiers had taught the people of Ta-yuan or Ferghana how to cast iron weapons.[142] Sites of iron foundries datable between the first and third centuries have been found at Niya, one of the states in the Western Regions.[143] It is even more interesting to note that the iron industry in the Western Regions, which had been initiated under the influence of Han China,[144] was already so sufficiently developed by the Western Chin period (265–316) that implements of the so-called "barbarian iron" began to be imported back to the Chinese troops stationed on the frontier from some of the countries there.[145] Along with the techniques of iron casting, it may be safely assumed that Han iron must also have been brought across the Chinese border to the Central Asian states. The above examination of both historical and archaeological evidence assures us that the Inner Asian barbarians did have direct access to Chinese iron during our period. But, as far as Pliny's statement is concerned, since it was made in the second half of the first century A.D., it can be considered true, if ever, only for Later Han China.

Finally, brief mention must be made of other kinds of Han articles found outside China as a result of archaeological excavations. Once more let us begin with the Noin-ula finds. First, the group of burial objects of indubitable Han origin are lacquer works.[146] Second, among the bronze articles, archaeologists generally believe that many are imported from Han China.[147] But, due to the similarity of chemical contents, it is, however, not always possible to make a clear distinction between the Han imports and the

---

[142] *HS*, 96A:8b.

[143] *HCKTKKSH*, p. 89.

[144] Huang Wen-pi, pp. 71–72.

[145] Henri Maspero, *Les Documents chinois de la troisième expédition de Sir Aurel Stein en Asie Centrale*, p. 68; Lo chen-yü and Wang Kuo-wei, *Liu-sha chui-chien, k'ao-shih*, 2:44b. See the interesting discussion in Lien-sheng Yang's review article, *HJAS*, 18 pp. 148–149.

[146] Umehara Sueji, *Mōko Noin-Ura hakken no ibutsu*, pp. 28–34 and *Kodai hoppō kei bumbutsu no kenkyū*, pp. 1–14; Alfred Salmony, "The Small Finds of Noin-Ula," *Parnassus*, pp. 18–19.

[147] Rudenko, p. 62; Salmony, *op. cit.*, p. 18.

local Hsiung-nu products, with, of course, the sole exception of Chinese mirrors.[148] Third, jade ornaments of various sorts have been generally considered to be from Han China,[149] especially those of better quality.[150] The Japanese expert, Umehara, has even been able to identify —quite convincingly—the only jade human figurine from Noin-ula to be the Chinese *Weng-chung*.[151]

These three kinds of Han products—lacquer, bronze and jade, it may be noted, have been continually coming to light from many sites in the Western Regions.[152] For instance, Han lacquer works similar to those found in Lo-lang were discovered in the Lop Nor region by Huang Wen-pi in 1930.[153] Han bronze mirrors and jades also have a wide archaeological distribution outside China, especially in northern Asia.[154] The route along which Han mirrors and jade ornaments were gradually brought to the various western countries is still traceable, to some extent, in light of modern archaeological discoveries.[155] As in the case of Han silk, some of these articles may have been originally gifts to the nomads from the court. For instance, it has been suggested that an inscribed Former Han mirror found in west Siberia early in the eighteenth century was probably an imperial gift to a certain Hsiung-nu leader, possibly the famous Chih-chih *Shan-yü* who moved to some place in west Siberia during the middle of the first century B.C.[156] But there can be little doubt that a great many of them must have found their way to the west through trade. It is rather significant to find that

---

[148] Rudenko, p. 62.

[149] Umehara, *Mōko Noin-Ura hakken no ibutsu*, pp. 39–43; Salmony, "Die ersten Funde von Noin Ula," *Artibus Asiae*, p. 89.

[150] Salmony, "The Small Finds of Noin-Ula," p. 20.

[151] Umehara, *Mōko Noin-Ura hakken no ibutsu*, p. 39. Cf., also, Rudenko, p. 115.

[152] *Seikai kōkogaku taikei*, 9:95–111.

[153] Huang Wen-pi, pp. 97–99, 150–151; and Ch'en Chih, *Liang-Han ching-chi shih-liao lun-ts'ung*, p. 109.

[154] See a map showing the archaeological distribution of Han mirrors in Egami Namio, p. 288.

[155] Umehara, *Kodai hoppō kei bumbutsu no kenkyū*, pp. 40–68.

[156] Egami Namio, p. 291. Cf. Lien-sheng Yang, "An Inscribed Han Mirror Discovered in Siberia," *TP*, pp. 330–340.

probably even as early as Han times there were already foreign imitations of Chinese bronze mirrors and jade ornaments, an unmistakable indication of a strong market demand of these commodities beyond the Chinese frontiers.[157]

Han China, of course, also received many kinds of precious articles from the western countries in return through both tribute and trade. For convenience, I have not touched upon them in the present chapter, but shall, however, turn to that aspect of the Sino-barbarian economic intercourse at another juncture toward the end of this study.

---

[157] Umehara, *Kodai hoppō kei bumbutsu no kenkyū*, pp. 54–56, 64–65, 67–68.

chapter seven

Overseas Trade

Of overseas trade in Han China we know extremely little. To begin with, however, let us translate a much quoted and studied passage from the *Han Shu,* which is by far the most important single record about Chinese sea-trade during the Former Han period:

By boat, it takes five months to travel from Hsü-wen and Ho-p'u on the border of Jih-nan to the country named Tu-yüan, then from Tu-yüan it takes four months to reach the country known as I-lu-mo, and further on more than twenty days to that of Shen-li. After arriving at Shen-li, however, one [has to] travel on foot. In more than ten days he comes to the country Fu-kan-tu-lu. From there he again [has to] travel by boat and in about two months he reaches Huang-chih, where the local custom is somewhat similar to that of Chu-yai (Hainan Island). It is a big land with large population, and has many curious products, which have been presented [to the court] as tribute since the time of Emperor Wu.

Previously there was a Chief Interpreter of the office of *Huang-men* (Yellow-Gate of the Palace), who, together with those summoned by the government for overseas adventures, went to sail to the sea with the purpose of purchasing pearls, beryl, curious stones and other precious things. They brought with them gold and silk of various shades. Wherever they went they were provided with both food and women. The trading boats of the barbarians which carried them from one place to another were also engaged in trade as well as in rapacity. It was a great danger to sail on these boats. Besides, the seas were rough and often times they perished on the sea. It took those who did not quit the round trip several years to return [to China]. [They brought back] large pearls with a circumference of slightly below two inches. During the Yuan-shih period of Emperor P'ing [A.D. 1–6] Wang Mang was in power. As he was bent on displaying his influence and virtue, he sent envoys to the King of Huang-chih with rich gifts and asked the latter to return the favor by dispatching envoys to present live rhinoceroses [to the court as tribute]. It takes eight months to sail from Huang-chih to P'i-tsung and two months to the border of Hsiang-lin in Jih-nan. South of Huang-chih is the country called I-ch'eng-pu whence the Han interpreter-envoys started their returning trip.[1]

Many problems involved in this passage have not yet been satisfactorily solved. First of all, there is the difficulty of identifying the place names. For our purpose here, however, it would suffice to follow the generally accepted identifications. According to the Japanese authority, Fujita Toyohachi,[2] Tu-yüan was probably somewhere on the north coast of Sumatra, I-lu-mo a Han transliteration of Arramaniya, near Thatung, at the mouth of the Salman in south Burma, Shen-li that of Sillah in the neighborhood of the Burmese city Pugan, Fu-kan-tu-lu that of Pugandhara, the ancient city of Pugan (or Pagan), in the vicinity of today's Tagaung on the left bank of the Irrawaddy, and P'i-tsung is now known as Pulaw Pisan, an island to the south-western end of the Malayan Peninsula. Fujita identifies I-ch'eng-pu with Courtllum or Kitul in southwestern India, but modification of later scholars has generally taken it to be Ceylon.[3] The most controversial of all the identifications is that of Huang-chih. Many wrong guesses had been made before G. Ferrand and Fujita came to the conclusion that Huang-chih was Kancipura, which is now known as Conjeveram, in southeastern India.[4] Since then various new attempts have been made to reopen the discussion,[5]

---

[1] *HS*, 28B:17b. For discussions of this passage see Gungwu Wang, "The Nanhai Trade, A Study of the Early History of Chinese Trade in the South China Sea," pp. 16–30 and Paul Wheatley, *The Golden Khersonese*, pp. 8–13.

[2] Fujita Toyohachi, *Tōzai kōsho-shi no kenkyū, Nankai hen*, pp. 95–135.

[3] Fujita Motoharu, "Kansho chirishi tsū Kōshikoku kō," *Shirin*, pp. 45–47; Kuwata Rokurō, "Nanyō jōdai-shi zakkō," *Ōsaka daigaku bunga-kubu kiyō*, p. 9; Su Chi-ch'ing, "Han-shu ti-li-chih I-ch'eng-pu Kuo chi Hsi-lan shuo," *Nan-yang hsüeh-pao*, pp. 1–4; and Miyazaki Ichisada, *Ajiashi kenkyū*, 2:473.

[4] G. Ferrand, "Le K'ouen-louen et les anciennes navigations inter-océaniques dans les mers du sud," *Journal Asiatique*, pp. 45–46. Cf. Kuwabara Jitsuzō, "Sui-T'ang shih-tai Hsi-yü jen Hua-hua k'ao," *Wu han Ta-hsüeh wen-che chi-k'an*, p. 424.

[5] For instance see Kuwata Rokurō, pp. 9–10; T'an Pi-an, "Han-tai yü Nan-hai Huang-chih Kuo ti chiao-t'ung," *She-hui ching-chi yen-chiu,*

but Fujita and Ferrand's theory is still generally accepted among experts.[6] With these place names tentatively identified, it is certainly amazing to see that China had already established trading relations, not only with peoples of Southeast Asia, but also with those of India, through a sea route, well before the beginning of the Christian era.

In this important passage, there are two interesting points concerning foreign trade of the Han times to be observed. First, the fact that overseas trade was put under the charge of an Interpreter of the Office of *Huang-men,* or Palace Gate-keeper, seems to indicate that the Han emperor, as an individual, also developed considerable interest in foreign trade. The Office of *Huang-men,* it may be noted, belonged to the *Shao-fu* or Small Treasury,[7] which was so to speak, the emperor's purse as distinguished from the empire's purse.[8] Thus the Interpreter's trading trip in this case must have been made on behalf of the emperor. Here we already see the beginning of the tradition in imperial China that overseas trade was often entrusted to the care of officials of the Inner Court, as later in the T'ang (618–907) and Sung (960–1279) times, although in this case the Han official was not necessarily a eunuch.[9] Second, it is also worth noticing that the Chinese trading party

---

2, pp. 111–143; Su Chi-ch'ing, "Huang-chih Kuo chiu-tsai Nan-hai ho-ch'u," *Nan-yang hsüeh-pao,* pp. 1–5.

[6] For instance, see Fujita Motoharu, pp. 43–44; Feng Ch'eng-chün, *Chung-kuo Nan-yang chiao-t'ung shih,* pp. 2–3; Chi Hsien-lin, *Chung-Yin wen-hua kuan-hsi shih lun-ts'ung,* p. 167; Chang Sun, *Wo-kuo ku-tai ti hai-shang chiao-t'ung,* p. 14; and Ts'en Chung-mien, *Sui-T'ang shih,* p. 568.

[7] *HS,* 19A:4b.

[8] Lien-sheng Yang, *Studies in Chinese Institutional History,* p. 89. Gungwu Wang is right in saying that the *Huang-men* were appointed by the emperor to purchase luxury goods for the court, but whether the *Huang-men* in this case can be identified with the eunuchs is rather open to doubt (pp. 22–23). Wheatley also takes the *Huang-men* to be "Department of Eunuchs" (p. 8, n. 3).

[9] Feng Ch'eng-chün, p. 2; Yao Pao-yu, *Chung-kuo ssu-chüan hsi-ch'uan shih,* pp. 14–15. It may be added that in the Former Han period, also under the *Shao-fu,* there was an office known as *Chūng-huang-men* or Office of Inner Palace Gate-keeper, which, according to Yen Shih-ku consisted of only eunuchs (*HS,* 19A:4b).

brought with it gold and silk for exchange for foreign rarities. This is certainly the earliest record about the exportation of Han silk to the South Seas. Moreover, it also furnishes an important clue in addition to the overland Silk Road, as to the existence of an overseas silk route between China and the West, with India as the intermediary. A considerable part of Han China's silk trade with India and Rome was probably conducted along the sea route. As has been well summarized in the *Sung Shu*,

> As regards Ta-Ch'in [Rome] and T'ien-chu [India], far out on the western ocean, we have to say that, although the envoys of the two Han dynasties have experienced the special difficulties of this road, yet traffic in merchandise has been effected, and goods have been sent out by way of Chiao-pu (Tongkin), the force of winds driving them far away across the waves of the sea. . . . All the precious things of land and water come from there, as well as the gems made of rhinoceros' [horn] and king-fishers' stones, *she-chu* [serpent pearls] and asbestos cloths, there being innumerable varieties of these curiosities; . . . all this having caused boats to sail along this [sea] route one after another as well as the exchange of both envoys and merchants.[10]

In the case of Rome, it is very clear that when the so-called Roman envoy first came to the Han court in A.D. 166 and a Roman merchant named Ch'in Lun later arrived in South China in 226, both travelled by sea via Jih-nan (Annam) and Chiao-chih (Tongkin) respectively. Another Chinese source also relates that during the Han period Roman merchants frequently visited Fu-nan (Cambodia),[11] Jih-nan and Chiao-chih.[12] Moreover, in the conception of the Han Chinese, Rome was always a maritime country, sometimes referred to as Hai-hsi Kuo or Country West of the Sea.[13] *The Periplus of the Erythraean Sea* also shows that Roman merchants were very active in the South Sea during the first century A.D., which further points to the possibility of the existence of an overseas Sino-Roman

---

[10] *Sung Shu*, T'ung-wen edition, 97:23; translation adapted with alterations from F. Hirth, *China and the Roman Orient*, p. 46.

[11] On Fu-nan see Paul Pelliot, "Le Fou-nan," *BEFEO*, pp. 248–303.

[12] *Liang Shu*, T'ung-wen edition, 54:17a; Hirth, *op. cit.*, p. 47.

[13] *HHS*, 116:9a; 118:4b.

silk trade.[14] Taking all these facts into account, it seems safe to conclude that, at least in the Later Han times, the indirect economic intercourse between China and the Roman Empire, if any, was carried on also along the sea route.

If we accept the identification of Huang-chih as Kanci-pura, then as early as during the Former Han times there already existed a sea route between China and India in addition to the land route discussed in the previous chapter.[15] According to a Chinese scholar, this early use of a sea route is also attested in ancient Indian sources. In the Pali text, *Milindapanha,* which is a dialogue between King Menandros (ca. 125–95 B.C.) and the monk Nagasena, the latter, Nagasena, actually mentions something to the effect that Indian cargo ships went as far as to China.[16] During the decades from Wang Mang's time to the early years of the Later Han, in which relations between China and the Western Regions were generally interrupted, Sino-Indian overseas silk trade probably became more flourishing as a result of the cutting off of the overland trade route. During this period, there seems to have been even some increase of Chinese silk in the Roman market, which, it is believed, was due to more frequent use of the sea route by the Indian intermediary.[17] It may further be conjectured that the growth of the overseas silk trade between the east and the west resulted partly also from the fact that both sides found it desirable to avoid the Parthian monopoly. At any rate, it is beyond doubt that in Later Han times Sino-India economic intercourse often resorted to the sea route. Another important piece of evidence which lends support to this general observation is the use of the sea route by envoys

[14] See Murakara Kentarō, "Erythraeikai annaiki ni mietaru kigen isseiki no Nankai bōeki," *Tōzai kōshō shiron,* 1:101–155.

[15] Cf. Feng Ch'eng-chün, p. 8. Lao Kan, however, is of the opinion that before the reign of Emperor Ho (89–105 A.D.) only land routes were available between China and India. *CYYY* 16, pp. 89–90. Lao's theory, which is based on his own interpretation of the various place-names in the above-quoted passage of the *Han shu,* has been vigorously refuted by Ts'en Chung-mien, *Sui-T'ang shih,* pp. 575–577.

[16] Chi Hsien-lin, p. 167.

[17] Kung Chün, *Wen-shih tsa-chih,* 2:5–6, pp. 24–25.

from India. For instance, in 159 and 161 Indian envoys twice came to the Han court to pay tribute. In both cases it is reported that they took the sea route by way of Jih-nan (Annam).[18]

In Later Han China, overseas trade seems to have gained much progress. In this respect, both Jih-nan and Chiao-chih played a very important role by serving as a link of intercourse between China and the various maritime countries. We have just seen that Indian and Roman envoys, as well as merchants, came to China by way either of Jih-nan or of Chiao-chih. Other maritime states who sent envoys to China via Jih-nan included the well-known Yeh-tiao, a state possibly in Java or Ceylon.[19]

The prosperity of Chiao-chih (Tongkin) as a seaport during the Later Han period particularly deserves attention. Chiao-chih was known especially for the production of such curiosities as pearls, ivory, tortoise shell, incense, and so forth, from which its immense wealth derived. This made it difficult for most of the governors there to keep their personal integrity. They exacted money, not only to fill their own purses, but also to bribe influential officials in the central government. Whenever they thought they had enough, they requested transfer to some other post, presumably for the sake of avoiding running any further risk. Such exactions often resulted in the rebellion of the natives.[20] Severe punishment occasionally befell an official who knew no limit to his corruption. For instance, Chang Hui was executed because of taking bribes while serving as Provincial Governor of Chiao-chih sometime during the

---

[18] *HHS*, 118:5b. Cf. Feng Ch'eng-chün, p. 8; Henry Yule, *Cathay and the Way Thither*, 1:66.

[19] An envoy from Yeh-tiao is reported to have come to send tribute to the court in 131 A.D. (HHS, 6:3b and 116:4a). For its identification with Java or Ceylon, see Fujita Toyohachi, pp. 653–694.

[20] *HHS*, 61:8a. It is interesting to note that this tradition of official corruption was carried on well into the Chin period (265–420) in which both the Governor-General of Chiao Chou and the governor of Jih-nan always illegally took 20 to 30 percent of the tribute sent by the maritime countries to the court. (*Chin Shu*, T'ung-wen edition, 97:15b–16a). For a study of the governors of Chiao-chih in the Later Han period, see the article by Ozaki Yasushi, in *Shigaku*, pp. 139–166.

reign of Emperor Ming (58–76). All his spoils were accordingly confiscated by the government and the emperor ordered them to be distributed among the high-ranking officials at the court as imperial gifts. One official, however, refused to take his share of pearls on the moral ground that they were originally bribes.[21] This story also reveals that pearls, the famous product of Chiao-chih, must have been among the objects of illegal exaction of all the corrupt governors of Chiao-chih. The pearl trade in Chiao-chih was then so lucrative that one memorialist even proposed to Emperor Chang (76–89) that the government should take the opportunity of the annual tour of report of the Provincial Accountant from Chiao-chih to the capital to trade in pearls and other precious articles as a means of securing additional revenue for the state treasury.[22] On the other hand, it is also highly significant that toward the end of the Later Han period when the famous Shih Hsieh (136–226) was Governor of Chiao-chih, the streets of Tongkin were filled with barbarians, presumably barbarian merchants.[23] All these facts can be properly comprehended only against the commercial background of Chiao-chih at that time. I can think of no better explanation than overseas trade that can account at the same time for both the prosperity of Chiao-chih and the frequent presence of foreigners there.[24]

On the south China coast, P'an-yü (modern Canton) was the oldest, as well as the most important, port.[25] Early in the Former Han period, P'an-yü already flourished as a center of overseas trade. As our Grand Historian says, "P'an-yü was also a capital and a center, the center for trade in pearls, round and otherwise, rhinoceros horns,

---

[21] HHS, 71:5a–b; Tung-kuan Han-chi, pp. 153–154; Hui Tung, Hou-Han Shu pu-chu, Ts'ung-shu chi-ch'eng edition, 4:437; Yao Chih-yin, Hsieh-shih Hou-Han-shu pu-i, 3:1b.

[22] HHS, 73:2a.

[23] SKC, Wu, 4:9a–b. Cf. Lao Kan, op. cit., p. 90.

[24] The importance of Chiao-chih in overseas trade during the Later Han period is also noted in the following works: Li Cheng-fu, Chün-hsien shih-tai chih An-nan, pp. 37–38 and Tamura Jitsuzō, Tōyōshi kenkyū, pp. 33–34.

[25] Fujita Toyohachi, pp. 643–652.

tortoise shells, *tai-mao,* fruits (such as *lung-yen* or *long-an* and *li-chih* or *litchi*), and textiles woven from vegetable fibers." [26] Pan Ku further informs us that merchants who went to P'an-yü to trade in these products from interior China mostly obtained riches there.[27] Throughout the Han period, P'an-yü served, as in later times, as the port of entry for those coming to China from the maritime countries of the South Sea as well as from farther west. Commodities from such countries normally first reached P'an-yü and then spread to various parts of inland China. This situation can be seen even from the introduction of certain foreign plants to China. It has been reported that jasmine was brought over from western countries by the barbarians and was first planted in Kwangtung sometime in the third century A.D. At the same time envoys and merchants who visited China from the Roman Orient, India or Parthia along the sea route also often first stopped at P'an-yü.[28]

The importance of P'an-yü in the overseas trade of Han China has been recently attested by archaeology. Precious articles of foreign origin including glass, amber, agate, and so forth, have been found in considerable quantity in many Han tombs at Canton and Ch'angsha. Some of them must have been imported from the South Sea.[29] As Ch'angsha is adjacent to Kwangtung, the discovery of large numbers of glasswares as well as beads of various rare stones there is even taken by archaeologists as a confirmation of the important passage quoted at the very beginning of the present chapter.[30] The case of amber is even more interesting. Amber is found not only in Ch'angsha, but also in Canton [31] and Kuei Hsien, Kwangsi.[32] As has been discussed

[26] *SC*, 129:6a. Translation by Nancy Lee Swann, *Food and Money in Ancient China,* p. 446.

[27] *HS*, 28B:17a.

[28] Fujita Toyohachi, pp. 649–652. As for the introduction of jasmine to south China, see also the critical view of B. Laufer, *Sino-Iranica,* pp. 329–330.

[29] *HCKTKKSH*, p. 82.

[30] Chung-kuo K'o-hsüeh Yuan K'ao-ku Yen-chiu So, *Ch'ang-sha fa-chüeh pao-kao,* p. 166.

[31] *Wen-wu ts'an-k'ao tzu-liao,* 1955, 6, p. 63.

[32] *KKTH*, 1957:2, p. 58.

in Chapter V, one possible source of the amber supply in
Han China was the Yunnan-Burma border area. Another
possible source was the Baltic. Both sources were known to
the Han Chinese.[33] If the latter was the case, then it could
come only through overseas trade, with P'an-yü as a port of
entry. It must also be pointed out, however, that amber
articles discovered at different places are not of the same
quality. Therefore, the two possibilities are by no means
mutually exclusive.[34]

There are even traces of overseas slave trade in recent
archaeological findings. From Han tombs in Canton are
found quite a few pottery human figurines, both male and
female of typical barbarian contenance. They were buried
together with the dead, obviously as servants of the latter.
Archaeologists believe that this very fact possibly reflects the
fashion of the day when aristocratic and powerful families
used foreign slaves as household servants. And the geographical location of these discoveries, Canton, further
indicates that these slaves were most likely bought from
some overseas markets.[35]

Another important port in coastal Kwangtung was Ho-
p'u, a place known particularly for its pearl trade.[36]
Under the Former Han dynasty, however, Ho-p'u was still
an underdeveloped frontier area to which families of
guilty officials were often exiled,[37] but even then the pearl
trade of Ho-p'u was already very lucrative. For instance,
during the reign of Emperor Ch'eng (32–7 B.C.), the wife
and children of Wang Chang were sent to Ho-p'u after he
died in imprisonment. A few years later when the government allowed them to return home, they had been able to
accumulate an immense fortune through pearl fishery.[38]
In Later Han times, the pearl trade of Ho-p'u grew more

---

[33] Chang Hung-chao, *Shih-ya*, pp. 58–63.

[34] Chung-kuo K'o-hsüeh Yuan K'ao-ku Yen-chiu So, *Ch'ang-sha fa-chüeh pao-kao*, p. 166.

[35] Li Chin, "Kuang-chou ti Liang-Han mu tsang," *Wen-wu*, 1961:2, pp. 47–53.

[36] See the careful study of Edward H. Schafer, "The Pearl Fisheries of Ho-p'u," *JAOS*, pp. 155–168.

[37] For instance, see *HS*, 76:13b and 93:4b.

[38] *HS*, 76:13b–14a.

prosperous owing largely to the effort of a *hsün-li* or model offical, Meng Ch'ang, who served as Governor of Ho-p'u sometime during the middle of the second century A.D. The story runs as follows:

> The Province [of Ho-p'u] did not produce grain or fruit, but the sea gave forth pearls and treasures [or, its treasure of pearls]. Its borders were coterminous with Chiao-chih, and there was regular communication [with that place] by merchants and peddlers who went there to buy cereals. In earlier times, the governors had all been, by and large, avaricious and corrupt, and required people to gather and search [for pearls] without regard to any limit. Consequently the pearls gradually migrated to the confines of Chiao-chih Province. Henceforth the travellers did not come, people were without resources, and the destitute died of starvation on the road. When Ch'ang took up his office he radically altered the earlier evil practices, and sought out what was advantageous to the populace. Before the expiration of a year, the departed pearls returned again, the folk went back to their profession of pearl fishery, and commerce circulated. This was said to be a miracle.[39]

Actually there was nothing miraculous about this miracle. The so-called "migration of pearls" was but a result of the fact that when avaricious officials forced the gathering of the maximum possible crops of pearls the oyster harvest was quickly reduced. And the "return of pearls" can also be easily explained on the ground that pearl production was restored to its normal course when necessary limitations were put on gathering.[40] From this passage we know not only of the prosperity of the pearl trade of Ho-p'u but also of the existence of a keen competition in the trade between Ho-p'u and Chiao-chih. Moreover, the fact that merchants of Ho-p'u regularly went to Chiao-chih to import cereals also reveals a close economic intercourse between the two areas conducted through coastal trade. This economic tie between Chiao-chih and China proper may be considered

---

[39] *HHS*, 106:6b. Translation taken from Schafer, pp. 156–157 with a few alterations. It may be added that the pearl trade in Ho-p'u continued to be prosperous in the period of the Three Kingdoms and the people there still followed the old Han practice of using pearls to buy rice from outside. But this time the Wu government found it desirable to monopolize the trade in order to increase the state revenue. *Chin Shu,* 57:10b–11a; cf. T'ao Yüan-chen, *San-kuo shih-huo chih,* p. 113.

[40] Schafer, p. 157.

archaeologically confirmed by the discovery of a large number of the Han *wu-shu* coins in North Vietnam.[41]

At this juncture it may be relevant to point out that Chinese expansion to the south, especially in Vietnam, also owed much to trade. As early as Ch'in Shih-huang's time, according to a second century B.C. source, the First Emperor's campaigns against the Yuehs were motivated by "the expected gains from the lands of the Yueh with their rhinoceros horns, ivory, kingfisher feathers, and pearls." [42] It seems quite possible that these Yueh products first became known to the Chinese through trade. Archaeology tends to show that commercial relations between China and parts of Vietnam must have been established at the end of the third century B.C., or the beginning of the second. For instance, in Thanh-hoa, the Han site of Chiu-chen province, there have been found Chinese objects of Ch'in and early Han date, which are referred to by archaeologists as the Huai Valley style. Since permanent Chinese settlers did not arrive the Chiu-chen area in any significant number until about two centuries later, it has been suggested that these Huai style pieces may have been brought there by trade. "It can be assumed that the first Chinese who ventured into the country and mingled with the natives were journeying merchants or artisans. . . . In the wake of these tradesmen certainly came the civil and military mandarins, accompanied by the less welcome tax-collectors, and by the political refugees." [43] In other words, as in other cases, Chinese expansion to Vietnam was ushered in by trade.

Finally, brief mention must also be made of trade in the East China sea. Navigation in the East Sea is of very ancient origin, traceable probably even to prehistoric times.[44] It was, however, from the fourth century B.C. on-

---

[41] Tamura Jitsuzō, p. 35.

[42] *Huai-nan tzu*, 18:21b. Cf. Leonard Aurousseau, "La première conquête chinoise des pays annamites (IIIᵉ Siècle avant notre ère)," *BEFEO*, pp. 137–264; Gungwu Wang, pp. 8–15; Lü Shih-p'eng, *Pei-shu shih-ch'i ti Yüeh-nan*, p. 22.

[43] Olov R. T. Janse, *Archaeological Research in Indo-China*, vol. 1, p. xvi.

[44] Chang Sun, pp. 1–2; Cheng Te-k'un, *Prehistoric China*, p. 127; Kwang-chih Chang, "Chinese Prehistory in Pacific Perspective: Some Hypotheses and Problems," *HJAS*, p. 134.

ward that coastal as well as outer sea sailing in this area developed to an unprecedented degree. This was closely related to the rise of the Taoist cult of physical immortality. The belief in the existence of the Three Divine Mountains, the reputed residence of *hsien* immortals, somewhere in the east seas had led many princes of Ch'i and Yen to send Taoist immortalists to search for it. Under the unified Ch'in and Han empires, the imperial quest for "immortality drugs" in the east seas was carried out even on a much larger scale.[45] The best known Taoist immortalist, Hsü Fu, during the reign of the First Emperor of Ch'in even brought with him to the seas three thousand boys and girls, together with seeds of five types of grains as well as various kinds of craftsmen. He is reported to have made himself king presumably on a certain large island and never returned to China.[46]

At any rate, in Han times, China not only established close relations with Korea but also began to have contact with Japan and other islands in the East Sea. Coastal sailing from the Shantung Peninsula to Korea was fairly common. For instance, in 109 B.C., when Korea rose in arms, a Chinese army of 5,000 soldiers was sent there from Shantung by crossing the Gulf of Pohai.[47] In this period, it is also reported that Chinese merchants visited Korea to such an extent that they even corrupted the native social customs.[48] We can safely assume that not a few of them must have gone there by the sea route. It is certainly no wonder that numerous Chinese objects, notably silk, *wu-shu* coins, weapons, lacquer works, bronze mirrors, and so forth have been unearthed in large quantity in North Korea, the Han site of Lo-lang Province.[49] Throughout the Later

---

[45] Ying-shih Yü, "Life and Immortality in the Mind of Han China," *HJAS*, p. 97.

[46] *SC*, 118:5b; Burton Watson, *Records of the Grand Historian of China*, 2:374–375. It may be noted that a vigorous attempt has been made by Wei T'ing-sheng to establish the thesis that Hsü Fu eventually settled down in Japan. See his *Jih-pen Shen-wu T'ien-huang k'ai-kuo hsin-k'ao*, and *Hsü Fu yü Jih-pen*.

[47] *SC*, 115:1b; Watson, 2:259. Mistaking the reign title *Yuan-shou* for *Yuan-feng*, Fujita Toyohachi gives the wrong date of 121 B.C. (p. 634).

[48] *HS*, 28B:14a.

[49] For an up-to-date general survey see *Sekai kōkogaku taikei*, 7:112–117.

Han period, tributary relations between China and the various tribes and states in Korea were generally well maintained. In extending the tributary system to this area, the role played by the Governor of Liao-tung was of decisive importance. Its full establishment in the early years of the Later Han, for instance, was due almost entirely to the conscientious work of a single individual, Ts'ai T'ung, who served as Governor there for more than thirty years under the first two emperors. His tactful use of both force and gifts induced most barbarians in the east seas, including tribes from Japan, to come to present tribute in the court. Before A.D. 107, as we are told, exchange of envoys between China and these tribes, or states, was very active.[50] Needless to say, there must also have been considerable tributary, as well as private trade, going along with the exchange of envoys through coastal sailing. Toward the very end of the Later Han period, the entire Liao-tung area, including part of North Korea, fell under the control of another important governor, Kung-sun Tu (died A.D. 204). The Kung-sun family ruled Liao-tung in three successive generations over a period of almost fifty years (189–237), until it was eventually conquered by the Kingdom of Wei. This half-century witnessed an unprecedented advance in overseas trade between China and the Liao-tung coastal regions. For instance, in one case the Kingdom of Wu sent no less than one hundred ships, loaded with commodities, to trade along the coast of Liao-tung. Both people and officials there showed much interest in such an exchange trade.[51] In another case we are again told that some seven to eight thousand people were sent by the Wu government along the sea route to establish commercial relations with Liao-tung.[52] It is true that behind these trading activities there was an obvious political motivation on the part of the

---

[50] *HHS*, 50:5b–6a. For general studies of Sino-Korean relations in the Han period see Shiratori Kurakichi and Yanai Wataru, "Kandai no Chōsen," *Manshū rekishi chiri*, 1:1–111; Ikeuchi Hiroshi, "Rakurō Gun kō," *Man-Sen chiri rekishi kenkyū hōkoku*, pp. 1–77; Wada Sei, *Tōa shi kenkyū, Manshū hen*, pp. 1–21.

[51] *Wei Lüeh*, quoted in *SKC, Wei*, 8:14b.

[52] *Ibid.*, 15a–b.

Wu to seek the alliance of the Kung-sun family against the Wei.[53] On the other hand, it must be emphasized that the Wu also had a genuine interest in the overseas trade, as such. In both cases, it may be noted, the Wu showed anxiety to obtain horses from Liao-tung. Direct tributary and commercial relations were even established between the Wu and Koguryo. In 223–234, Koguryo presented 1,000 sable furs and other local products to the Wu as tribute, and, in return, the Wu court sent envoys to confer on the king of Koguryo the title of *Shan-yü*, together with the gift of clothes and other precious articles. In their returning trip, the Wu envoys also brought with them eighty horses from Koguryo.[54] This instance further indicates the Wu's interest in overseas horse trade.

Further to the east in the seas, relations with the various tribes of Japan were gradually established. Under the Former Han dynasty it is already reported that more than one hundred small states of the Wo-jen in the sea of Lo-lang (Korea) regularly came to present tribute to China.[55] Scholars generally believe that the so-called Wo-jen probably were then the residents of northern Kyūshū.[56] Down to the Later Han times, Sino-Japanese relations continued to improve. It is clearly recorded in the *Hou Han Shu* that, in 57 and 107 respectively, the state of Wo sent tribute to the Han court. In the first case, Emperor Kuang-wu is even said to have given an official seal to the king of the Wo.[57] With the rapid growth of overseas trade in the East China Sea in the early third century came also the close economic, as well as political intercourse, between Wei China and Japan. Within a short span of ten years (238–247), four times envoys from the state of Wo arrived in China and twice the Wei sent envoys to return their calls. For

[53] Lien-sheng Yang, *Studies in Chinese Institutional History*, pp. 130–131.

[54] *Wu-shu*, quoted in *SKC, Wu*, 2:23b.

[55] *HS*, 28B:14a. Later sources indicate, however, only some thirty of the hundred states came to pay homage to the Han emperor. *HHS*, 115:5b; *SKC, Wei*, 30:23b–24a.

[56] Kimiya Yasuhiko, *Nisshi kōtsūshi*, 1:20.

[57] *HHS*, 115:6a. Cf. Ho Ch'ang-ch'ün, "Ku-tai Chung-Jih wen-hua chiao-liu shih-hua erh-tse," *Chung-hua wen-shih lun-ts'ung*, pp. 285–286.

tributary exchange, Chinese gifts including gold, silk, bronze mirrors, and so forth, were matched by Japanese local products, especially white pearls.[58] Sino-Japanese intercourse during the Han period, as recorded in old Chinese sources, seems to have been fully borne out by modern Japanese archaeological findings. Bronze mirrors as well as other metal objects, including iron utensils of Han date, have continuously come to light in archaeological excavations at many sites in Japan. Even copper coins cast under the reign of Wang Mang were found at many sites in northern Kyūshū, which unmistakably indicates the overseas trade between China and Japan. What is more significant, however, is the discovery in 1784 of a gold seal of the king of Wo-nu state given by Han China, which completely confirms the above-mentioned statement of the *Hou Han Shu*. Previously some doubt has been cast on the authenticity of the seal. But in light of the recent discovery of a similar Han seal given to the king of Tien or Yunnan, it seems that the doubt can now be reasonably removed.[59]

In concluding this chapter, a word may be said about the unsolved problem of I-chou and T'an-chou, two large islands somewhere in the East China Sea. According to the *Hou Han Shu*, Hsü Fu and his several thousand boys and girls eventually settled in either I-chou or T'an-chou in the east. In the Later Han period, people from this island often came to Kuei-chi, an important port on the Chekiang coast, to trade with the Chinese.[60] Later in the period of the Three Kingdoms, the ruler of the Wu, Sun Ch'üan, was told the same story. In 230, the Wu sent a force of ten thousand people to the sea in search of both places. They failed to locate the whereabouts of T'an-chou, but did reach I-chou and brought several thousand people

---

[58] *SKC, Wei*, 30:27a–28b. Cf. T'ao Yüan-chen, pp. 87–88.

[59] Kimiya Yasuhiko, pp. 21–30; *Seikai kōkogaku taikei*, 2:113–116; and Wang Chung-shu, "Shuo Tien-wang chih yin yü Han Wo-nu kuo-wang yin," *K'ao-ku*, pp. 573–575. For a most recent discussion of the seal of King of Wo-nu see the article by Okabe Nagaaki in *Suzuki Shun Kyōju Kanreki Kinen Tōyōshi ronsō*, pp. 117–145.

[60] *HHS*, 115:6b. See also *K'ua-ti chih* quoted in *SC*, 118:5b.

of the island back to the Wu.[61] In spite of the fact that the
two places remain yet to be identified the story nevertheless
serves our purpose well because it points to another direction in the east seas toward which Han China's overseas
trade was developed.

[61] *SKC*, *Wu* 2:20a–b. I-chou has generally been taken as today's Taiwan.
For a recent different view, see Liang Chia-pin, "Lun Sui-shu Liu-ch'iu
wei T'ai-wan shuo ti hsü-kou ti kuo-ch'eng chi ch'i ying-hsiang—Chien-
lun Tung-Wu I-chou wei Liu-ch'iu," *Tung-hai hsüeh-pao*, pp. 101–148.

chapter eight

Conclusions: Trade and Expansion in Historical Perspective

In the above, we have analyzed various aspects of trade and expansion in Han China within the institutional context of the time, with their political implications emphatically indicated whenever and wherever necessary. For it is the basic structure which gives meaning and unity to the historical facts concerning Sino-barbarian economic relations, not the facts as such, that we have been concerned with throughout this study. Now, by way of conclusion, we must bring forth for discussion a few problems of major political, economic, and cultural significance in their broad historical perspective.

1 Political and Economic Interests Within the Tributary System

Throughout this study, the pervasiveness of the tributary system as a dominating factor in the domain of foreign relations has been fully exposed. With the sole exception of contraband trade, almost all kinds of Sino-barbarian economic relations were harnessed to this system, directly or indirectly. Not only the exchange of tribute and gift was inherent in it, but private trade between the Chinese and the barbarians was also an inseparable part of it. Even the non-tributary trade among barbarians beyond the Han imperial frontiers, as has been shown in the case of the silk trade, is found to have had a possible Chinese tributary origin. In this connection it is necessary to reexamine the

very nature of the tributary system in our period through a
discussion of its theoretical basis.

In a sense, the political principle behind the system may
be understood as the acceptance of the Han imperial rule by
the barbarians. The exchange of tribute and gift, the essential part of the system, was but a ritualistic expression of
such political relations between the imperial government
and the barbarians in economic terms. But under such an
understanding we would, however, find it inadequate to
interpret the system simply as the very mechanism through
which Sino-barbarian economic relations were regulated. In
other words, the tributary system functioned not merely in
the domain of foreign relations. Rather it was an important aspect of the entire Han imperial system concerning
not only the barbarians, but the Chinese as well. This point
is clear when we bear in mind the fact that "local products"
of various Chinese provinces were also required to be presented to the court annually as tribute from the Chinese
people. On the other hand, it was an equally common
practice for imperial gifts, from time to time, to be
made to both Chinese meritorious officials as well as
model citizens. This, of course, does not mean that the
Chinese and barbarians were equally treated under the
tributary system. As a matter of fact, the so-called "acceptance of imperial rule" involved not only different levels
of "acceptance" but also different categories of "rule,"
varying generally from one group of people to another. It
was from this point of view that the Chinese were distinguished from the barbarians and the inner barbarians
from the outer ones. The ultimate goal of the tributary
system was to achieve political stability through the establishment of a lasting imperial order in which proper relations between the state and the people could always be
maintained. Trade and expansion therefore necessarily fell
under the general purview of this all-embracing system.

In this system we also discern at work the Confucian
principle of extension from the closest to the remotest: the
closer a particular group of people stood in relation to the
nucleus of the imperial power the greater was the atten-

tion given to it. In the light of this underlying principle, it seems, then, not too difficult to see why the inner barbarians, like the Hsiung-nu, and the Ch'iang were a much more immediate concern of the Han court than the outer ones, like those of the Western Regions; why of the same Hsiung-nu people the southern group was treated with kindness and generosity at the expense of the northern branch; and, to some extent, also why overland trade on the whole, as our study has amply shown, was much better developed than overseas trade. Thus the Han tributary system, with its dominant political character, had its strength as well as weakness as far as trade and expansion were concerned. On the one hand, it seems that in the long run the system was capable of fully absorbing the fruits of trade and expansion by keeping the various barbarian groups in a state of relative equilibrium at every stage of historical development. On the other hand, the system also inevitably set limitations on trade and expansion because neither endless search of wealth by acquisitive merchants, nor unlimited pursuit of territories by expansionist emperors or generals, if serving no useful purpose of the empire, could expect to receive much encouragement under the system. In either case, however, the system displayed its rationality to a remarkably high degree.

Previously it has been pointed out that under the tributary system two levels of Sino-barbarian economic intercourse may be conveniently distinguished. At the state level the intercourse was always a loss to China whereas at the personal level it did bring benefits to various kinds of individual Chinese. In the earlier discussions I have clearly shown why and how the tributary economic intercourse was a liability rather than an asset for Han China as far as it affected the state finances. Scholars have generally noticed that in the exchange between Chinese imperial gifts and barbarian tribute the economic value of the former always greatly exceeded that of the latter.[1] But this is only a small part of the whole story. As the case of

---

[1] Owen Lattimore, *Manchuria, Cradle of Conflict*, p. 111; T. F. Tsiang, "China and European Expansion," *Politica*, pp. 3-4.

Han China has shown, we must take into account not only military expenditure involved in wars of conquest but also administrative and other expenditures required by the maintenance of the imperial rule in the newly-conquered areas. Both were prerequisites for the establishment of tributary relations. On the other hand, Sino-barbarian economic intercourse at the personal level needs further elaboration.

To begin with, let us quote a very interesting, but much neglected, passage from the *Yen-t'ieh lun* or *Discourses on Salt and Iron*. In defense of the government policy of encouraging foreign trade, the Imperial Secretary argued:

> Ju Han gold and other insignificant articles of tribute are means of inveigling foreign countries and snaring the treasures of the Ch'iang and Hu [i.e. Hsiung-nu]. Thus, a piece of Chinese plain silk can be exchanged with the Hsiung-nu for articles worth several pieces of gold and thereby reduce the resources of our enemy. Mules, donkeys and camels enter the frontier in unbroken lines; horses, dapples and bays and prancing mounts, come into our possession. The furs of sables, marmots, foxes and badgers, colored rugs and decorated carpets fill the Imperial treasury, while jade and auspicious stones, corals and crystals, become national treasures. That is to say, foreign products keep flowing in, while our wealth is not dissipated. Novelties flowing in, the government has plenty. National wealth not being dispersed abroad, the people enjoy abundance.[2]

The importance of this passage to our discussion can hardly be exaggerated. In the first place, it reveals a contemporary Chinese conception of Sino-barbarian economic intercourse in purely economic terms. According to this conception, the intercourse was always to Han China's advantage because it was precisely through the exchange trade that China was enriched by treasures of the various barbarians. In the second place, although the argument gives us the impression that the state was also greatly benefited by such intercourse, it was in the final analysis, as we shall see later, some individual Chinese, including the emperor, who were the real beneficiaries. And third, the passage also gives a preliminary account of the various

[2] *Yen-t'ieh lun*, p. 4; translation by Esson Gale, *Discourses on Salt and Iron*, pp. 14–15.

kinds of foreign commodities imported to Han China, which will serve as a basis for the discussion of the nature of foreign trade in this period.

Let us begin with the emperor's personal interest in expansion and trade. As we have seen, the conquest of Vietnam by Emperor Ch'in Shih-huang was primarily motivated by his desire to obtain such rarities as rhinoceros horns, ivory, and pearls of that region. It is certainly interesting that similar remarks were also made by historians of the period of the expansionist Emperor Wu of Han. Ssu-ma Ch'ien already related his expansion to the southwest to the discovery of the *chü* berry sauce in Canton and of bamboo canes in Bactria.[3] Pan Ku further elaborated the point roughly as follows: "In Emperor Wu's time, the Empire was rich and powerful. Therefore, when the Emperor saw rhinoceros horns and tortoise shells, he was able to set up seven provinces in the south including Chu-yai (Hainan Island). Inspired by the *chü* berry sauce and bamboo canes, the southwest was opened up. Having heard about the Heavenly Horses, he eventually succeeded in establishing relations with Ferghana and Bactria. From that time on, precious articles like shining pearls, rhinoceros horns, tortoise shells and emeralds overflowed in the inner palace, four best kinds of horses filled the palace gates, and giant elephants, lions, fierce dogs, and big birds were fed in the Imperial garden. In short, rare things of various places came from all directions."[4] It would seem that the Han emperor certainly had a strong economic interest in expansion as well as in the inclusion of more barbarians into the tributary system. Concerning the imperial interest, however, two points must be made. First, all these precious articles mentioned above were undoubtedly luxuries, which were economically valuable only as far as the emperor enjoyed them in his private life. In no way did they enrich China at the state finance level. Rather the contrary was the case. In

---

[3] *SC*, 116:3b; Burton Watson, *Records of the Grand Historian of China*, 2:296.

[4] HS, 96B:10a–b.

refutation of the above view of the Imperial Secretary about foreign trade, sharp criticism presented by the literati may also be found in the *Yen-t'ieh lun:*

> Now mules and donkeys are not as useful as cattle and horses. Sable and marmot furs, wool and felt goods do not add substance to silk. Beautiful jades and corals come from mount K'un. Pearls and ivory are produced in Kuei Lin. These places are more than ten thousand *li* distant from Han. Calculating the labor for farming and silk raising and the costs in material and capital, it will be found that one article of foreign import costs a price one hundred times its value, and for one handful, ten thousand weight of grain are paid. As the rulers take delight in novelties, extravagant clothing is adopted among the masses. As the rulers treasure the goods from distant lands, wealth flows outward. Therefore, a true King does not value useless things, so to set an example of thrift to his subjects; does not love exotic articles, so to enrich his country.[5]

Significantly enough, the criticism was also made on solid economic ground, and argued even more realistically against tributary exchange with the barbarians. It is clear what the Imperial Secretary cherished as "treasures" of the barbarians were in reality luxuries that practically added nothing to the wealth of the empire at the state finance level. Just as the literati said, to a conscientious ruler these luxuries were useless things. This is exactly what happened to Sun Ch'üan, King of the Wu, during the Three Kingdoms period. In A.D. 221, Emperor Wen of Wei sent an envoy to the Wu asking for such precious articles as pearls, ivory, rhinoceros horns, tortoise shells, and peacocks. Officials at the Wu court all proposed turning down the unreasonable request. But Sun Ch'üan eventually decided to comply with the request because these luxuries, in his own words, "to me are no more than tiles and stones." [6] Again in 235, the Wei sent envoys to the south with horses to trade for similar luxuries. Sun Ch'üan granted the trade and said "I have no use for all these things and yet I get horses out of them. Why shouldn't I allow such an exchange?" [7] This attitude of Sun Ch'üan seems to have fully justified the criticism of the literati.

---

[5] *Yen-t'ieh lun,* p. 5; Gale, pp. 15–16.
[6] *Chiang-piao chuan* quoted in *SKC, Wu,* 2:10a.
[7] *SKC, Wu,* 2:24a–b.

But, it must also be pointed out, the emperor's interest in foreign rarities was not just because he valued them as luxuries, as such. This leads directly to our second point, namely, rare products as tributary articles from the barbarians also had prestige value for the emperor. Tribute symbolized submission. Therefore, the extent to which the Chinese imperial rule was accepted by the barbarians was often judged by the variety of exotic curiosities in the emperor's possession. This explains why in Han fu, or "rhyme-prose" writings, which often have a political purport,[8] the Han rule is praised among other things, for the possession of precious tributary articles including both jewelry and animals.[9] Even the critical philosopher, Wang Ch'ung, of the first century A.D., also, on several occasions compared the Han favorably to the Chou Dynasty on the ground that the former had more valuable tribute from far away barbarians.[10] It is no wonder that each time when Emperor Ho (89–105) received some rare tributary articles he ordered Pan Chao, the famous woman scholar and sister of Pan Ku, to write a fu to eulogize the event.[11]

This strong imperial interest in foreign rarities had its repercussions in the Han high society. Following the emperor's example, officials and aristocrats also began to search for similar exotic luxuries. In several of Pan Ku's letters to his brother, General Pan Ch'ao in the Western Regions, we are told that a certain Mr. Tou, presumably an imperial in-law, bought various kinds of luxuries from the Western Regions. One letter says that Tou had once sent some 800,000 cash there with which more than ten

---

[8] On the political nature of fu of the Han period, see Helmut Wilhelm, "The Scholar's Frustration: Notes on a Type of *Fu*," *Chinese Thought and Institutions*, pp. 310–319.

[9] Examples are many. See especially Pan Ku's *fu* on the two Han capitals, *CHHW*, 24:3b and 7b. It may be further noted that these tributary treasures are also mentioned in Chang Heng's fu on the East Capital, but the author urges that the emperor should value worthy people more than rare animals and grain more than luxuries, *CHHW*, 53:5b.

[10] Liu P'an-sui, *Lun-heng chi-chieh*, pp. 391, 395–396.

[11] *HHS*, 114:2a.

pieces of rugs were purchased. Another letter is to notify his brother that Tou was forwarding 700 pieces of colored silk fabrics and 300 pieces of plain white silk to the Western Regions to buy such luxuries as the Yüeh-chih horses, *Su-ho* incense, and woolen fabrics.[12] These two fragments not only reveal how much aristocrats of the Later Han period were interested in foreign goods but also bear importantly on our discussion of foreign trade. At least two points may be made. First, that some ten rugs, costing 800,000 cash, shows the extreme expensiveness of the imported commodities. Second, in the Sino-barbarian trade, both coins and silk were used by the Chinese as media of exchange. The second instance also indicates another important channel through which Han silk was brought beyond the Chinese frontiers.

In chapter VII we have seen that the Han emperor sometimes sent envoys abroad with gold and silk to acquire precious articles. This practice was also followed by the aristocrats. The powerful imperial in-law of the second century A.D., Liang Chi, for instance, is reported to have dispatched his private messengers to various foreign countries for the purpose of seeking excessively rare products.[13] Apart from regular trade, officials, as well as other powerful people of the time, also obtained precious foreign goods by taking presents from the barbarians. During the reign of Emperor Chang, for example, when Li Hsün served as the Deputy *Chiao-wei* of the Western Regions, the barbarian hostage princes, as well as merchants, had several times presented him as gifts, slaves, Ferghana horses, gold, silver, incenses, and carpets.[14] Although Li refused to accept any of them because of his moral principle and integrity, the example, nevertheless, seems to indicate that it must have been a well-established custom for the barbarians to present such treasures to the Chinese

---

[12] *CHHW*, 25:4a. It is not clear what was exactly the *su-ho* incense. F. Hirth has, however, identified it with Storax (*China and the Roman Orient*, pp. 263–266).

[13] *HHS*, 64:6a.

[14] *HHS*, 81:1a.

officials who had direct control over them.[15] The same custom also prevailed among corrupt Chinese officials. A certain Meng T'o of Emperor Ling's time (168–188) was even able to receive the appointment of Circuit-Intendant of Liang-chou after he won the favor of the notorious powerful eunuch, Chang Jang, by presenting to the latter a bottle of grape wine imported from the Western Regions, which, in turn it is interesting to add, was among the gifts he took from others.[16] This story fully reveals the extent to which foreign luxuries were cherished by the Chinese.

At this juncture it seems necessary to further clarify the nature of foreign trade in Han China by attempting a general classification of the various commodities imported from foreign lands. It has been rightly suggested that long-range Sino-barbarian trade in early imperial China was largely confined to the exchange of luxuries.[17] This was especially the case with the trade with such places as the Roman Orient, the Western Regions, and the overseas countries. Of the luxuries, two general categories may be conveniently distinguished: living commodities and all other products. By living commodities, I mean not only the curious animals, such as elephants, lions, big birds, horses of the finest quality, and rhinoceroses, which filled the imperial zoo as well as gardens of the aristocrats in the capital,[18] but also human beings including slaves and jugglers. In chapter VII we have seen that archaeology has shed some light on the importation of foreign slaves to China, possibly by sea route. From the case of Li Hsün,

---

[15] Another instance can be cited to illustrate the point. Ch'en Shan was appointed Governor of Liao-tung in Emperor An's time (107–125) when the Northern Hsiung-nu were active in that region. Since Ch'en treated these barbarians reasonably, they were grateful to him and presented their precious articles to him before they migrated to other places. *HHS*, 81:2a.

[16] Wang Wen-t'ai, ed., *Ch'i-chia Hou-Han shu*, 5:13a; *HHS*, 108:10a and commentary.

[17] Owen Lattimore, *Inner Asian Frontiers of China*, pp. 174–175.

[18] See Ch'en Chu-t'ung, *Liang-Han ho Hsi-yü teng ti ti ching-chi wen-hua chiao-liu*, pp. 12–13.

just cited, above, we further know that slaves, both male and female, also came to China from the Western Regions. Although on the whole the number of foreign slaves in Han China does not appear to have been very significant, it can, nevertheless, be safely concluded that they did find their way to China as commodities and had considerable prestige value among the rich and powerful families of the time.[19] Whether jugglers were also commodities, comparable to the slaves, during this period is difficult to say because of the lack of sufficient evidence. What is certain is the fact that they were often presented to the Han court as tribute by the barbarian states such as Parthia[20] and Shan.[21] However, as these jugglers are always indicated as have originally come from Li-kan or Ta-Ch'in, probably referring to the Roman Orient, it would then seem that they were possibly bought from the slave market in the Roman Empire. Otherwise it would be hard to explain how Roman jugglers could be used by other states as a tributary article. Foreign jugglers of various kinds not only amused the Han emperor, but also entertained people in the big cities. According to a first century A.D. description of the Western Capital, Ch'ang-an, they held their circus performances in large squares.[22] It is not clear whether these performances were open to the public. At least the aristocrats must have shared in the enjoyment of the display of all kinds of barbarian skills with the emperor. Possibly some of the aristocratic families also had foreign jugglers of their own.

Of the other types of foreign luxuries, numerous items are mentioned in the Chinese sources. In the interest of clarity, however, only a few important samples will be discussed below. First of all, let us turn to the Roman

---

[19] On the problem of foreign slaves in Han China see also Martin Wilbur, *Slavery in China during the Former Han Dynasty*, pp. 95–96; Chien Po-tsan, *Li-shih wen-t'i lun-ts'ung*, pp. 158–160.

[20] Hirth, *op. cit.*, pp. 35, 36.

[21] *Ibid.*, pp. 36–37.

[22] *CHHW*, 52:10b–11a; cf., also, Ch'en Chu-t'ung, pp. 22–24 and Liu Kuang-i, "Ch'in-Han shih-tai ti pai-chi tsa-hsi," *Ta-lu tsa-chih*, pp. 24–26.

Empire. In Chinese sources, the list of articles taken as
Roman products is often amazingly long.[23] But some
remain yet to be identified and some have been incorrectly
identified.[24] Generally speaking glass, textiles of wool and
linen, corals and pearls from the Red Sea, amber from the
Baltic, and various precious stones are believed to have
been imported to Han China from the West by the Roman
merchants.[25] Among these reported Roman imports, only
two may be considered as being more or less confirmed by
archaeology: glass and amber. The problem of amber has
already been touched upon previously and needs no repe-
tition here. Glasswares of possible Roman origin are reported from time to time to have been found not only in
China but also in Korea and Central Asia.[26] Some of the
glass fragments found in Honan have led scholars to
believe that Roman glass did reach China in this period.[27]
More recently, some glassware has been excavated from
tombs of Han date at Ch'angsha. Archaeologists have noted
the fact that there seems to have been both a considerable
increase in quantity and improvement in quality in glass
articles toward the end of the Former Han period, and
have suspected that this phenomenon may have had something to do with the prosperity of overseas trade at that
time.[28] If this was the case, the possibility that some of
them came from the Roman Empire certainly cannot be
overlooked.

Imports from Central Asia and the Western Regions
consisted mainly of two large categories; delicacies such as
raisins and grape wines, and a great variety of luxuries,
among which furs and woolen textiles occupied a particularly important place. They came to Han China either as
tribute or as articles of trade from various peoples and

---

[23] For instance, see Hirth, *op. cit.,* pp. 41–42; 73–74.

[24] Ch'i Ssu-ho, *Chung-kuo ho Pai-chan-t'ing Ti-kuo ti kuan-hsi,* pp. 25–32.

[25] G. F. Hudson, *Europe and China,* pp. 96–98.

[26] Mortimer Wheeler, *Rome Beyond the Imperial Frontiers,* p. 175.

[27] C. G. Seligman, "The Roman Orient and the Far East," pp. 556–557.

[28] Chung-kuo K'o hsüeh Yuan K'ao-ku Yen-chiu So, *Ch'ang-sha fa-chüeh pao-kao,* pp. 127–128, 129, 166.

places including the Hsiung-nu, Wu-sun, Parthia, and India.[29] Mention must also be made of jade of the period, which had important religious significance in addition to its decorative value.[30] Although Han China also produced its own jade, it was nevertheless the jade from the Western Regions that was especially cherished by the Chinese.[31] Many letters of the period, written on wooden slips, discovered at Niya near Khotan, reveal that it was quite common for Chinese residents in the Western Regions to buy jade there and send it home to be presented to their relatives and friends.[32] Archaeological excavations further show that Khotan jade was imported to Han China in great quantity.[33] As Stein has rightly pointed out, the famous *Yü-men Kuan*, or the Barrier of the Jade Gate, "took its significant name from that precious jade (Yü) of Khotan which from early down to modern times formed an important article of trade export from the Tarim Basin to China." [34]

From the various maritime countries came precious sea products, notably pearls and tortoise shells. As personal ornaments, pearls were especially popular among the aristocrats as well as the rich commoners. Reasons for the popularity of pearls are not far to seek. In the first place, there was a very wide range of difference in the quality of pearls.[35] Therefore, even a moderately well-to-do family could afford to have some pearls of inferior quality. In the

---

[29] Ch'en Chu-t'ung, pp. 7–9.

[30] See the comprehensive study by Berthold Laufer, *Jade, A Study in Chinese Archaeology and Religion*, esp. pp. 296–297 on the religious implications of jade in the Han period. See, also, an interesting article on jade and pearls in ancient China including the Han period by Matsuda Hisao, "Gushi no gyoku to Kōkan no shu," *Tōzai kōshō shiron*, 1:157–186.

[31] Yao Pao-yu, *Chung-kuo ssu-chüan hsi-ch'uan shih*, pp. 12–13.

[32] Lo Chen-yü and Wang Kuo-wei, *Liu-sha chui-chien, k'ao-shih* 3:5a–6a.

[33] Aurel Stein, *Ancient Khotan: Detailed Report of Archaeological Explorations in Chinese Turkestan*, 1:132–133; and his *Sand-Buried Ruins of Khotan*, p. 252.

[34] Stein, *On Ancient Central Asian Tracks*, p. 166.

[35] For instance, under the Chin dynasty the pearls of Ho-p'u were classified into three different grades and were taxed at different rates (*Chin Shu*, 57:10b–11a). This difference in quality must have been true for pearls of the Han times too.

second place, compared to other luxuries of the time, the source of supply of pearls was more constant and less exhaustible. Although people of the time generally valued pearls from remote places like Central Asia and the Roman Orient, their prime source, however, must have been the nearby South Sea areas.[36]

While Han China's economic intercourse with remote barbarians was largely confined to luxuries, that with the neighboring barbarians was rather conducted on the basis of daily necessities. The various "barbarian markets" on the frontiers where the Hsiung-nu, Ch'iang, Hsien-pi, and Wu-huan came regularly to trade with the Chinese may be taken as the best proof of the exchange of necessities in Sino-barbarian trade during the period. In the city of Ku-tsang (in modern Kansu), as we have seen in chapter V, the "barbarian markets" even met four times a day—a fact which fully indicates the mutual need for the exchange of necessities. It was in this kind of Sino-barbarian trade that even the poor Chinese also had their share. Due to lack of records, it is now impossible to know exactly what were the barbarian goods that were available in such markets. So far as we can judge from our previous discussions of the frontier trade, it seems that such living commodities as cattle, horses, sheep, mules, and donkeys were staples that China received from her barbarian neighbors. The exchange trade between Chinese silk and barbarian horses particularly deserves our attention. It was probably the most important type of transaction that was always carried on at both state and personal levels, thus characterizing much of the Sino-barbarian economic intercourse not only in Han China but also in later times down, at least, to the Sung dynasty. Exchange of other commodities between the Chinese and the northern nomads, it may be added, can only be considered as supplementary to this trade.[37] As to mules and donkeys, the above-quoted criticism of the literati that they were of little use, however, proved to be a

---

[36] Cf. E. Schafer, "The Pearl Fisheries of Ho-p'u," p. 158.

[37] Matsuda Hisao, "Ken-ba kōeki kansuru shiryō," *Nairiku Ajia-shi ronshū*, pp. 1–14. Cf., also, Lu-chin-k'o, *K'ao-ku hsüeh-pao*, 2:43.

bit unfair. In fact, as has been shown at the end of chapter II, donkeys became, as time went on, a favorite animal of the Chinese, especially under the Later Han dynasty. Moreover, they were used extensively by the common people for a variety of purposes.[38]

From the above brief analysis, it is clear that various kinds of individual Chinese, from the emperor down to the commoner, all developed their personal interests in the Sino-barbarian economic intercourse under the tributary system. It is impossible to know whether the totality of all such individual gains derived from the intercourse counterbalanced the financial losses of the state involved in the establishment and maintenance of the entire system. But this is rather beside the point. What is important is the fact that the two did not belong to the same category or level, so to speak. At any rate the gains of the individuals did not help the losses of the state in any direct way. Moreover, the state always tended to keep the individual's pursuit of barbarian wealth within a limit. We have seen that even the emperor was not free from criticism if he over-developed his addiction in the acquisition of foreign rarities; that normal exchange trade between the Chinese and barbarians was a strictly state-regulated matter; and that, it hardly needs to be added, economic exactions imposed on the barbarians by individual Chinese officials or powerful local people on the frontiers, though not uncommon in the period, were nevertheless forbidden by the state. Sometimes the state also even took part in foreign trade at the expense of the gains of the individuals. For instance, during the period of the Three Kingdoms, Wu monopolized the pearl trade of Ho-p'u [39] and Wei also monopolized the selling of a certain foreign commodity known as "barbarian powder." [40] Here, we see clearly the conflict between the interests of the state and that of the individual. Although Confucianism generally disapproved of the par-

---

[38] *HHS*, 23:3b.

[39] *Chin Shu*, 57:10b–11a.

[40] *Ch'üan San-kuo wen*, 32:7b. According to the Later Han dictionary, *Shih-ming*, 36a, the "barbarian powder" was used for face-painting. Cf. also W. Eberhard, *Localkulturen im alten China*, pp. 219–221.

ticipation of the state in competition with the people for profits, in practice, however, this Confucian principle was not always followed. It is true that there were also cases in which the officials encouraged the development of trade of the people, such as Meng Ch'ang's contribution to the pearl fishery of Ho-p'u.[41] But in so doing they considered that they were promoting, not the gains of the individuals, but the welfare of the people in general, which could be partially identified with the interests of the state.

The following interesting instance throws further light on our present discussion: During the T'ai-ho era (227–233) under the Wei, Ts'ang Tz'u was Governor of Tun-huang. Previously, whenever the barbarian merchants of the Western Regions came to China for trade, they were always cheated and oppressed in their dealings with the powerful Chinese natives. It was Ts'ang Tz'u who eventually rectified the situation by using goods in the possession of the local government to trade with the barbarian merchants as well as by extending full protection to them.[42] In this case, Ts'ang Tz'u not necessarily loved the barbarian any more than his own fellow countrymen. Rather, he typified the conscientious Chinese official who always placed the interests of the state above that of the individual.

2 *Sinicization, Barbarization and Commercialization— Some Historical Consequences of Trade and Expansion.*

As we all know, in only about a century after the disintegration of the Han empire, that is, at the beginning of the fourth century, China witnessed the great explosion of barbarian uprisings, known in history as "the invasion of China by five barbarian tribes."[43] Even before the end of the third century, sporadic barbarian rebellions already

---

[41] We may cite another instance. During the reign of Emperor Ling (168–188), when Chou Ching served as Governor of Kuei-yang, he made many efforts to facilitate overseas trade of that region. See *CHHW*, 103: 2b–3a.

[42] *SKC, Wei*, 16:22b–23a.

[43] The five tribes are the Hsiung-nu, Hsien-pi, Ch'iang, Ti and Chieh. For a general survey see W. Eberhard, *Kultur und Siedlung der Rand-*

occurred in many parts of the Chinese empire. Since at
that time the newly-unified Western Chin dynasty was
still militarily powerful enough, all these rebellions were
quelled one after another.[44] People of the time generally
held the Kingdom of (Ts'ao) Wei responsible for having
included too many barbarians into the Chinese territory.[45] But, as our study has shown, the roots of the barbarian disaster of Chin China were struck deep in the Han,
especially the Later Han, period. Of the submissive, or
surrendered, barbarians of Han times a general distinction
can be made between the outer ones and the inner ones.
The latter always lived inside the empire. Based partly on
the belief in the miraculous assimilative power of the
Chinese civilization, the Han policy was to include, step by
step, the surrendered barbarians in the Chinese imperial
system and eventually transform them into fully civilized
Chinese subjects. Early in the Former Han, we have already seen that some of the Ch'iang people were thus
brought inside the empire and lived face to face with the
Chinese. Under the inclusive policy of the Later Han
government, we find more and more barbarians inside the
Chinese frontiers. In the course of development in the second and third centuries, surrendered barbarians were
brought, in an increasingly rapid pace, under the direct
control of the Chinese local administration, which deprived the original barbarian tribal leaders of all the
power to rule over their people except empty titles.[46]
According to a late third century estimate, in the Kuan-
chung (Shensi) area alone, out of a population of over a
million, half were barbarians.[47] The inclusion of so many
barbarians into the empire immediately put the lofty
Confucian theory of assimilation to serious test. Subse-

völker Chinas, pp. 35–87 and Wang I-t'ung, "Wu-Hu t'ung-k'ao," *Chung-
kuo wen-hua yen-chiu hui-k'an*, pp. 57–79. For an excellent detailed study
of the nature of these barbarian uprisings see T'ang Chang-ju's article
in his *Wei-Chin Nan-pei Ch'ao shih lun-ts'ung*, pp. 127–192.

[44] T'ang Chang-ju, *op. cit.*, pp. 142–145.
[45] See the various memorials collected together in Lü Ssu-mien, *Liang-
Chin Nan-pei Ch'ao shih*, 1:25–27.
[46] Cf. T'ang Chang-ju, *op. cit.*, pp. 134–138.
[47] *Chin Shu*, 56:5b.

quent history proved that the actual process of Sinicization of the barbarians, instead of being smooth, was a very difficult and painful one. It took China several centuries to digest all the barbarian elements, and moreover, in accomplishing the historical task of civilizing the inner barbarians, China also encountered innumerable setbacks in its political, economic, and cultural developments throughout the period of disunity from the third century to the sixth.

This was so, not so much because the inclusive policy itself was inadequate, as because the policy was inadequately executed at the hands of local officials, as well as the powerful local Chinese. Excessive individual Chinese exploitation was already reported to the Han court early in the first century B.C. as the basic cause of internal barbarian rebellions. With the increase of barbarians inside the empire such exploitations also grew in intensity and scale. We have seen that at least in the early third century many surrendered barbarians already began to develop settled agricultural life of their own under the encouragement of the Chinese government. In many cases, they were required to pay land tax to the Chinese government more or less like the regular Chinese subjects. But on the other hand individual barbarians sometimes were also forced to work for the Chinese landlords as serfs. This was especially true under the Western Chin dynasty (265–316). In the T'ai-yuan area (in modern Shansi), for instance, several thousand surrendered Hsiung-nu were employed by the powerful Chinese families as tenants.[48] Shih Lo, a famous barbarian leader in the early third century, was sold in his youth, together with many of his fellow tribesmen, into slavery in Shantung. Since Shih later worked in the field for his Chinese master, we may assume that most, if not all, of these barbarians must have been turned into agricultural slaves.[49] These two instances show not only the extent to which the surrendered barbarians were exploited

---

[48] *Chin Shu*, 93:3b.

[49] *Chin Shu*, 104:1b–2a. Cf. Yi-t'ung Wang, "Slaves and Other Comparable Social Groups During the Northern Dynasties (386–618)," *HJAS*, p. 320.

by the Chinese, but also the fact that they had already been transformed from nomads into farmers by then.[50]

Enslavement alone probably would not have made the inner barbarians dangerous. The danger of barbarian uprisings was directly created by the fact that along with enslavement a large number of them were also relied upon by the Chinese government as armed forces for either border defense or military expeditions against rebellious outer barbarians under the general policy of "using barbarians to fight against barbarians." Especially, during the period of the Three Kingdoms, Wei, Shu and Wu all strived to strengthen their military power by introducing more barbarian soldiers into the armies. This fact probably also explains the rapid increase of barbarians in China in the third century.[51] With the inner barbarians enslaved on the one hand and armed on the other, barbarian uprisings were but to be expected. The danger was already keenly sensed at an earlier date by some Chinese officials who were familiar with barbarian affairs. For instance, sometime around 250, the well-known general, Teng Ai, suggested to the Wei court that the various barbarians who lived face to face with the Chinese should be gradually moved out of China.[52] About a half-century later, Chiang T'ung wrote a famous treatise in which the idea of transferring all the inner barbarians beyond the Chinese frontiers was further elaborated.[53] It is obvious that the very roots of barbarian uprisings of the fourth century must be traced back to the treatment of the surrendered barbarians under the Han dynasty.

It is highly interesting to note that the dissolution of the Chinese Empire in the early fourth century amidst barbarian uprisings bears remarkable resemblance to the fall of the Roman Empire in the West in the fifth century in face of the Gothic invasions.[54] If we looked into the mat-

[50] Cf. T'ang Chang-ju, *op. cit.*, pp. 150–151.

[51] *Ibid.*, pp. 128–132.

[52] *SKC, Wei,* 28:18b.

[53] *Chin Shu,* 56:1a–8b.

[54] For instance, Arthur Waley has compared the fall of Lo-yang in 317 into the hands of barbarians, to the Gothic sack of Rome in 410. See his article "The Fall of Lo-yang," *History Today,* pp. 7–10.

ter a little more deeply, we would find even more interesting similarities in details. The barbarian policy of the Roman Empire, if any, seems also to have been to absorb the Germans into its frontier provinces with a view to eventually civilizing them.[55] Like the *shu-kuo* or subject states of the Han, Rome also allowed these inner barbarians to organize themselves into separate units known as Federates. As one historian succinctly puts it, "Under the name of Federates they kept their chiefs, their customs and their language; they were not placed under the laws of the Empire." [56] Like the inner barbarians in Han China, the Federates also guarded the Roman frontiers from within against the inroads of other barbarians, or even their kinsfolk, in return for Roman pay or lands.[57] The barbarian, especially German, infiltration into the Roman army hardly needs mention. Early in the second and third centuries the auxiliaries were already recruited from the barbarians living beyond the frontiers. Later, even the legions had to rely on the barbarians as a source of supply of men. In the middle of the fourth century, soldier, *miles*, became the synonym of *barbarus*.[58] In order to procure the military service of the barbarians, the Romans also offered opportunities to the nomadic barbarians to be settled within the empire as farmers. These barbarian settlers, known as *laeti* in the Belgic provinces and as *gentiles* in Italy and Gaul, it must be pointed out, were not free people (*laeti* being a German word applied to the half-free). They were bound to military service of an hereditary kind, namely, their children were subject to the same service as the parents. On the other hand, however, they were entitled to hereditary use of the *laeti* lands.[59] This policy especially reminds us of the general trend, beginning in Later Han times, of encouraging the inner

[55] Harold Mattingly, *Roman Imperial Civilization*, p. 114.

[56] Ferdinand Lot, *The End of the Ancient World and the Beginnings of the Middle Ages*, p. 196.

[57] H. St. L. B. Moss, *The Birth of the Middle Ages, 395–814*, pp. 17–18.

[58] Lot, p. 232; Moss, p. 21.

[59] J. B. Bury, *History of the Later Roman Empire from the Death of Theodosius to the Death of Justinian*, 1:40, 98–99; Lot, p. 106.

barbarians to develop settled agricultural life in order to
render military and labor services to the Chinese government on a regular basis. Under the Western Chin dynasty,
as has been just shown above, thousands of barbarians were
also enslaved as serfs and many of these barbarian serfs
were even sold to the Chinese landlords by the government.[60] No wonder such amazingly parallel developments
in the Roman Empire led also to similar consequences. As
in the case of the Chinese Empire, the Roman Empire, in
the words of J. B. Bury, "was to be dismembered, not only
or chiefly by the attacks of professed enemies from without,
but by the self-assertion of the barbarians who were admitted within the gates as Federates and subjects." [61]

In Roman history, there are problems of the Romaniza-
tion of the barbarians as well as the barbarization of the
Romans, both of important historical significance. Parallel
problems may also be found in Chinese history: Sinicization of the barbarians and barbarization of the Chinese.
Although they did not become acute problems until after
the fourth century, especially in North China, their very
origins can nevertheless be traced back at least to the Han
times.

Let us first take a look at the Sinicization of the barbarians. Under the political, economic, and cultural in-
fluences of Han China, both outer and inner barbarians
tended to take steps toward Sinicization. Of the outer
barbarians we may cite two small tributary states in the
Western Regions as illustration. In 65 B.C., the king of
Kucha came to the Han court to pay tribute with his wife,
a princess from Wu-sun who had earlier studied Chinese
music in Ch'ang-an. The royal couple were well received
and imperial gifts, including honorary titles, various kinds
of fine silk and other precious articles showered on them.
They stayed in China for about a year. Since both of them
became thoroughly Sinicized and were extremely fond of
Han clothes and institutions, when they returned home
they followed the Han imperial style of life in mimicry. It

<hr>

[60] T'ang Chang-ju, *op. cit.*, pp. 150–152.
[61] Bury, 1:97–98.

is interesting to note, however, that their imitation immediately exposed them to the mockery of many other neighboring barbarians, who said: "The king of Kucha is neither a donkey nor a horse, but a mule." [62] Another case of Sinicization is to be found in the state of Sha-ch'a (Yarkand). During Wang Mang's reign, Sha-ch'a was one of the few states in the Western Regions that refused to accept the usurper's rule. As we are told, this was because its king had spent his early years in the Han capital as a hostage prince and therefore had become, since then, a great admirer of Chinese civilization. He even adopted some of the Han political and legal institutions in his country and always taught his sons to keep allegiance to the Han dynasty.[63] His reason for defying Wang Mang's authority, that is, loyalty to the Imperial House of Liu, may well have been more apparent than real. Nevertheless, it can hardly be denied that at least this barbarian king knew how to rationalize his action in a Sinicized way. This instance also tells us that long-time stay in China must have Sinicized many hostage princes from the various tributary states and thus helped, to a considerable extent, to expand Chinese civilization beyond the Han frontiers.[64]

Sinicization of the Hsiung-nu outside Han China also calls for some further remarks. First of all, the Hsiung-nu developed agriculture under the Chinese influence. Systematic excavations of Gorodisce at the confluence of the lower Ivolga and the Selenga rivers in 1949 and 1950 by Russian archaeologists, uncovered, among other Hsiung-nu remains, millets and a plowshare, which can be dated to the early Han period. Archaeologists believe that the Hsiung-nu themselves carried on agriculture and used Chinese prisoners of war to cultivate their lands.[65] Seeds

---

[62] *HS*, 96B:6a. This famous mockery, it may be noted, later found its way into the Chinese language and today the phrase "neither donkey nor horse" is still used to indicate all kinds of unsuccessful or immature imitations.

[63] *HHS*, 118:6a.

[64] Cf. Ise Sentarō, *Seiiki keiei-shi no kenkyū*, p. 59.

[65] Karl Jettmar, "Hunnen und Hiung-nu—ein archäologisches Problem," *Archiv für Völkerkunde,* pp. 170–171.

of millet have also been unearthed from the Hsiung-nu graves at Noin-ula in Mongolia.[66] These finds seem to fit very well with the Chinese sources that report that the Hsiung-nu already planted certain kinds of millet at least in the early first century B.C.[67] In spite of the archaeological confirmation, it must be pointed out, however, that the role of agriculture in the economic life of the Hsiung-nu was probably not very significant. As Rudenko has remarked, "in any case, the demand for millets substantially suppressed the possibility of the cultivation of them, and the Hsiung-nu obtained millets as well as rice primarily from China." [68]

In the light of archaeological discoveries, it may be concluded that the material culture of the Hsiung-nu was Sinicized, to greater or lesser degrees, in all its essential aspects. For instance, they wore Chinese silk, ate Chinese rice with chopsticks made of bone, sheltered themselves in a Chinese type of semi-mud huts, as well as imitated Chinese carts. Thus, in all the four major categories of daily life, that is, clothing, food, dwelling, and transportation (collectively known to the Chinese as *i-shih-chu-hsing*) the Chinese influence was deeply felt by the Hsiung nu. Rudenko even believes that the Hsiung-nu followed the Han example of using registers for the census of the population and of domestic animals for the purpose of levying taxes.[69]

---

[66] S. I. Rudenko, *Kul'tura khunnov i noinulinskie kurgany*, p. 28.

[67] *HS*, 94A:15a and Yen Shih-ku's commentary.

[68] Rudenko, p. 29.

[69] *Ibid.*, p. 114. With regard to the Chinese type of building it may be noted that in the Minussinsk region a Chinese house was discovered by Russian archaeologists at Abakan some decades ago. The house was probably built toward the end of the Former Han, as far as we can judge from the Chinese inscriptions on the typical Han tiles. Russian archaeologists believe that it was the residence of Li Ling, the famous general who surrendered to the Hsiung-nu in 99 B.C. (Jettmar, *op. cit.*, p. 170). Recently a Chinese archaeologist has suggested that the building in question was most possibly occupied by the eldest daughter of Wang Ch'iang (Chao-chün), one of the best known women in Chinese history, who was married to *Shan-yü* Hu-han-yeh in 33 B.C. in the capacity of a Han princess. See Chou Lien-k'uan, "Su-lien nan Hsi-po-li-ya so fa-hsien ti Chung-kuo shih kung-tien i-chih," *K'ao-ku hsüeh-pao*, pp. 55–66. Cf. also a long note on this problem by Tsunoda Bunei in *Kodaigaku*, 6:1 (April, 1957), pp. 87–95.

The inner barbarians were Sinicized at a still higher level. Theirs, so to speak, was one of assimilation rather than imitation.[70] As has been shown above, politically the surrendered barbarians, especially from the Later Han times on, were either under the supervision or some sort of direct control of the Chinese government, whereas, economically, they also took steps toward agriculturalization. Thus their very way of life became increasingly Sinicized. But their Sinicization was manifested also in many other aspects. For instance, like the latinization of the barbarian names under the Roman Empire, surrendered barbarians from the Han times on generally assumed Chinese names, whose barbarian origin can now be identified only through careful studies.[71]

The case of Liu Yuan, the great Hsiung-nu rebel leader of the early fourth century, and his sons may best be taken to illustrate the extent to which the inner barbarians had been exposed to the influence of Chinese culture. In the first place, the adoption of Liu, the imperial surname of the Han dynasty, as their own is sufficient proof of their inclination toward Sinicization. Moreover, the use of this surname was not started by Liu Yuan, but had been chosen by his ancestors far back in the Han period. Secondly, from his case we also know that at least by the third century, the Hsiung-nu nobility must have already received much Chinese education. In his youth, Liu Yuan liked learning and studied Chinese classics and history under a well-known Confucian master. During his years in Lo-yang as a hostage prince at the end of Wei and the beginning of Chin, he also made many friends among Chinese officials and scholars.[72] Two of his sons, Liu Ho and Liu Ts'ung, are described as equally versed in Chinese classics and history, and the latter was even an excellent calligrapher as well as a poet.[73] Further examination of the biographical infor-

---

[70] See a recent discussion by Huang Lieh, "Wu-Hu Han-hua yü Wu-Hu cheng-ch'üan ti kuan-hsi," *LSYC*, pp. 131–142.

[71] See the excellent study by Yao Wei-yüan, *Pei-ch'ao Hu-hsing k'ao*, *passim*.

[72] *Chin Shu*, 101:1a–3b.

[73] *Ibid.*, 101:9b–10a; 102:1a–b.

mation of the Hsiung-nu leaders who helped Liu Yuan to found the first barbarian dynasty in Chinese history reveals that almost all of them had a good background of Confucian education.[74] This very fact explains why the Hsiung-nu at the beginning of their rebellion professed to continue the imperial rule of the Han dynasty and named their empire after it.[75]

Other barbarians like the Ch'iang, Hsien-pi and Ti also underwent a similar process of Sinicization ever since their inclusion into China in Han times.[76] Thus, parodoxically enough, on the one hand, it was the Han inclusive barbarian policy that led to the general barbarian uprisings in the early fourth century and the subsequent barbarization of North China in the next three centuries, but, on the other hand, it was also due to the same policy that gradually brought about the Sinicization of all the inner barbarians until they eventually submerged in the Chinese population beyond identification under the reunified Sui and T'ang China.

Close Sino-barbarian intercourse, especially, economic intercourse, also affected the way of life of the Chinese of our period to some extent, which, for brevity, is here referred to as "barbarization." From the historical point of view, it seems that the Later Han society was far more barbarized than the Former Han society. This, however, need not occasion surprise because acceptance of foreign things always takes time.

Barbarization resulted not only from the continuous introduction of foreign commodities into China, of which a brief account has been given above, but also from the increasing visits to China by foreigners, especially the merchants. Little trace, if any, of activities of the foreign merchants in China can be found in the Former Han period. But down to the Later Han, there was obviously considerable advancement in the Chinese knowledge of the so-called "barbarian merchants," especially those from

---

[74] *Ibid.,* 101:10b–11a; 102:25a; 103:1a–b.

[75] Cf. Wang I-t'ung, "Wu-Hu t'ung-k'ao," p. 60.

[76] *Ibid.,* pp. 62–66.

the Western Regions. Foreign merchants at this time penetrated into interior China even as far as Lo-yang, the Later Han capital. Early in A.D. 58, when Emperor Kuang-wu died, all the barbarian merchants from the Western Regions in the capital together established a shrine and made sacrificial offerings to the emperor.[77]

In the middle of the second century, one Western Region barbarian merchant by mistake killed a rabbit from the private zoo of the powerful imperial in-law, Liang Chi. As a result, more then ten barbarians were accused and put to death.[78] In the early third century, Ts'ang Tz'u, Governor of Tun-huang, issued *kuo-so* passports to all barbarian merchants of the Western Regions who wanted to go to Lo-yang for trade.[79] As these three instances show, throughout the Later Han period, barbarian merchants never ceased to visit China—a further indication of the prosperity of Sino-barbarian trade. The last instance is particularly worth noticing because it tells us that the barbarians also used the same *kuo-so* passports for travel in China as required of the Chinese subjects. The Later Han Chinese were so familiar with the pattern of behavior of the Western Region barbarian merchant that they even compared the famous General Ma Yuan of the first century to him because this Chinese general also had the habit of stopping at every place he happened to pass by.[80]

Such constant contacts with barbarian people and commodities inevitably left an imprint of barbarization on the Han society in many aspects. Historians and archaeologists alike generally discern in the Han civilization a heavy barbarian touch.[81] With details we are not here concerned. The following three selected instances will suffice to serve the purpose of illustration. First, let us begin with the emperor and the aristocracy. Emperor Ling (168–

---

[77] *Tung-kuan Han-chi, Kuo-hsüeh chi-pen ts'ung-shu* edition, p. 143.

[78] *HHS*, 64:6b.

[79] *SKC, Wei*, 16:23a.

[80] *HHS*, 54:6a. On Ma Yuan see Henri Maspero, "L'expédition de Ma Yuan," *BEFEO*, pp. 11–18.

[81] See Tz'u-kung, "Liang-Han chih Hu-feng," *Shih-hsüeh nien-pao*, pp. 45–54; *Seikai kōkogaku taikei*, 7:143–146.

188) is reported to have been thoroughly barbarized in his daily life. He liked not only barbarian clothes, curtains, beds, chairs, rice but also barbarian music and dance. This imperial example of barbarization, as we are told, was in turn followed by all the nobles in the capital.[82]

Our second instance concerns the literati class alone. It is well known that the Chinese literati, during the long period of disunity under Wei, Chin and the Southern and Northern dynasties (220–589), indulged in narcissism to such an extent that they generally painted their faces with white powder. So far as our knowledge goes, this practice had its beginning at least in the second century A.D. During the reign of Emperor Chih (146–147), Li Ku, a top-ranking minister at the court, was accused of, among other things, painting his face with "barbarian powder" on the occasion of an imperial funeral service.[83] Previously, we have seen that the Wei government in the period of the Three Kingdoms even found it lucrative to monopolize the selling of "barbarian powder," which indicates that there was a considerable market demand for this particular foreign commodity. Whether or not the face-painting practice of the Chinese gentlemen was started under some foreign influence is not known. Nevertheless, the use of "barbarian powder" itself is undoubtedly an act of barbarization.

Our last instance falls into the realm of religion which affected the life of people of all classes from the emperor down to the commoners. Buddhism, the barbarian religion, was introduced to China, as scholars now tend to agree, sometime around the beginning of the Christian era.[84] The arrival of this religion was closely related to the

---

[82] *HHS*, 23:3b. On the so-called "barbarian beds," actually chairs, see Fujita Toyohachi, *Tōzai kōshō-shi no kenkyū, Seiiki hen*, pp. 143–185; C. P. Fitzgerald, *Hu-ch'uang or Barbarian Beds*, and W. Eberhard, *Localkulturen im alten China*, pp. 22–23.

[83] *HHS*, 93:5a. For a discussion of the narcissism of the literati during this period see Yü Ying-shih, "Han-Chin chih chi shih chih hsin tzu-chüeh yü hsin ssu-ch'ao," *Hsin-Ya hsüeh-pao*, pp. 56–58.

[84] Modern discussions on the problem of the introduction of Buddhism are numerous. For brief but succinct accounts in English, see the following two recent works: E. Zürcher, *The Buddhist Conquest of China*, 1:

Sino-barbarian economic intercourse of Han times, because the former found its way to China exactly along the same trade routes used by the barbarian merchants. The Buddist infiltration from the Northwest, for instance, is believed to have been made by using the famous Silk Road.[85] The connection between foreign trade and the spread of Buddhism to China would become at once clear when we bear in mind the fact that under the Later Han dynasty Lo-yang was, on the one hand, a place, where, as has been shown, there was always a community of "barbarian merchants from the Western Regions," and, on the other hand, the most important center of Buddhism. This connection is concretely shown in the case of An Hsüan from Parthia. He first arrived in Lo-yang in A.D. 181 as a merchant, but later worked enthusiastically for the propagation of Buddhism in China.[86]

Buddhism also came to south China via sea routes with which barbarian merchants from various maritime countries were then familiar. That the earliest reference to the existence of Buddhism in China is made in an imperial decree of A.D. 65 in connection with Prince Ying of Ch'u in the south seems to point to the possibility of its being related also to overseas trade of the time.[87] As we have seen in the last chapter, Sino-Indian trade during the Later Han period mostly took the sea routes. It is certainly legitimate to conjecture that among the Indian merchants, who visited coastal China from Tongkin to Canton,[88] were undoubtedly Buddhist converts.[89]

The relationship between Sino-barbarian trade and the religious barbarization of China in Han times can further be seen from the historical process through which

---

18–43; Kenneth Ch'en, *Buddhism in China*, pp. 27–53. The best account in Chinese may be found in T'ang Yung-t'ung, *Han Wei Liang-Chin Nan-pei Ch'ao fo-chiao shih*, esp. 1:47–86.

[85] Zürcher, pp. 22–23.

[86] Zürcher, p. 34; K. Ch'en, p. 40; Arthur Waley, "Life under the Han Dynasty," *History Today*, 2:92.

[87] Zürcher, p. 26.

[88] For barbarian merchants in such places in the early third century, see Lao Kan, "Han-tai ti lu-yün yü shui-yün," p. 90.

[89] K. Ch'en, p. 38.

Buddhism was gradually accepted by the Chinese. According to Fan Yeh, the author of the *Hou Han Shu,* Prince Ying of Ch'u was the first Chinese every converted to Buddhism. His conversion led many others to turn to this barbarian religion for salvation. Later on Emperor Huan (147–167) made sacrificial offerings to both Lao Tzu and Buddha. Thereafter, the commoners also began to develop their Buddhist faith and Buddism thus flourished in China.[90]

This general observation, which is of great importance from the point of view of social history, is confirmed at least by the bits of evidence concerning Later Han Buddhism now at our disposal. The first clear indication of the existence of Buddhism, as has been pointed out, is found in the imperial decree of A.D. 65 with reference to Prince Ying of Ch'u.[91] Emperor Huan's worship of Buddha is also authenticated by Hsiang K'ai's memorial of A.D. 166.[92] But the earliest description of popular Buddhism in China is dated A.D. 193 or 194, much later than the other two.[93] Putting aside such details as whether Prince Ying of Ch'u was the earliest Chinese Buddhist convert, Fan Yeh's statement is undoubtedly true as far as the historical process of Buddhist conquest of China was concerned, namely, it began with the nobility and then infiltrated into the masses. In other words, it was a development from the upper scale of the society to the lower. That the Buddhist conquest of Han China should take this particular course can best be understood against the background of Sino-barbarian trade of the time. As the above discussion has revealed, foreign trade, especially trade between China and Central Asia, was essentially one of luxuries. It was the nobility, not the common people, who could afford to buy foreign luxuries and therefore were much more exposed to foreign influence. By the same

---

[90] *HHS,* 118:6a.

[91] *HHS,* 72:3a.

[92] *HHS,* 60B:10b.

[93] *HHS,* 103:6a; *SKC, Wu,* 4:2b–3a. For further discussions see T'ang Yung-t'ung, 1:71–73; Zürcher, p. 28.

token, barbarian merchants in China must also have had far closer contact with the nobility than with the commoners. It would then seem quite natural that religious barbarization began with the upper classes in Han China.

Before I bring my study to an end, it may be further noted that the Chinese high society toward the end of this period not only was considerably barbarized but also allowed itself to be exposed to heavy commercial influence, which, again for the sake of brevity, will be referred to as commercialization. This growing commercialization of the Han high society must be, however, understood against the historical background that trade, including foreign trade, was far more flourishing under the Later Han than under the Former Han. This point can be further seen in the contemporary descriptions of the life and activities of the merchant class by the social critics. It is true that in the early days of the Former Han the merchants were also very active and were often described as "drifting all around like water flowing over the empire." [94] It was, nevertheless, in Later Han times that we encounter in literature detailed and picturesque descriptions of the life of merchants. For illustration, I offer the translation of the following two interesting passages, which speak for themselves. Writing in the middle of the second century A.D., Wang Fu portrayed his time thus:

> The fashion of the present is to quit agriculture and sericulture for trade. It has resulted in having oxen, horses, carts and carriages blocking the roads and cities swarming with loafers. Few people are engaged in the fundamental profession and many make their living on floating occupations. . . . A glance at the situation in Loyang would show that traders are ten times as many as farmers, while loafers are ten times as many as traders.[95]

A more lively description comes from the pen of Chung-ch'ang T'ung (180–220):

> Since the Han arose there have been numerous people who are themselves commoners and yet use their wealth to oppress others. On the other hand people of purity and integrity who suffer hard-

---

[94] *SC*, 129:4a, 118:6b; *HS*, 45:3b. Cf. N. L. Swann, *Food and Money in Ancient China*, p. 437.

[95] *Ch'ien-fu lun*, *SPTK so-pen*, p. 18.

ship under the shelter of thatched roofs have no influence whatsoever on the customs of the society. As for the wealthy people, they
have hundreds of towered buildings stretched in rows, fertile lands
all over the countrysides, thousands of male and female slaves, as
well as followers counted by tens of thousands. Engaging in commercial pursuits in every corner of the country, their boats ply on all
waters and carts roll along every road. Cities are full of their ware-
houses with stored commodities. Jades and other precious articles in
their possession are beyond the capacities of even big rooms; and, as
for their horses, oxen, sheep, and pigs, there is no pasture large
enough to graze them. Bewitching boys and beautiful concubines fill
up their decorated chambers, and singers and entertainers attend on
[them] in deep halls. Guests waiting to see them dare not leave and
horses and carriages encountering them on road dare not move forward. [Leftover] meats of all kinds often become rotten [and there-
fore] inedible, while [superfluous] sweet wines are kept too [long] as
to turn petrified and therefore undrinkable. People [around them]
follow the directions as they turn their eyes, and read their mind as
their facial expressions reveal pleasure or anger. All these are either
the enjoyments that properly belong only to lords and marquises, or
the privileges that are exclusively granted to kings and princes. But
today they can be obtained by those who just know how to use guile
and practice fraud! And, moreover, those who obtain them in this
way are not even condemned for the sin [of presumptuousness].[96]

That in this passage there must be some degree of intended exaggeration concerning the details of the life of
the mercants of the day is easily discernible. Nevertheless,
the general picture that emerges from such a vivid description leaves little room for doubt.

Under such circumstances, some degree of commercialization of the upper classes can only be considered natural.
a few examples will suffice to illustrate the close connection between the Later Han upper classes and trade: In
A.D. 159, when Emperor Huan is reported to have made an
imperial tour to such places as Yü-chung (in Kansu) and
Tai (in Shansi), he was followed by a great merchant of
Lo-yang who brought with him money and commodities.[97] In the middle of the second century, both aristo-

---

[96] *HHS,* 79:7b; *CHHW,* 88:3b. A different English translation may be
found in E. Balazs, *Chinese Civilization and Bureaucracy,* pp. 219–220.

[97] *Shui-ching chu,* 1:24a. There is a small point concerning this piece
of information which needs elucidation. Based obviously on a different
edition of *Shiu-ching chu,* T'ang Chang-ju takes this Emperor Huan to

crats and eunuchs plunged into the private inn business because of its growing profit.[98] According to another second century source, landlord classes of the day generally engaged in trade of various kinds nine months out of a year.[99]

By way of conclusion, it is particularly revealing to see, in the case of the barbarized Emperor Ling, a touch of commercialization in the Han imperial life. He is reported to have several times played the merchant game with his court ladies in the Western Garden. He asked the ladies to play the role of hostesses of private inns while he himself impersonated a travelling merchant stopping at every "private inn" to enjoy the entertainment of the "hostess." [100] This story reveals at least two interesting facts about the Han society at the end of the second century. First, it indicates the general commercial prosperity of the time, which even made the emperor familiar with the life of the merchant. Second, it confirms our previous observation that the growth of private inns resulted largely from

---

be a Hsien-pi chieftain of the early fourth century, because his edition gives "in the 11th year (A.D. 305) of Emperor Huan of the Imperial (To-pa) Wei." (*Wei-Chin Nan-pei Ch'ao shih lun-ts'ung*, p. 194.) But my edition, which is a photolithographic reproduction of the *Yung-lo ta-tien* edition, gives "formerly in the 13th year of Emperor Huan of Han." I believe the *Yung-lo ta-tien* version is probably more reliable for the following reasons: 1) The so-called 13th year of Emperor Huan is the 2nd year of Yen-hsi (A.D. 159) and in that year Emperor Huan did make a tour of imperial inspection to Ch'ang-an, although Yü-chung and Tai are not mentioned as having been included in the trip (*HHS*, 7:5b). 2) If the Emperor Huan in question was a Hsien-pi chieftain, it would be difficult to understand how possibly he could be followed by a rich Lo-yang merchant as early as in A.D. 305 when the Western Chin dynasty still maintained its control over a unified China. As far as I can judge from the text, this merchant obviously followed the emperor all the way from Lo-yang. Of course my version also leaves a point unsolved, namely, why it gives "the 13th year of Emperor Huan" instead of "the 2nd year of Yen-hsi." Needless to say, the entire passage must have suffered some sort of corruption. Nevertheless, when we compare the two different versions against the historical background, mine undoubtedly fits the circumstances much better.

[98] *HHS*, 66:9a.

[99] *CHHW*, 47:1a–8a. Cf. Lien-sheng Yang, "Tung Han ti hao-tsu," *CHHP*, pp. 1028–1029.

[100] *HHS*, 23:4a.

the increase of travelling merchants, which in turn points unmistakably to the existence of a far more flourishing trade under the Later Han dynasty. Thus, most significant of all, we see in the person of a Han emperor the unity and embodiment of the twin historical forces of barbarism and commercialism.

Abbreviations

BEFEO: *Bulletin de L'École française d'Extrême-Orient*

BMFEA: *Bulletin of the Museum of Far Eastern Antiquities*

CHHP: *Ch'ing-hua hsüeh-pao* 清華學報

CHHW: *Ch'üan Hou-Han wen* 全後漢文 , in Yen
K'o-chün 嚴可均 , *Ch'üan Shang-ku San-tai Ch'in-Han San-kuo Liu-ch'ao wen* 全上古三代秦漢三國六朝文

CYYY: *Chung-yang Yen-chiu Yüan Li-shih Yü-yen Yen-chiu So chi-k'an* 中央研究院歷史語言研究所集刊

HCKTKKSH: *Hsin Chung-kuo ti k'ao-ku shou-huo* 新中國的考古收穫

HHS: *Hou Han Shu* 後漢書

HJAS: *Harvard Journal of Asiatic Studies*

HS: *[Ch'ien] Han Shu* [前] 漢書

JAOS: *Journal of the American Oriental Society*

KKTH: *K'ao-ku t'ung-hsün* 考古通訊

LSYC: *Li-shih yen-chiu* 歷史研究

SC: *Shih Chi* 史記

SKC: *San-kuo Chih* 三國志

SPTK: *Ssu-pu ts'ung-k'an* 四部叢刊

TP: *T'oung Pao*

WYWK: *Wan-yu wen-k'u* 萬有文庫

Bibliography

Note: In an historical study of the scope and nature of this one, it would be a forlorn enterprise to attempt what may be called an exhaustive bibliography. The following list indicates no more than the primary and secondary sources that have been directly consulted in the writing of this book.

I CHINESE WORKS

An Chih-min. "Kuan-yü Nei-Meng-ku Cha-lai-no-erh ku-mu ch'ün ti tsu-shu wen-t'i," *Wen-wu*, 1964:5.

Chan-kuo ts'e, WYWK edition.

Chang Cheng-lang. "Han-tai ti t'ieh-kuan t'u," *Li-shih chiao-hsüeh*, 1951:1.

Chang Hsing-lang. *Chung-Hsi chiao-t'ung shih-liao hui-pien*, Shih-chieh shu-chü reprint, Taipei, 1962. 6 vols.

Chang Hung-chao. *Shih-ya*. Peking, 1927.

Chang Sun. *Wo-kuo ku-tai ti hai-shang chiao-t'ung*. Shanghai, 1956.

Chang Wei-hua. *Lun Han Wu-ti*. Shanghai, 1957.

Ch'en Chih. *Liang-Han ching-chi shih-liao lun-ts'ung*. Sian, 1958.

———. "Han-Chin kuo-so t'ung-k'ao," *LSYC*, 1962:6.

Ch'en Chu-t'ung. *Liang-Han ho Hsi-yü teng ti ti ching-chi wen-hua chiao-liu*. Shanghai, 1957.

Ch'en Meng-chia. "Han-chien so-chien Chü-yen pien-sai yü fang-yü tsu-chih," *K'ao-ku hsüeh-pao*, 1964:1.

Ch'en Yin-k'o. *T'ang-tai cheng-chih shih shu-lun kao*. Shanghai, 1947.

Cheng Lung. "Nei Meng-ku Cha-lai-no-erh ku-mu ch'ün tiao-ch'a chi," *Wen-wu*, 1961:9.

Cheng Shao-tsung. "Jeh-ho Hsin-lung fa-hsien ti Chan-kuo sheng-ch'an kung-chü chu-fan," *KKTH*, 1956:1.

Ch'eng Shu-teh. *Chiu-ch'ao lü k'ao*. Reprint, Taipei, 1965. 2 vols.

Cheng Te-k'un. *Ssu-ch'uan ku-tai wen-hua shih*. Chengtu, 1946.

———. "P'o-jen k'ao," *Shuo-wen yüeh-k'an*, 4 (May, 1944).

Chi Hsien-lin. *Chung-Yin wen-hua kuan-hsi shih lun-ts'ung*. Peking, 1957.

Ch'i Ssu-ho. *Chung-kuo ho Pai-chan-t'ing Ti-kuo ti kuan-hsi*. Shanghai, 1956.

Chia I. *Hsin shu, Ssu-pu pei-yao* edition.

Ch'iang Ju-hsün. "Han chou-chün-hsien li-chih k'ao," *Chung-kuo hsüeh-pao,* 1:6 (1913).

Ch'ien Mu. "Hsi-Chou Jung-huo k'ao." *Yü-kung,* 2:4 (October, 1934) and 2:12 (February, 1935).

———. "Chou-kuan chu-tso shih-tai k'ao," *Yen-ching hsüeh-pao,* 11 (June, 1932); reprinted in *Liang-Han ching-hsüeh chin-ku wen p'ing-i.* Hong Kong, 1958.

———. *Kuo-shih ta-kang.* Taipei, 1953. 2 vols.

———. *Ch'in-Han shih.* Hong Kong, 1957.

Chien Po-tsan. *Li-shih wen-t'i lun-ts'ung.* Revised edition, Peking, 1962.

Ch'ien Ta-hsin. *Nien-erh shih k'ao-i,* Commercial Press edition.

Chin Shu. T'ung-wen edition.

Chou-li. Shih-san ching chu-shu edition. Nan-ch'ang, 1815.

Chou Lien-k'uan. "Su-lien nan Hsi-po-li-ya so fa-hsien ti Chung-kuo shih kung-tien i-chih," *K'ao-ku hsüeh-pao,* 1956:4.

Chu Chieh-ch'in. "Hua-ssu ch'uan-ju Ou-chou k'ao, *Chung-Hsi wen-hua chiao-t'ung shih i-ts'ui,* Shanghai, 1939.

Ch'ü Shou-yüeh. "Chung-kuo ku-tai ti tao-lu," *CHHP,* n. s. 2:1 (May, 1960).

Ch'un-ch'iu Kung-yang chu-shu, Shih-san ching chu-shu edition. Nan-ch'ang, 1815.

Chung-kuo K'o-hsüeh Yuan K'ao-ku Yen-chiu So. *Hsin Chung-kuo ti k'ao-ku shou-huo.* Peking, 1961.

———. *Ch'ang-sha fa-chüeh pao-kao.* Peking, 1957.

Fang Hao. *Chung-Hsi chiao-t'ung shih.* Vol. 1. Taipei, 1953.

Feng Ch'eng-chün. *Chung-kuo Nan-yang chiao-t'ung shih.* Shanghai, 1937.

[*Ch'ien*] *Han Shu.* Commercial Press, 1927.

Ho Ch'ang-ch'ün. "Feng-sui k'ao," *Kuo-hsüeh chi-k'an,* 6:3 (December, 1939).

———. *Ku-tai Hsi-yü chiao-t'ung yü Fa-hsien Yin-tu hsün-li.* Wuhan, 1956.

———. "Tung-Han keng-i shu-i chih-tu ti fei-chih," *LSYC,* 1962:5.

———. "Ku-tai Chung-Jih wen-hua chiao-liu shih-hua erh-tse," *Chung-hua wen-shih lun-ts'ung,* 6 (August, 1965).

———, translator. *Hsi-yü chih Fo-chiao,* by Hatari Ryōtei. Shanghai, 1956.

Hou Han Shu. Commercial Press, 1927.

Hsi-Han hui-yao, Chung-hua shu-chü edition.

Hsia Nai. "Hsin-chiang fa-hsien ti ku-tai ssu-chih p'in," *K'ao-ku hsüeh-pao,* 1963:1.

———. "Hsin-chiang ch'u-t'u Han-T'ang chin tz'u-hsiu," *Wen-wu ching-hua,* 2, Peking, 1963.

Hsü Chung-shu. "Pa-Shu wen-hua ch'u-lun," *Ssu-ch'uan Ta-hsüeh hsüeh-pao, She-hui k'o-hsüeh,* 1959:2.

Hu Chao-hsi. "Lun Han-Chin ti Ti-Ch'iang ho Sui-T'ang i-hou ti Ch'iang-tsu," *LSYC*, 1963:2.

Hu Chi-ch'uang. *Chung-kuo ching-chi ssu-hsiang shih.* Shanghai. Vol. 1, 1962; vol. 2, 1963.

Hua-yang Kuo chih, SPTK edition.

Huai-nan tzu, Che-chiang shu-chü edition.

Huang Lieh. "Wu-Hu Han-hua yü Wu-Hu cheng-ch'üan ti kuan-hsi," *LSYC*, 1963:3.

Huang Sheng-chang. "Kuan-yü O-chün Ch'i chieh chiao-t'ung lu-hsien fu-yüan wen-t'i," *Chung-hua wen-shih lun-ts'ung,* 5 (1964).

Huang Wen-pi. *Lo-pu-nao-erh k'ao-ku chi.* Peking, 1948.

Hui Tung. *Hou-Han Shu pu-chu, Ts'ung-shu chi-ch'eng* edition.

K'ao-ku hsüeh-pao, Peking, 1953–.

K'ao-ku, Peking, 1959–.

Ku Chi-kuang. "Chan-kuo Ch'in-Han chien chung-nung ch'ing-shang chih li-lun yü shih-chi," *Chung-kuo she-hui ching-chi shih chi-k'an,* 7:1 (June, 1944).

Ku Yen-wu. *Jih-chih lu, chi-shih* edition by Huang Ju-ch'eng.

Kuang-hsi Sheng Wen-wu Kuan-li Wei-yuan-hui. "Kuang-hsi Kuei-hsien Han-mu ti ch'ing-li," *K'ao-ku hsüeh-pao,* 1957:1.

Kung Chün. "Liang-Han yü Lo-ma ti ssu mao-i k'ao," *Wen-shih tsa-chih,* 2:5/6 (June, 1942).

Kuo Mo-jo. "Kuan-yü O-chün Ch'i chieh ti yen-chiu, *Wen-wu ts'an-k'ao tzu-liao,* 1958:4. Reprinted in *Wen-shih lun-chi.* Peking, 1961.

Kuo Pao-chün. *Chung-kuo ch'ing-t'ung ch'i shih-tai.* Peking, 1963.

Kuo-yü, WYWK edition.

Jui I-fu (Ruey Yih-fu). "P'o-jen k'ao," *CYYY,* 23:1 (1951).

Lao Kan. "Ts'ung Han-chien so-chien chih pien-chün chih-tu," *CYYY,* 8:2 (1939).

———. "Han-chien chung ti Ho-hsi ching-chi sheng-huo," *CYYY,* 11 (1944).

———. "Han-tai chih lu-yün yü shui-yün," *CYYY,* 16 (1947).

———. "Shih Han-tai chih t'ing-chang yü feng-sui," *CYYY,* 19 (1948).

———. "Han-tai ti t'ing-chih," *CYYY,* 22 (1950).

———. "Han-tai ti Hsi-yü Tu-hu yü Wu-chi Chiao-wei," *CYYY,* 28:1 (1956).

———. *Chü-yen Han-chien k-ao-shih.* Taipei, 1960.

Li Cheng-fu. *Chün-hsien shih-tai chih An-nan.* Chungking, 1945.

Li Chia-jui. "Liang-Han shih-tai Yünnan ti t'ieh-ch'i," *Wen-wu,* 1962:3.

Li Chien-nung. *Hsien-Ch'in Liang-Han ching-chi shih kao.* Peking, 1957.

Li Chin. "Kuang-chou ti Liang-Han mu-tsang," *Wen-wu,* 1961:2.

Li Shao-ming. "Kuan-yü Ch'iang-tsu ku-tai shih ti chi-ko wen-t'i," *LSYC,* 1963:5.

Liang Chia-pin. "Lun Sui-shu Liu-ch'iu wei T'ai-wan shuo ti hsü-kou ti kuo-ch'eng chi ch'i ying-hsiang—Chien-lun Tung-Wu

I-chou wei Liu-ch'iu," *Tung-hai hsüeh-pao* 1:1 (June, 1959).

Liang Shu, T'ung-wen edition.

Ling Ch'un-sheng. "T'ai-wan ti hang-hai chu-fa chi ch'i ch'i-yüan," *Min-tsu-hsüeh Yen-chiu So chi-k'an,* 1 (1956).

Liu Hsi. *Shih-ming, SPTK* edition.

Liu Kuang-i. "Ch'in-Han shih-tai ti pai-chi tsa-hsi," *Ta-lu tsa-chih,* 22:6 (March, 1961).

Liu P'an-sui. *Lun-heng chi-chieh.* Shanghai, 1957.

Lo Chen-yü and Wang Kuo-wei. *Liu-sha chui-chien.* 1914.

Lu-chin-k'o (S. I. Rudenko). "Lun Chung-kuo yü Ah-erh-t'ai pu-lo ti ku-tai kuan-hsi," *K'ao-ku hsüeh-pao,* 1957:2.

Lü Shih-p'eng. *Pei-shu shih-ch'i ti Yüeh-nan.* Hong Kong, 1964.

Lü Ssu-mien. *Hsien-Ch'in shih.* Shanghai, 1941.

————. *Ch'in-Han shih.* Shanghai, 1947.

————. *Liang-Chin Nan-pei Ch'ao shih.* Shanghai, 1948.

————. *Yen-shih cha-chi.* Shanghai, 1937.

Ma Ch'ang-shou. *Pei-Ti yü Hsiung-mu.* Peking, 1962.

————. *Wu-huan yü Hsien-pi.* Shanghai, 1962.

Ma Tuan-lin. *Wen-hsien t'ung-k'ao, T'u-shu chi-ch'eng* edition.

Pai Shou-i. *Hsüeh-pu chi.* Peking, 1961.

Pai Shou-i and Wang Yü-ch'üan. "Shuo Ch'in-Han tao Ming-mo kuan shou-kung-yeh ho feng-chien chih-tu ti kuan-hsi," *LSYC,* 1954:5.

P'eng Hsin-wei. *Chung-kuo huo-pi shih.* Revised edition, Shanghai, 1958.

San-kuo Chih, T'ung-wen edition.

Shang Ch'eng-tsu. "O-chün Ch'i chieh k'ao," *Wen-wu ching-hua,* 2, Peking, 1963.

Shang-chün shu, WYWK edition.

Shih Chi, Chung-hua t'u-shu kuan edition.

Shih-shuo hsin-yü, Ch'ung-wen shu-chü edition.

Shui-ching chu, photolithographic reprint of the *Yung-lo ta-tien* edition. Peking, 1955.

Su Ch'eng-chien. *Hou-Han shih-huo chih ch'ang-pien.* Shanghai, 1947.

Su Chi-ch'ing. "Han-shu ti-li chih I-ch'eng-pu Kuo chi Hsi-lan shuo," *Nan-yang hsüeh-pao.* 5:2 (December, 1948).

————. "Huang-chih Kuo chiu-tsai Nan-hai ho-ch'u," *Nan-yang hsüeh-pao,* 7:2 (December, 1951).

Sun Shou-tao. "Hsiung-nu Hsi-ch'a-kou wen-hua ku-mu ch'ün ti fa-hsien," *Wen-wu,* 1960:7/8.

Sun Yü-t'ang. "Hsi-Han ti ping-chih," *Chung-kuo she-hui ching-chi shih chi-k'an,* 5:1 (March, 1937).

————. "Han-tai ti chiao-t'ung," *ibid.,* 7:1 (June, 1944).

————. "Chan-kuo Ch'in-Han shih-tai fang-chih-yeh chi-shu ti chin-pu," *LSYC,* 1963:3.

Sung Shu, T'ung-wen edition.

T'an Ch'i-hsiang. "O-chün Ch'i chieh ming-wen shih-ti," *Chung-hua wen-shih lun-ts'ung,* 2 (1962).

————. "Tsai lun O-chün Ch'i chieh ti ta Huang Sheng-chang T'ung-chih," *ibid.*, 5 (1964).

T'an Pi-an. "Han-tai yü Nan-hai Huang-chih Kuo ti chiao-t'ung," *She-hui ching-chi yen-chiu,* 2 (September, 1951).

T'ang Chang-ju. *Wei-Chin Nan-pei Ch'ao shih lun-ts'ung.* Peking, 1955.

————. *Wei-Chin Nan-pei Ch'ao shih lun-ts'ung hsü-pien.* Peking, 1959.

T'ang Yung-t'ung. *Han-Wei Liang-Chin Nan-pei Ch'ao Fo-chiao shih.* Peking, 1955. 2 vols.

T'ao Yüan-chen. *San-kuo shih-huo chih.* Shanghai, 1935.

Ts'ai Chung-lang wen-chi, SPTK so-pen.

Ts'ao Ts'ao chi. Peking, 1962.

Ts'en Chung-mien. *Sui-T'ang shih.* Peking, 1957.

Tseng Yung. "Liao-ning Hsi-ch'a-kou ku-mu ch'ün wei Wu-huan i-chi lun," *K'ao-ku,* 1961:6.

T'ung Chu-ch'en. "K'ao-ku-hsüeh shang Han-tai chi Han-tai i-ch'ien ti tung-pei pien-chiang," *K'ao-ku hsüeh-pao,* 1956:1.

Tung-Han hui-yao, WYWK edition.

Tung-kuan Han-chi, Kuo-hsüeh chi-pen ts'ung-shu edition.

Tzu-chih t'ung-chien, Ku-chi ch'u-pan she. 1956.

Tz'u-kung. "Liang-Han chih Hu-feng," *Shih-hsüeh nien-pao,* 1 (1929).

Wang Chung-shu. "Han-tai wu-chih wen-hua lüeh-shuo," *KKTH,* 1956:1.

————. "Shuo Tien-wang chih yin yü Han Wo-nu kuo-wang yin," *K'ao-ku,* 1959:10.

Wang Fu. *Ch'ien-fu lun, SPTK so-pen.*

Wang Hsien-ch'ien. *Han-shu pu-chu,* Hsü-shou t'ang edition.

Wang I-t'ung. "Wu-Hu t'ung-k'ao," *Chung-kuo wen-hua yen-chiu hui-k'an,* 3 (September, 1943).

Wang Nien-sun. *Tu-shu tsa-chih, WYWK* edition.

Wang Wen-t'ai, editor. *Ch'i-chia Hou-Han Shu.*

Wang Yü-ch'üan. "Han-tai t'ing yü hsiang-li pu-t'ung hsing-chih pu-t'ung hsing-cheng hsi-t'ung shuo," *LSYC,* 1954:2.

————. *Wo-kuo ku-tai huo-pi ti ch'i-yüan ho fa-chan.* Peking, 1957.

Wang Yü-hu. "Ch'in-Han ti-kuo chih ching-chi chi chiao-t'ung ti-li," *Wen-shih tsa-chih,* 2:9/10 (October, 1943).

Wei T'ing-sheng. *Jih-pen Shen-wu T'ien-huang k'ai-kuo hsin-k'ao.* Hong Kong, 1950.

————. *Hsü Fu yü Jih-pen.* Hong Kong, 1953.

Wen wu. Peking, 1959–.

Wen-wu ts'an-k'ao tzu-liao. 1950–1958.

Wu Cho-hsin. *Han-shu Ti-li chih pu-chu, Erh-shih-wu shih pu-pien* edition.

Yang K'uan. *Chan-kuo shih.* Shanghai, 1955.
Yang Lien-sheng. "Tung-Han ti hao-tsu," *CHHP,* 11:4 (1936).
Yao Chih-yin. *Hsieh-shih Hou-Han-shu pu-i,* Kuo-hsüeh t'u-shu kuan. 1931.
Yao Pao-yu. *Chung-kuo ssu-chüan hsi-ch'uan shih.* Chungking, 1944.
Yao Wei-yüan. *Pei-ch'ao Hu-hsing k'ao.* Peking, 1962.
Yen Keng-wang. *Chung-kuo ti-fang hsing-cheng chih-tu shih, shang-pien.* Vols. 1–2, Taipei, 1961.
Yen K'o-chün. *Ch'üan Shang-ku San-tai Ch'in-Han San-kuo Liu-ch'ao wen,* Shih-chieh shu-chü. Taipei, 1963.
Yen-t'ieh lun. Commercial Press, 1936.
Yin Ti-fei. "Anhui Sheng Shou-hsien An-feng-t'ang fa-hsien Han-tai cha-pa kung-ch'eng i-chih," *Wen-wu,* 1960:1.
Yin Ti-fei and Lo Ch'ang-ming. "Shou-hsien ch'u-t'u ti O-chün Ch'i chin-chieh," *Wen-wu ts'an-k'ao tzu-liao,* 1958:4.
Ying Shao. *Feng-su tung-i, SPTK* edition.
———. *Han kuan-i,* in Sun Hsing-yen, *Han-kuan ch'i-chung.*
Yu Chung. "Han-Chin shih-ch'i ti Hsi-nan I," *LSYC,* 1957:12.
Yü Chia-hsi. *Yü Chia-hsi lun-hsüeh tsa-chu.* Peking, 1963. 2 vols.
Yü Ching-jang. "Hu-chiao ch'eng-ch'ieh pi-po chü-chiang," part 2, *Ta-lu tsa-chih,* 17:8 (October, 1958).
Yü Ying-shih. "Tung-Han cheng-ch'üan chih chien-li yü shih-tsu ta-hsing chih kuan-hsi," *Hsin-Ya hsüeh-pao,* 1:2 (1956).
———. "Han-Chin chih chi shih chih hsin tzu-chüeh yü hsin ssu-ch'ao," *Hsin-Ya hsüeh-pao,* 4:1 (1959).
Yüan Hung. *Hou-Han chi, SPTK* edition.
Yünnan Po-wu Kuan. *Yünnan Chin-ning Shih-chai Shan ku-mu ch'ün fa-chüeh pao-kao.* Peking, 1959.

II JAPANESE WORKS

Egami Namio. *Yūrashiya kodai hoppō bunka.* Kyoto, 1948.
Fujita Motoharu. "Kansho chirishi tsū Kōshikoku kō," *Shirin,* 24:4 (October, 1939).
Fujita Ryōsaku. *Chōsen kōkogaku kenkyū.* Kyoto, 1948.
Fujita Toyohachi. *Tōzai kōshō-shi no kenkyū, Nankai hen; Seiiki hen.* Tokyo, 1943.
Hamaguchi Shigekuni. "Kandai no densha," *Tōyō gakuhō,* 22:4 (August, 1935).
———. "Kandai no den," in *Wada Hakase koki kinen Tōyōshi ronsō.* Tokyo, 1961.
Harada Yoshito and Tawaza Kingo. *Lo-Lang.* Tokyo, 1930.
Hibino Takeo. "Kyōteiri ni tsuite no kenkyū," *Tōyōshi kenkyū,* 14:1/2 (July, 1955).
Ikeuchi Hiroshi. "Rakurō Gun kō," *Man-Sen chiri rekishi kenkyū hōkoku,* 16 (1941).

Inoue Yasushi and Iwamura Shinobu. *Seiiki*. Tokyo, 1963.
Ise Sentarō. *Seiiki keiei-shi no kenkyū*. Tokyo, 1955.
Kamada Shigeo. "Kandai no Junri to Kokuri," *Shigaku zasshi*, 59:4 (1950).
————. *Shin-Kan seiji seido no kenkyū*. Tokyo, 1962.
Katō Shigeshi. *Shina keizaishi kōshō*. Tokyo, 1952. 2 vols.
Kimiya Yasuhiko. *Nisshi kōtsūshi*. *Tokyo, 1926*. 2 vols.
Kurihara Tomonobu. *Kodaigaku*, 8:1 (March, 1959).
Kuwabara Jitsuzō. "Sui-T'ang shih-tai Hsi-yü jen Hua-hua k'ao," *Wuhan Ta-hsüeh wen-che chi-k'an*, 5:1 (1936).
————. *Tōzai kōtsūshī ronsō*. Tokyo, 1933.
Kuwata Rokurō. "Nanyō jōdai-shi zakkō," *Ōsaka daigaku bungakubu kiyō*, 3 (1954).
Matsuda Hisao. "Gushi no gyoku to Kōkan no shu", *Tōzai kōshō shiron*. Vol. 1. Tokyo, 1939.
————. *Tōa ronsō*, 3 (September, 1940).
————. "Ken-ba kōeki kansuru shiryō", *Nairiku Ajia-shi ronshū*. Tokyo, 1964.
————. *Kodai Tenza no rekishi chirigaku teki kenkyū*. Tokyo, 1956.
Miyazaki Ichisada. *Ajiashi kenkyū*. Vol. 1, Kyoto, 1957; vol. 2, Kyoto, 1959.
————. "Shina no tetsu ni tsuite," *Shirin*, 40:6 (November, 1957).
Murakawa Kentarō. "Erythraeiki annaiki ni mietaru kigen isseiki no Nankai bōeki," *Tōzai kōchō shiron*, Vol. 1. Tokyo, 1939.
Ōba Osamu. "Kandai no sekisho to pasupōto, *Kansai Daigaku Tōzai gakujutsu kenkyū ronsō*, 16 (1954).
————. "Kan no shoku-fu," *Tōyōshi kenkyū*, 14:1/2 (July, 1955).
Okabe Nagaaki. "Nu no kokuō kin-in mondai hyōron," *Suzuki Shun Kyōju Kanreki Kinen Tōyōshi ronsō*. Tokyo, 1964.
Ozaki Yasushi. "Gōkan Kōchi shishi ni tsuite," *Shigaku*, 33: 3/4 (1961).
Seikai kōkogaku taikei. Tokyo. Vol. 2 (1960); vol. 7 (1959); vol. 8 (1961); vol. 9 (1962).
Shiratori Kurakichi. *Seiiki shi kenkyū*. Tokyo, 1944. 2 vols.
Shiratori Kurakichi and Yanai Wataru. "Kandai no Chōsen," *Manshū rekishi chiri*. Vol. 1, Tokyo, 2nd printing, 1940.
Sogabe Shizuo. "Kandai ni okeru yū-tei haichi no kankaku ni tsuite," *Bunka*, 20:6 (November, 1956).
Tamura Jitsuzō. "Kandai ni okeru Kanton-Futsuin chihō no kaitaku," *Tōyōshi kenkyū*, 9:5/6 (1942).
Uchida Gimpū, "Gōkan Kōbutei no tai-Minami Kyōdo seisuku ni tsuite," *Shirin*, 17:4 (October, 1932); 18:1 (January, 1933).
————. "Gōkan makki yori Gokoran boppatsu ni itaru Kyōdo gobu no josei ni tsuite," *Shirin*, 9:2 (April, 1934).
————. "Kyōdo seii nempō," *Tōyōshi kenkyū*, 2:1 (1936).
————. "Shūdai no mōkyō," *Tōyōshi kenkyū*, 4:4/5 (1939).
————. "Ugan zoku ni kansuru kenkyū," *Man-Mō shi ronsō*, 4 (1943).

———. *Kodai no Mōko,* Tokyo, 1940.

Umehara Sueji. *Kodai hoppō kei bumbutsu no kenkyū.* Kyoto, 1938.

———. *Mōko Noin-Ura hakken no ibutsu.* Tokyo, 1960.

Utsunomiya Kiyoyoshi. *Kandai shakai keizai shi kenkyū.* Tokyo, 1955.

Wada Sei. *Tōa-shi kenkyū, Manshū hen.* Tokyo, 1955.

Yoneda Kenjirō. "Kandai no hengun soshiki," *Tōyōshi kenkyū,* 12:3 (1953).

III WESTERN WORKS

Ackerman, P. "Textiles through the Sassanian Period," in A. U. Pope, editor. *A Survey of Persian Art.* Vol. 1. Oxford, 1938.

Aurousseau, L. "La première conquête chinoise des pays annamites (IIIᵉ siècle avant notre ère)," *BEFEO.* 1923.

Bailey, C., editor. *The Legacy of Rome.* Oxford, 1923.

Balazs, Etienne. *Chinese Civilization and Bureaucracy.* Yale, 1964.

Bielenstein, Hans. *Emperor Kuang-wu and the Northern Barbarians.* The 17th Ernest Morrison Lecture in Ethnology. The Australian National University, Canberra, 1956.

Borovka, G. "Die Funde der Expedition Koslow in der Mongolei, 1924/25," *Jahrbuch des deutschen Archäologischen Instituts,* XLI (1926).

Bury, J. B. *History of the Later Roman Empire from the Death of Theodosius to the Death of Justinian,* Dover Publications, New York, 1958. 2 vols

Cammann, Schuyler. "Review of P. C. Bagchi's 'India and China: A Thousands Years of Cultural Relations'," *The Far Eastern Quarterly,* 12:1 (November, 1952).

———. "Archaeological Evidence for Chinese Contacts with India During the Han Dynasty," *Sinologica,* 5:1 (1956).

———. "Review of H. H. Dubs' 'A Roman City in Ancient China'," *The Journal of Asian Studies,* 21:3 (May, 1962).

Carter, Dagny. *The Symbol of the Beast.* New York, 1957.

Chang, Ch'un-shu. *The Colonization of the Ho-hsi Region—A Study of the Han Frontier System.* Unpublished Ph.D. thesis. Harvard University, 1963.

———. "Military Aspects of Han Wu-ti's Northern and Northwestern Campaigns," *HJAS,* 26 (1966).

Chang, Kwang-chih. "Chinese Prehistory in Pacific Perspective: Some Hypotheses and Problems," *HJAS,* 22 (1959).

———. *The Archaeology of Ancient China.* Yale, 1963.

Charleston, R. J. "Han Damasks," *Oriental Art,* 1:2 (Autumn, 1948).

Charlesworth, M. P. *Trade-Routes and Commerce of the Roman Empire.* Cambridge, 1924.

———. "Some Notes on the Periplus Maris Erythraei," *The Classical Quarterly,* 22 (1928).

———. "Roman Trade with India," in P. R. Coleman-Norton, editor, *Studies in Roman Economic and Social History, in Honor of Allan Chester Johnson*. Princeton, 1951.

Chavannes, Edouard. "Trois généraux chinois de la dynastie des Han Orientaux," *TP*, 2:7 (1906).

———. "Les pays d'Occident d'après le Heou Han Chou," *TP*, 2:8 (1907)

———. *Les documents chinois découverts par Aurel Stein dans les sables du Turkestan oriental*. Oxford, 1913.

Ch'en, Kenneth. *Buddhism in China*. Princeton, 1964.

Cheng Te-k'un. *Prehistoric China*. Cambridge, 1959.

Creel, H. G. "The Role of the Horse in Chinese History," *The American Historical Review*, LXX:3 (April, 1965).

Dabbs, Jack A. *History of the Discovery and Exploration of Chinese Turkestan*. The Hague, 1963.

Dittrich, Edith, "Das Motiv des Tierkampfes in der Altchinesischen Kunst," *Asiatische Forschungen*, 13 (1963).

Dubs, H. H. *The History of the Former Han Dynasty*. Baltimore and London, 1938–1955. 3 vols.

———. *A Roman City in Ancient China*. London, 1957.

Duyvendak, J. J. L. *The Book of Lord Shang*. London, 1928.

Eberhard, W. *Kultur und Siedlung der Randvölker Chinas*, Supplement, *TP*, 36 (1942).

———. *Localkulturen im alten China*, Supplement, *TP*, 37 (1942).

Fairbank, J. K. and S. Y. Teng. "On the Ch'ing Tributary System," *HJAS*, 6:2 (June, 1941).

Ferrand, G. "Le K'ouen-louen et les anciennes navigations interocéaniques dans les mers du Sud," *Journal Asiatique*, 13 (1919).

Fitzgerald, C. P. *Hu-ch'uang or Barbarian Beds*. London, 1964.

Gale, Esson M. *Discourses on Salt and Iron*. Leiden, 1931.

Goodrich, Carrington L. "Trade Routes to China," in J. Labatut and W. J. Lane, editors, *Highways in Our National Life*. Princeton, 1950.

Haloun, Gustav. "Zur Ue-tsi-Frage," *Zeitschrift der Deutschen Morgenländischen Gesellschaft*, 91 (1937).

———. "The Liang-chou Rebellion, 184–221 A.D.," *Asia Major*, n. s. 1:1 (1949).

Hirth, Friedrich. "The Story of Chang K'ien, China's Pioneer in Western Asia," *JAOS*, 37 (1919).

———. *China and the Roman Orient*. Shanghai, 1885.

Hsu, Cho-yun. *Ancient China in Transition*. Stanford, 1965.

Hudson, G. F. *Europe and China*. London, 1931.

Hulsewé, A. F. P. *Remnants of Han Law*. Vol. 1. Leiden, 1955.

———. "Han-time Documents," *TP*, 45 (1957).

Janse, Olov R. T. *Archaeological Research in Indo-China*. Harvard. Vol. 1, 1947; vol. 2, 1951.

Jettmar, Karl. "The Altai before the Turcs," *BMFEA*, 23 (1951).

———. "Hunnen und Hiung-nu—ein archäologisches Problem," *Archiv für Völkerkunde*, 6/7 (1951/52).

Kuhn, H. "Zur Chronologie der Sino-Sibirischen Bronzen," *Ipek*, 1934.

Lattimore, Owen. *Manchuria, Cradle of Conflict*. New York, 1932.

———. *Inner Asian Frontiers of China*. Beacon Press, Boston, 1962.

———. *Studies in Frontier History*. London, 1962.

Laufer, Berthold. "Historical Jottings on Amber in Asia," *Memoirs of the American Anthropological Association*, 3 (February, 1907).

———. *Jade, A Study in Chinese Archaeology and Religion*. Chicago, 1912.

———. *Sino-Iranica, Chinese Contributions to the History of Civilization in Ancient Iran*. Chicago, 1919.

Legge, James, translator. *The Ch'un Ts'ew with the Tso Chuen*, in *The Chinese Classics*. Reprint, Hong Kong, 1960.

———. *The Shoo King or Book of Historical Documents. Ibid.*

———. *The Works of Mencius. Ibid.*

Loewe, Michael. "Some Notes on Han-time Documents from Chüyen," *TP*, 47 (1959).

———. "Some Military Despatches of the Han Period," *TP*, 51 (1964).

Lot, Ferdinand. *The End of the Ancient World and the Beginnings of the Middle Ages*. A Harper Torchbook, New York, 1961.

Majumdar, R. C. *An Advanced History of India*. London, 1950.

Mänchen-Helfen, O. "Zur Geschichte der Lackkunst in China," *Wiener Beiträge zur Kunst- und Kultur- Geschichte Asiens*, 11 (1937).

———. "From China to Palmyra," *The Art Bulletin*, 25:4 (December, 1943).

Maspero, Henri. "L'expédition de Ma Yuan," *BEFEO*, 18 (1918).

———. *Les Documents chinois de la trosième expédition de Sir Aurel Stein en Asie Centrale*. London, 1953.

Mattingly, Harold. *Roman Imperial Civilization*. New York, 1957.

Maverick, Lewis A. *Economic Dialogues in Ancient China, Selections from Kuan-tzu*. Carbondale, 1954.

Minns, Ellis H. "The Art of the Northern Nomads," *Proceedings of the British Academy*, 28 (1942).

Miyakawa, Hisayuki. "The Confucianization of South China," in Arthur Wright, editor, *The Confucian Persuasion*. Stanford, 1960.

Moss, H. St. L. B. *The Birth of the Middle Ages, 395–814*. Oxford, 1935.

Palmer, J. A. B. "Periplus Maris Erythraei: The Indian Evidence as to the Date," *The Classical Quarterly*, 41 (1947).

Parker, Edward Harper. "The Old Thai or Shan Empire of Western Yünnan," *China Review*, 20 (1890).

———. "The History of the Wu-wan or Wu-hwan Tunguses of the

First Century; Followed by That of Their Kinsmen the Sien-pi," *ibid.*, 20 (1892–1893).

Pelliot, Paul. "Le Fou-nan," *BEFEO*, 3 (1903).

Pfister, R. "Les Soieries Han de Palmyre," *Revue des Arts asiatiques*, 13:2 (1941).

Pirenne, Jacqueline. "Un problem-clef pour la chronologie de l'Orient: la date du 'Périple de la Mer Erythrée'," *Journal Asiatique*, CCXLIX (1961).

Pokora, Timotcus, "The Life of Huan T'an," *Archiv Orientalni*, 31 (1963).

Postan, M. M. and H. J. Habakkuk, editors. *The Cambridge Economic History of Europe*. Vol. 2. Cambridge, 1952.

Rawlinson, H. G. *Intercourse Between India and the Western World*. Cambridge, 1926.

Rudenko, Serg Ivanovich. *Kul'tura khunnov i noinulinskie kurgany*. Moscow, 1962.

Salmony, A. "Die ersten Funde von Noin Ula," *Artibus Asiae*, 4 (1930).

———. "The Small Finds of Noin-Ula," *Parnassus*, 8:2 (February, 1936)

Schafer, Edward H. "The Pearl Fisheries of Ho-p'u," *JAOS*, 72:4 (December, 1952).

Schoff, W. H. (annotated and translated) *The Periplus of the Erythraean Sea*. New York, 1912.

———. "The Transcontinental Silk Trade at the Christian Era," *Proceedings of the Numismatic and Antiquarian Society of Philadelphia*, 27 (1913).

———. *Parthian Stations by Isidore of Charax*. Philadelphia, 1914.

———. "The Eastern Iron Trade of the Roman Empire," *JAOS*, 35 (1915).

———. "As to the Date of the Periplus," *Journal of the Royal Asiatic Society of Great Britain and Ireland*, 1917.

Seligman, C. G. "The Roman Orient and the Far East," *Annual Report of the Smithsonian Institution*. 1938.

Stein, Sir M. Aurel. *Sand-Buried Ruins of Khotan*. London, 1903.

———. *Ancient Khotan: Detailed Report of Archaeological Explorations in Chinese Turkestan*. Oxford, 1907. 2 vols.

———. *Ruins of Desert Cathay*. New York, 1912. 2 vols.

———. *Serindia*. Oxford, 1921. 5 vols.

———. *Innermost Asia*. Oxford, 1928. 4 vols.

———. *On Ancient Central Asian Tracks*. New York, 1933.

———. "Central Asian Relics of China's Ancient Silk Trade," *Hirth Anniversary Volume*. London: Probsthain (1922?).

Stein, R. A. "Remarques sur les mouvements du Taoisme Politicoreligieux au IIe siècle ap. J-C," *TP*, 50:1–3 (1963).

Swann, Nancy Lee. *Food and Money in Ancient China*. Princeton, 1950.

Tarn, W. W. *The Greeks in Bactria and India*. Cambridge, 1938.
————. *Hellenistic Civilization*. 3rd edition. London, 1952.
Teggart, Frederick J. *Rome and China, A Study of Correlations in Historical Events*. Berkeley, 1939.
Trevor, Camila. *Excavations in Northern Mongolia*. Leningrad, 1932.
Tsiang, T. F. "China and European Expansion," *Politica*, 2:5 (March, 1936).
Waley, Arthur. "Life under the Han Dynasty," *History Today*, 3 (1953).
————. "The Fall of Lo-yang," *ibid.*, 4 (1954).
Wang, Gungwu. "The Nanhai Trade, A Study of the Early History of Chinese Trade in the South China Sea," *Journal of the Malayan Branch of the Royal Asiatic Society*, 31:2 (June, 1958).
Wang, Yi-t'ung. "Slaves and Other Comparable Social Groups During the Northern Dynasties (386–618)," *HJAS*, 16 (1953).
Wang, Yü-ch'üan, "An Outline of the Central Government of the Former Han Dynasty," *HJAS*, 12 (1949).
Warmington, E. H. *The Commerce Between the Roman Empire and India*. Cambridge, 1928.
Watson, Burton, translator. *Records of the Grand Historian of China*. Columbia, 1961. 2 vols.
Weber, Max. *General Economic History*. Translated by Frank Knight. Reprint, The Free Press, 1950.
Wheatley, Paul. *The Golden Khersonese*. Kuala Lumpur, 1961.
Wheeler, Sir Mortimer. *Rome Beyond the Imperial Frontiers*. London, 1954.
Wilbur, Martin, C. *Slavery in China During the Former Han Dynasty*. Chicago, 1943.
Wilhelm, Helmut "The Scholar's Frustration: Notes on a Type of Fu," in J. K. Fairbank, editor, *Chinese Thought and Institutions*. Chicago, 1957.
Willetts, William. *Chinese Art*. Penguin Books, Baltimore, 1958. 2 vols.
Wittfogel, Karl A. *Oriental Despotism, A Comparative Study of Total Power*. Yale, 1957.
Wylie, A. "History of Heung-noo in Their Relation with China," *The Journal of the Royal Anthropological Institute*, 3:3 (January, 1874); 5:1 (July, 1875).
Yang, Lien-sheng. "An Inscribed Han Mirror Discovered in Siberia," *TP*, 42 (1953).
————. "Notes on Maspero's *Les Documents chinois de la troisième expédition de Sir Aurel Stein en Asie Centrale*," *HJAS*, 18 (June, 1955).
————. *Topics in Chinese History*. Harvard, 1950.
————. *Money and Credit in China*. Harvard, 1952.
————. *Studies in Chinese Institutional History*. Harvard, 1961.

————. *Les aspects économiques des travaux publics dans la Chine impériale.* Collège de France, 1964.

Yetts, Perceval. "Discoveries of the Kozlov Expedition," *Burlington Magazine,* 48 (April, 1926).

Yule, Sir Henry. *Cathay and the Way Thither,* Vol. 1. London, 1915.

Yü, Ying-shih. "Life and Immortality in the Mind of Han China, 206 B.C.–A.D. 220," *HJAS,* 25 (1964–1965).

Zürcher, E. *The Buddhist Conquest of China,* Leiden, 1959. 2 vols.

Glossary

The following glossary is a highly selective one. It includes only technical terms and some proper names which are discussed either in the text or in the notes. Place names and personal names are generally not given.

Ch'ang-shui Chiao-wei 長水校尉
Chi chiao-wei 己校尉
chi-wei 己未
Ch'iang 羌
ch'ien 錢
chieh 節
chih-kuan 質館
Chih-shih 織室
chin 津
chin 錦
ch'iung-lu 穹廬
chü 拘
chü-chung nei-fu 舉衆內附
chü-kuo lai-fu 舉國來附
chü-pu lai-fu 舉部來附
chü-t'u nei-shu 舉土內屬
chuan 傳
chuan-she 傳舍
chün 郡
chün-hsien 郡縣
chün-shih 軍市
chün-shih ling 軍市令
Chung-hang Yüeh 中行説
Chung Huang-men 中黃門

erh-yeh 二業

fang-p'ai 坊箄
fu 賦、箄
fu-ch'ien 賦錢

ho-ch'in 和親
Hsi Chih-shih 西織室
Hsi-yü Tu-hu 西域都護
hsien 仙
hsien 縣
hsien-kuan 縣官
Hsien-pi 鮮卑
Hsin 新
Hsin shen ling kuang ch'eng shou wan nien 新神靈廣成壽萬年
Hsiung-nu 匈奴
hsün-li 循吏
Hu 胡
hu 斛
Hu Ch'iang Chiao-wei 護羌校尉
hu-tiao 戶調

235

Hu Wu-huan Chiao-wei 護烏桓校尉

Hu-shih 胡市

Huang-men 黃門

i 億

i-wan 億萬

i-i-chih-i 以夷制夷

i-i-fa-i 以夷伐夷

i-mi 義米

i-shih-chu-hsing 衣食住行

I-ts'ung Hu 義從胡

I-wu ssu-ma 伊吾司馬

ju-ku-shih 如故事

Jung 戎

kan (chien) ch'u-wu 間出物

kan-lan 間闌

kan-lan ch'u-wu 間闌出物

k'ao-cheng 考證

k'ao-i 考異

K'ao-kung 考工

keng-fu 更賦

ko 戈

k'o-she 客舍

ku-shih 故事

kuan 關

kuan-she 館舍

kuan-shih 關市

kuo-so 過所

lan-ch'u sai 闌出塞

lan-ch'u ts'ai-wu 闌出財物

li 里

li-chih 荔枝

lou-ch'uan 樓船

lung-yen 龍眼

Man-i ti 蠻夷邸

Ming-tao 明刀

mu-mien 木棉

nei 內

nei-chün 內郡

nei-shu 內屬

ni-lü 逆旅

Nieh I 聶壹

Nieh Weng-i 聶翁壹

Pa 霸

pan-liang 半兩

Pan-tun 板楯

Pao-sai 保塞

Pao-sai man-i 保塞蠻夷

Pao-sai wai-man-i 保塞外蠻夷

p'i 匹

p'i-pi 皮幣

pien-hu 編戶

Po 燮

pu 郡

pu 布

pu-i 補遺

se-fu 嗇夫

Sha-ch'a 涑車

Shan 撣

Shan-yü 單于

shang 上

Shang-fang 尚方

Shao-fu 少府

she-chu 蛇珠

sheng 升

shih 石

Shih-che Chiao-wei 使者校尉

shih-jen 市人
shih-wen 釋文
shu-kuo 屬國
Shu-kuo Tu-wei 屬國都尉
Shu-pu 蜀布
so-pen 縮本
ssu-kuan 私館
Ssu-ma 司馬
Ssu-nung 司農
ssu-shih 私市
su-ho 蘇合
suan-fu 算賦
sui 隧
sui-chang 隧長

Ta-Ch'in 大秦
tai-mao 玳瑁
T'ai-p'u
tao 道
Ti 狄
Ti 氐
t'ing 亭
t'ing-chuan 亭傳
t'ing-shih 亭市
tou 斗
tsan 賛
tsu 卒
Tsung-pu 賨布

t'u 徒
Tu-hu 都護
Tu-wei 都尉
tui 隊
t'un-t'ien 屯田
Tung Chih-shih 東織室
Tung-Hu 東胡
T'ung-p'u 僮僕
T'ung-p'u Tu-wei 僮僕都尉

wai 外
wai-ch'en 外臣
wai-chün 外郡
wai-shih 外市
wei-chia ssu-shih 為家私市
weng-chung 翁仲
Wo-jen 倭人
Wu-chi Chiao-wei 戊己校尉
Wu Chiao-wei 戊校尉
Wu-huan 烏桓
wu-shu 五銖

Yeh-che 謁者
Yü-fu 御府
Yü-men Kuan 玉門關
Yüeh-chih 月氏
Yung-lo ta-tien 永樂大典

Index

agate, found in Han tombs, 179
agriculture, 17, 21–22; of Ch'iang, 88; of Hsiung-nu, 87, 208–209; of Wu-huan, 88, 107
Ai-lao, 113, 117
Ai-lao barbarians, 82, 117. *See also* Southwestern barbarians
Alexandria, 89
Altai region, 104
amber, 116–117; found in Han tombs, 179–180
An, Emperor, 78
An-hsi. *See* Parthia
An Hsüan (Parthian merchant-turned-Buddhist), 214
An-ting, 53, 67, 83, 91
Anhwei, 22, 124
aristocrats, interest in foreign rarities, 194–196; engaged in inn business, 217–218. *See also* high society
Arramaniya, 173
Artha'sastra, 152
asbestos cloths, 175
Assam, 166
Augustus, 158, 159. *See also* Roman Empire

Bactria, 94, 112, 114, 137, 153, 155, 192. *See also* Ta-hsia
Baltic, the, 180
bamboo canes, 94, 112, 192
barbarians, as revealed in Han documents on wood, 97–98; inner and outer distinction of, 68 ff. *See also* surrendered barbarians
"barbarian iron," 169. *See also* iron, iron industry

barbarian markets, 106, 107–108. *See also* border markets, *Hu-shih, kuan-shih*
"barbarian powder," 201 and n., 213
barbarian soldiers, 14, 83–85, 205. *See also* Han army, *shu-kuo* soldiers, *I-ts'ung Hu*
barbarian threat, in pre-Han period, 4; in Han China as observed by Fan Yeh, 55–56; in Later Han China, 75 n.
barbarization, 211–216
barbarus, 206
barrier markets. *See kuan-shih*
barriers (*kuan*), in Warring-States period, 123–124, 125; in Former Han period, 119–120, 126–128; in Later Han period, 132; criticism of Mencius, 124 n. *See also* passport system
Barygaza, 155
beryl, 172
Berytus, 158
boats, 31–32, 217
Bombax malabaricum, 113 n. *See also* tree-cotton
border markets, 95–96, 99–101. *See also* barbarian markets, *Hu-shih, kuan-shih*
Brahmaputra valley, 166
bronze mirrors, 26–27; found in: Inner Mongolia, 110, Japan, 186, Korea, 183, Noin-ula, 104, 169–170, Siberia, 170, Western Regions, 170, Yunnan, 116; foreign imitations, 171

CHINA AND THE BARBARIANS
UNDER THE LATER HAN DYNASTY

Caspian Sea

WESTERN

GREAT
REGIONS

Yü-

PARTHIA
YÜEH-
CHIH

SHEN-TU